Keeping Your Money

How to Avoid Taxes and Probate
Through Estate Planning

To Sylvia,
With my
best wishes
Charlie Plotnick
12-15-8

KEEPING YOUR MONEY

How to Avoid Taxes and Probate Through Estate Planning

Charles K. Plotnick

Stephan R. Leimberg

John Wiley & Sons, Inc.

New York • Chichester • Brisbane • Toronto • Singapore

Publisher: Stephen Kippur
Editor: David Sobel
Managing Editor: Ruth Greif
Editing, Design, and Production: Publications Development Co.

Portions of *Keeping Your Money* were originally published in hardcover by
Coward-McCann, Inc., as *Die Rich,* and in paperback by Stein and Day, Inc., as
Get Rich/Stay Rich. This edition has been updated and revised and is published
by arrangement with the authors.

This publication is designed to provide accurate and authoritative
information in regard to the subject matter covered. It is sold with the
understanding that the publisher is not engaged in rendering professional
advice. If professional advice or other expert assistance is required, the
services of a competent professional person should be sought.

Library of Congress Cataloging-in-Publication Data

Plotnick, Charles.

  Keeping your money.
  1. Estate planning—United States—Popular
works. 2. Inheritance and transfer tax—Law
and legislation—United States—Popular works.
I. Leimberg, Stephan R. II. Title.
KF750.Z9L45 1987   343.7305'3   87-6121
ISBN 0-471-63113-2   347.30353
ISBN 0-471-85948-6 (pbk.)

Printed in the United States of America

87 88 10 9 8 7 6 5 4 3 2 1

To Harriet,
from all of us who miss her.
—Charles K. Plotnick

To Jo Ann,
for my new found freedom.
—Stephan R. Leimberg

A special thanks to two good friends,
Russ Miller and Tom Brinker,
who have always graciously shared their knowledge and
expertise with the public, and whose personal friendship and
generous input is sincerely appreciated by the authors of this book.

Preface

This book is about thinking and caring and—most importantly—*doing*—for yourself and others. It is a practical step-by-step guide to estate planning, a process we define as the accumulation, conservation, and distribution of assets in the manner that most efficiently will accomplish your personal objectives.

You acquired this book because you care about others, because you are wise enough to know that if you don't take the action necessary to protect your own financial future, no one else will, and because in estate planning, time is of the essence—tomorrow may be too late, and plans put off are actions perhaps never begun.

Here's how to start:

1. Read this entire book quickly. Skip any chapters that have no relevance to your situation.
2. Reread those portions of the book that deal specifically with tools or techniques that could help you achieve your goals.
3. Take the appropriate actions to implement your plan.

The ideas and information contained in this book are practical and can be followed by anyone serious about living better and safeguarding his or her future.

This book contains ideas and information that can save you and your family thousands of dollars and, at the same time, provide you with peace of mind and a definite plan for your future.

Together, we have had a combined total of almost 50 years' experience dealing with all phases of estate planning. Our backgrounds include lecturing nationally to thousands of attorneys and accountants, teaching graduate college and tax masters law school courses, speaking to civic and social organizations, and guiding and advising individual and corporate legal clients. Because of the diversity of our contacts with the public, we gained an understanding of the very wide gap that continues to exist between what can be accomplished to best plan for the future and what is, in fact, actually being done.

This book is not designed to fill you with abstract concepts that very few people will understand, much less attempt to pursue. Rather, it is to advise you of the many ways in which careful estate planning can make both the present and the future much more enjoyable—for you, for members of your family who will share the future with you, and for your heirs.

Read this book and you will find there are countless ways in which you can improve your position today, and in the future, if you systematically and seriously attempt to do so. Please accept our invitation to increase your current financial security and the value of your property for your future. Make certain that those you love receive as much of this property as they can possibly get, without its being unnecessarily diluted, or even lost completely, because of lack of planning!

Charles K. Plotnick
Stephan R. Leimberg

Contents

Contents

Introduction

Although the title of this book is *Keeping Your Money*, the book is really about opportunity. About how you can take this opportunity to get the most for yourself and your family by taking advantage of the biggest change in tax laws in years. But like most opportunities, this will only prove advantageous if you take the time and make the plans to get the greatest possible benefits for your family and yourself.

Consider the case of John Stevens. The small company John owned always seemed busy, but John never realized a profit from it. He couldn't keep track of the business and was poorly organized. To improve his situation, John purchased a computer, but two years later, John's business was still in the same rut. John had failed to program the computer to solve the problems for which it was purchased.

The new tax law, like John's computer, will not solve your estate planning problems, unless you devise a plan to make the tax laws work for you. Unless you create a program that coordinates the new tax laws with the present laws and your own family situation, you will not be able to guarantee the future financial security of your family and yourself.

We firmly believe that those who have worked hard all of their lives deserve to have both security in the present and something to show for their life's efforts in the end. It is as simple as that. We will *not* attempt to tell you how to beat the system. It is enough to work within the system. The problem is that very few people understand what the system is all about. Our purpose in writing this book is to explain the system to you, tell you what you must know, and where you should go to get advice. This book is totally devoted to *estate planning*—the accumulation of property and the ability to transfer that property to whom you wish, in the time or manner that you want to give it, without having it taken away, dissipated or lost because things were not set up properly.

One caution: While we sincerely believe that no one can read this book without gaining information that can possibly be worth thousands of dollars to them and to their families, *merely reading* this book will not greatly improve your personal situation.

You must implement the many ideas in this book as they apply to your personal situation. To put these ideas into effect requires, in many cases, the services of a professional. However, we promise we will not stimulate you to action and then abandon you without giving you guidelines to help implement the ideas. We have, therefore, devoted part of this book to specific recommendations on how to choose the professionals: insurance agents, accountants, lawyers and bankers, if any or all are indicated, to help you complete your plans.

We have also tried to be as nontechnical as possible. Lawyers and accountants get reams of information daily on new tax laws and new cases that seem to show one how to get around each new law as it is passed. It is absolutely impossible in one short, easily readable book to tell you everything there is to know about tax planning and tax laws. However, we have tried to combine essential information about estate planning that everyone should be aware of, with some technical information and down-to-earth practical advice that should be of considerable benefit to almost anyone.

After you have read this book, you will be in a much better position to define the type of professional assistance and advice you need. Time is a very precious commodity. No matter how wealthy any of us are or how important we think we are in the scheme of life, we can never again recapture a lost minute. Life is the most important thing that we will ever have or could hope to possess. All of us owe it to ourselves and to our loved ones to take a little time to put our lives in order, so that when we come to the end of our lives, we will be able to feel in our hearts that we have really lived and made life better for ourselves and those people and institutions we love.

PART ONE

CREATING A PLAN TO KEEP YOUR MONEY

How to Prepare a Tailor-Made Plan for You and Your Family

1

Why You Need a Plan

Do I really need a plan? There are two ways to answer that question: first is that, whether or not you want one, you already *have* a plan—the one your home state drew for you. It's called Intestacy, and you may not like what the state has planned for you. We'll cover the disadvantages of intestacy in greater detail in Chapter 6.

The second answer to the question is an unequivocal *yes!* You really need a plan as long as there is any person, including yourself, in whom you have the slightest interest. Life is a continuing process, and whether one likes to think about it or not, we have no choice about certain events: if we live, we must eventually either retire, become disabled, or die. Death is the inevitable conclusion to life. All of us are now in the process of making our way through our own lives, and at some point in time, our lives will come to an end regardless of whether or not we have taken control back from the state government and made plans for ourselves and our families.

Death is inevitable, but taxes are not. You *can* reduce your tax burden. Many of us can legitimately avoid taxes altogether. However, a large part of your estate may be lost to taxes and other costs and won't go to your family or other beneficiaries if you don't have a plan. With a good estate plan, you can close the valves on losses to your estate. Figure 1 (adopted with the permission of realtor and nationally known radio commentator, Russ Miller) illustrates how the assets in your estate will literally "go down the drain" if you fail to plan.

Is Estate Planning Only for the Wealthy?

One of the most common misconceptions is that estate planning is only for the wealthy. Although planning is important for persons who have accumulated substantial property, estate planning is just as important, if not more so, for those of modest to moderate means. A needless loss of money to pay taxes or estate settlement costs hurts the survivors even more when the estate is small. Money saved by the use of a well-thought-out tax savings device, even if it's only putting the right title on a bank account, will have the greatest significance where the property

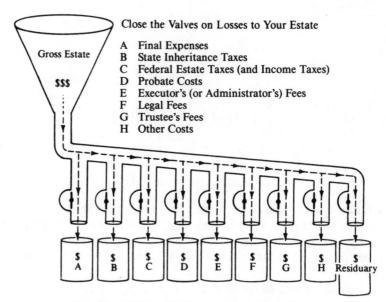

Close the Valves on Losses to Your Estate

A Final Expenses
B State Inheritance Taxes
C Federal Estate Taxes (and Income Taxes)
D Probate Costs
E Executor's (or Administrator's) Fees
F Legal Fees
G Trustee's Fees
H Other Costs

represents a proportionately larger part of the person's assets. Putting it more bluntly, the less wealth we have, the less those we love can afford our money management mistakes.

Uncontrolled Planning

What happens if you do not have an estate plan? Somewhere someone has a plan for you which will go into effect if you do not formulate one of your own.

If you do nothing about planning, the federal and state government will plan your estate for you. This is often called *uncontrolled* planning. The cost can be quite high. If you do nothing, you forfeit the right to give your property to whom you select in the manner that you choose, to select the people to administer your plan, to arrange your assets to minimize taxes, and, in general, the right to arrange for the disposition of your property and the reduction of taxes and other settlement costs.

People Planning

There are two reasons for an estate plan. The first, and most important, involves people.

Estate planning is extremely important for anyone who has (a) minor children (You wouldn't leave them home alone without a babysitter, and you wouldn't let a stranger decide who that babysitter would be—so how can you not choose a guardian?); (b) an exceptionally artistic or intellectually gifted family member (Have you provided the financial means for that person to develop and use his or her talent?); (c) a retarded, emotionally disturbed or physically handicapped child or other dependent (such a child may never be completely self-sufficient); (d) a spouse who cannot or does not want to handle money or securities or a business interest; or (e) parents or other relatives who depend on you, and finally, estate planning is important if you are single. (If you don't provide for yourself, who will?)

Asset Planning

While most people think of asset planning only in terms of large amounts of money, how your assets are titled can be very important. For example, in some states there are no state death taxes on property owned jointly by husband and wife. Therefore, if the only asset a family has is a $10,000 bank account, there would be no death taxes on this property if it were in the joint names of husband and wife. However, if the husband were to die and the same property was solely in his name, a tax would be imposed. Legal ownership of property is, therefore, an essential element of planning, and taxes can play a very important role in this area.

For federal death-tax purposes, from an asset-planning point of view, recent tax law changes mean you must rethink, review, and in many cases revise your plans. Estate planning is now indicated from an asset-planning perspective if you are single, widowed, or divorced, and have assets of over $600,000 (see the discussion of the unified credit on page 137). If you are married, it is now possible to pass an unlimited amount of property to your spouse, estate-tax free. This means that you must focus the thrust of your tax-savings planning at the death of the surviving spouse.

You will learn more about the unified credit and the marital deduction in the chapters dealing with the federal estate tax. At this point, it is important to appreciate the necessity of asset planning in any over-all estate plan. You will see that, while the amounts you can pass tax free at your death seem to be quite large, there are many cases in which, by planning now, additional taxes can be saved at the death of the surviving spouse. This will significantly increase the amount of property your beneficiary will ultimately receive. You will also see that the value of your property for estate-tax purposes can include all or part of your home, the proceeds of life insurance, and just about everything you have. There are also various forms of state death tax and administrative costs that can be minimized if you own a business or property in more than one state. Certainly, if you own your own business, you have an asset that needs individualized attention. Again, we have specifically considered the effects of planning for your business in Chapter 15.

"Do I need a plan?" The answer is yes! It is essential to consider those people, including yourself, whose future can be positively affected by proper planning, as well as to consider your assets and the tax implications of estate planning in regard to what will eventually happen to your property.

2

Overcoming Inertia

Quite often an estate breaks up not because the estate owner has done anything wrong—but because he or she hasn't done *anything*.

There are many reasons why people fail to take action and formulate a plan, causing a breakup in their estate and a loss of security for the future of themselves and their families. If you can recognize these obstacles, you should be able to overcome them and get your plan underway.

Where to begin? If you don't know where to start, you probably won't. One of the prime objectives of this book is to show you precisely where to start. The following chapters will provide you with this specific information, so that you can be on your way to a more secure future. We're going to start by considering why many people do not plan.

An Unpleasant Subject

For those who find planning for a death a fearful and distasteful matter, it might be helpful to balance these feelings with the knowledge of what their thoughts would be if they knew they were about to die and had made no plans. One of the most useful ideas we will offer you in this book is the importance of conducting a "financial firedrill" at least once a year. Sit down with your spouse and children and teach them what to do "if." Show them where important documents are located. Tell them who they should or should not rely on. Explain where to go for help. If you teach your wife to be your widow or your husband to be a widower, you remove much of death's financial sting. The time to educate your survivors is before they are survivors!

To overcome the problem of the limit on your available time, institute a system of priorities. If something is really important to you, it must be placed ahead of other tasks, even though they seem to be all-encompassing at the time. In this manner, the truly important items on your list will be accomplished, and you will find you still have time to take care of other more routine matters. There is no excuse for being too busy to plan for your future and your family's future. If you are worried about what might happen to you if you don't put money away for yourself for retirement, and if you think the possibility of your becoming ill and dying is a matter of so little consequence that it is near the bottom of your priority list, then you probably would not have had the interest to buy this book. However, if you are genuinely concerned about your family's future, as well as your own, planning your estate will become your number one priority.

Dislike of Professional Advisors

You are now ready to formulate your plan, but you are hesitant about contacting a lawyer, an insurance agent, a trust officer, or an accountant.

In Chapter 24, you will find specific advice on selecting personal advisors. However, if your hesitancy about planning is caused by an unwillingness to deal with specific advisors, then you must first overcome this reluctance. You are not only an important individual in your own right, but you are a potential client or customer. As such, you have the absolute right to select those individuals with whom you feel most comfortable and whose background, education, and experience indicate that they can be most helpful to you. You are not obligated to do business with the first individual with whom you come in contact, regardless of the importance of his/her position or background.

Be aware of the fact that you are the individual whose "business" is being solicited and whose sense of approval is desired by the professional. Since you are paying the freight, insist on driving the train. Demand the attention and respect to which you are entitled.

Unawareness of Tax Consequences

One reason people often give for failure to plan their future is they didn't perceive a need to plan. They were unaware, for example, that their children might have to pay a large federal estate tax because they did not set up a bypass trust (explained in Chapter 13). People don't understand that by their inaction they shift the problems to others less able to handle them.

At the very least, you should have your situation professionally evaluated if, after reading this book, you have even the slightest indication of a potential tax problem.

Unwillingness to Address Family Situations

It is easy to plan when you have a husband, wife, and child all living together in a happy, healthy, and loving environment. All families, however, are not created equal, and in some there are particular problems that need tough decisions. What do you do about providing for your spouse if you are separated, but your spouse is caring for your minor child? More than two-thirds of all children born in 1980 will live in a single-parent household by the time they are 19 years old. What estate plans should you make where you have three children, all of whom you love, but one of whom has a disability that will handicap him/her for the rest of his/her life? How do you make provisions in your will for your dependent mother when you know that your wife and mother have never gotten along well together? These are serious decisions requiring delicate but responsible solutions. They are the types of problems that so many people continually set aside for some future date, at which time (they hope) the problem will have disappeared. In fact, should something happen to you before the problem goes away, then you will have made what was a very difficult problem for you into a completely unmanageable problem for those you love. If these questions were hard for you to answer during your lifetime, how can you expect them to be logically and neatly solved if you are no longer here?

In short, the very reason that you might hesitate to take any action at this time is, in fact, the very reason that you *must* take action now. Otherwise, the difficult decisions that you have avoided making can result in a lifetime of difficulty for your surviving family members.

Belief in Lasting Health and Immortality

No one has done it. Yet, some people act as if they will live forever. Unfortunately, when you are old, it is usually too late to accomplish what otherwise could have been done. The time to save for your old age is when you are young. The time to buy life insurance is when it is cheap and you are young and insurable. The time to worry about disability is when you are well enough to buy disability insurance. And, of course, the time to make your will is now!

Life's Financial Problems

What are the financial problems we face in our lives? Let's use the word, L I V E S to describe them, standing for:

L Lack of Liquidity. Lack of liquidity caused by death-generated expenses means there isn't enough cash to pay death taxes and other estate settlement costs. Often, a lack of liquidity means our heirs will be involved in a forced sale—they will have to sell precious heirlooms, valuable assets, and perhaps even the family business to satisfy the demands for cash.

I Improper Disposition of Assets. Many people leave (a) the wrong things, (b) to the wrong people, (c) in the wrong manner, or (d) at the wrong time. It's obvious that a Porsche 911 should not be left to a teenager or an octogenarian.

But it's just as improper to leave large sums of money outright to someone ill-equipped to handle it or to leave a business interest to a spouse who can't (or doesn't want to) take the emotional and physical punishment of running it. It may be improper to leave equal shares of your estate to your children: one child may need or deserve more—or less—than another.

Ask yourself:

1. *Whom* do I want to benefit?
2. What *needs* does that person (or persons) have?
3. What manner (and timing) of distribution would meet those needs best?
4. Are there restrictions, limitations, or terms that should be placed on my gifts?

Inflation is a second "I" that often thwarts the best laid plans. We strongly suggest you discuss with a ChFC (Chartered Financial Consultant) or CFP (Certified Financial Planner) how to protect against the ravages of inflation through proper diversification.

Inadequate income and capital in the event of death, disability, retirement, or for special needs. There's an old but still true saying that the only difference between an old woman and an elderly lady is adequate income. Will you have adequate income if you are disabled? (If you haven't checked, how can you be sure?)

V Value. Most people have not stabilized or maximized the value of the assets they already have. For instance, we recommend the *Rule of 2*. For every person you have named in *any* dispositive document (such as a will, a trust, a life insurance policy, a pension, or profit-sharing plan), there should be two backups in case the one you named can't or wouldn't accept. Check your will to see if there are two backups for any trustee, guardian, or executor you named. Do you have a buy-sell agreement for your business so the value of your lifetime of efforts will survive your death? (A buy-sell is useless unless it is in writing *and* is adequately funded.)

E Excessive Transfer Costs. Most people will pay too much in taxes, too much in legal fees, and too much in other administrative costs to transfer wealth and provide security to those they love. A great deal of these costs can be reduced or eliminated (see the estate planning alphabet on page 119).

S Special Needs. Perhaps the single most important objective of estate planning is the solution to special needs. Such goals include the need to care for a spouse who can't handle money, property, or a family business; a physically handicapped, mentally retarded, or emotionally disturbed child; a relative who looks to you as the sole means of financial support; or a desire to assure the education or training of a particularly gifted family member or friend. Special needs also include the desire to give to schools, churches, synagogues, or other institutions or charities.

These are the estate-planning obstacles that must be overcome for any of us to enjoy more meaningful lives. Continue reading and we will show you—step by step—how to solve these problems.

4

The Importance of a Tailor-Made Plan

You are unique—you are separate and distinct from everyone else. That is not to say that you don't have things in common with other people. But, your likes and dislikes, your savings habits, your health, your outlook on life, your background, your ambition, and your goals for yourself and your family are all specific to you. Since this is so, why allow yourself to be placed into a group without having your personal wishes and desires considered? This is what you are doing if you do not have a "tailor-made" plan.

Demand Individualized Attention

Since you are different, you deserve to be treated as an individual, or as a family unit, with your own distinct property, goals, and objectives. Don't trust the estate planner who has the solution to your problem before you have finished outlining all of the facts (especially if that "solution" consists solely of the purchase of a product or service this "planner" is offering).

In Chapter 5 we will deal specifically with what information must be assembled and analyzed before any solutions can be recommended. Once all of the available information is known, you will be in a position to decide the best arrangements for you and your family. Then, and only then, can anyone else be in a position to offer you guidance to help you formulate your unique plan.

A simple and inexpensive but effective way of removing property from an estate is by transferring ownership of a life insurance policy. It is a tax-saving device often recommended by insurance agents and other estate planners to reduce estate taxes. However, simplistic solutions of this type made without inquiring into the many variables involved can result in unfortunate and unexpected consequences.

Don't rush to become involved in new tax-saving plans unless you are certain that you will, in fact, benefit from them. Savings plans, real estate, and stock plans that often promise higher returns after taxes may, in fact, deliver these "higher returns" only to those persons in a higher income tax bracket than you. And, of course, a major consideration must be: Does the plan in question help you achieve your goal—which may or may not be entirely financial. Do you want safety as opposed to the opportunity for the highest possible return?

Should the emphasis be on retirement, death benefits, or what you'll need next year to get by on? We each have different goals; therefore, allow no one else to substitute their goals and aspirations for yours.

Measure Your Worth

One of the first tasks you must accomplish in planning your estate is to see exactly where you are now. An accountant calls this a balance sheet—a measure of your assets, your liabilities, and your net worth. To start, you must break it down into several different categories. For example:

1. What are you worth today, assuming that you keep working at what you are now doing and your assets remain fairly constant?
2. What will your worth be if you project a growth in your assets at a conservative rate over 5, 10, 15, and 20 years?
3. What are you worth if you were not to consider your earned income but had to rely *solely* on the return from your investments and capital?
4. What are you worth to your family if you died *or* became permanently disabled today?

There are only two sources of financial security—a person at work and wealth at work.

As a working individual, you receive a return for your work that is called *earned income*. The working individual has been compared to a machine, which is a capital investment that generates a certain return (earnings) as a result of the educational and practical experience put into the work performed. The return on that "machine" is paid to you in the form of your salary or in the form of the money that you take from a business that you own. In most cases this is by far the largest source of income presently available to you and your family.

The next category is the return on your capital or investments. Is the return you are receiving adequate? Can it be improved? Will it continue at the same level? To obtain these answers requires some work. There are forms at the end of this book which you can use to make an inventory of all your assets. In Chapter 5, the forms will be discussed in greater detail. In order for you to make a determination as to what you are really worth, you will have to gather all the information relating to your property. Use these forms to simplify assembling the data, and you can arrive at an amount that will represent the current market value of the assets that comprise your present estate. What is the real worth of these assets? The only way to make a determination as to the real value to you and your family of your "capital assets" is to review them so that you can arrive at a figure that would represent the amount of income that this property could generate for you and your family. In these days of rapidly changing interest rates, it is difficult to select an exact figure that would represent the amount of return you could expect to receive on your capital investments. For example, you add up all your assets arriving at a figure of $40,000. If this $40,000 could be converted to cash and invested, what after-tax return could you reasonably expect? Most planners would use a conservative 5 percent or closely related figure. Keep in mind that, if security is your goal, you should take a conservative approach to the amount of expected return. Otherwise, you risk overestimating the potential income that could be realized from your assets.

Therefore, if you hope to retire in 20 years, your plan must take into account the fact that at that point your earned income will stop. The return on your investments, plus whatever other retirement plan will be in effect at that time, must equal the amount of income you hope to receive at that time. Other retirement income would come from whatever company or individual retirement plan you might have (discussed in detail in Chapter 17) as well as any help you might receive from your government plan (covered in Chapter 18). If it looks as though you might fall short, then you will have to take steps to increase your income, utilizing the many saving techniques in this book, so that you can achieve your goal.

Lastly, if you were to die or become permanently disabled, what would you be worth to your family? Since the income derived as the result of your working would stop, it is necessary for you to arrange to offset this significant loss of income. Life insurance and social security, if applicable and available, can go a long way toward filling this gap. But today, right now, what are you worth to your family in the event of your death?

Take your assets, the amount of your insurance or other death benefits, use 5 percent or whatever conservative figure you select, and you will have the answer. If you have $50,000 in insurance, at a 5 percent after-tax return, your family will receive $2,500 a year; $100,000 in insurance and other benefits would produce an income of $5,000 per year; $250,000 invested at 5 percent would provide an annual income of $12,500. Of course, higher rates of return (in return for a higher risk of losing your capital) would necessitate accumulating a smaller amount of principal. But you are dealing with your future and your family's. So keep abreast of the current rates of return, but plan conservatively. Certainly, if you consider the potential decrease in purchasing power that inflation can bring, a conservative estimate would be closer to reality. In any event, it is always better to have a little too much than not quite enough. No widow ever complained she'd been left too much life insurance. No retired man or woman has ever said, "I'm sorry I invested as much or as well as I did," and no one who was disabled ever felt that more money coming in would have been too much.

5

Where Do I Stand Today?

In order to plan for the future, you must first know where you stand at the present time. Chances are you have already accomplished quite a bit, and whatever property you now have will serve as a base for future acquisitions.

What information do you need? How do you go about gathering it? In the appendix to this chapter, you will find *Your Financial Firedrill,* a form that will take less than one hour to complete and could save hundreds of hours (and thousands of dollars) for your family. The information requested should show you most, if not all, of what will be necessary to give a complete picture of your present situation. You are asked to complete information about yourself; your family; the names of your personal advisors; updated information as to present estate planning documents such as wills, marital agreements, trust, custodianships, social security information, and the like. It requires you to list specific information concerning your real estate, securities and mortgages, personal property such as household furnishings, automobiles, and jewelry. Information is requested about bank accounts, savings, checking, cash, and miscellaneous property. Space is provided for specific information about your life insurance and insurance on the lives of the members of your family. Information is requested about hospitalization insurance and disability coverage.

If you are employed, information is requested about your employee group insurance, qualified and nonqualified pension benefits, and other specific employee/employer arrangements.

Finally, you are asked to list the sources of your family income. You'll find that completing this form will be an enlightening experience. For example, by reviewing your insurance and company benefits thoroughly, you might find that they are not set up precisely as you thought they were and, in fact, might be set up improperly. Stock certificates that you thought were in joint names might be in your name or your wife's name alone. Deeds to property can sometimes be typed incorrectly, and beneficiary provisions of company-sponsored plans may be outdated. Quite often, business agreements may become outmoded, mostly from sheer neglect. It is better to discover any inaccuracies that may exist at this time, rather than at some point in the future when it might be too late to change them to accomplish the purposes for which they were originally made.

Now complete the *Financial Firedrill* form as accurately as possible.

Analyzing Your Needs

You now have a clear picture of what you have and how it is set up. You have essentially frozen a period in time and prepared a balance sheet of your family's current assets. Now let us look at your financial picture, not in terms of what you now have or do not have, but in terms of your continuing family finances. Do you live on a monthly budget? How much do you save annually? What methods of savings or investing do you prefer? In the next section, you will detail how your present family finances are conducted and analyze for yourself those forms of savings or investments that you now prefer.

Next, you are asked to state, in terms of your own priorities, the importance of adequate funds for disability, retirement, college education, or a specific need. Space is provided to detail any educational needs that your family might have.

Formulating a Plan

Now for the all-important task of formulating a preliminary plan. First, look at what your income and capital needs will be to give you financial independence without working. At what age would you like to retire, and what do you estimate your required monthly retirement income should be? (Write those figures down.) What sources of funds do you now have to fulfill the above requirements? (Write that amount down.) What is the difference between what you have and what you'll need? How do you propose to make up the difference between what you hope to have and what your present assets will provide?

A thorough plan must cover all contingencies. Therefore, you should include provisions for income and capital needs during any possible future disability. In such a case, what would you estimate your required monthly income to be, and what sources of funds at present are expected to fulfill these needs and requirements?

Last, what income and capital needs do you foresee following your death? What will your surviving spouse and dependent children require for their income during any adjustment period, until your youngest child is self-supporting, and what will it take to provide a life income for your surviving spouse after your youngest child is self-supporting? How about lump-sum needs? Should there be money set aside for emergencies, to cancel an outstanding mortgage, to clear up any outstanding notes and taxes, or for college or graduate school education? What sources of income will help satisfy these needs? What government benefit or company pension plans can you count on? What other sources of capital do you have? What can you expect from insurance or from the proceeds of business agreements?

Testing and Implementing Your Plan

A reliable plan must be tested against the many factors beyond your control that can affect you and your family's future. In order for your plan to be reliable, it must be able to withstand unexpected problems, expenses, and taxes. Therefore, before you can begin to implement the plan, you must be aware of the legal and tax implications of what can happen to your property in the course of transferring it to your family in the event of your death. The taxes and cost consequences can prevent your property from going to your family in the way you want it to. A large percentage may go either to the government by way of taxes or for unnecessary probate costs and other expenses that could have been avoided by planning. Therefore, you have to test your plan to see if it maximizes your tax advantages and reduces, to the greatest extent possible, any costs or expenses that will have to be paid. To do this you have to know what the federal estate tax and state death taxes are. (See Chapter 11.) You have to know how to keep up with your fringe benefits and to get the most from your government-sponsored plans, as indicated in Chapter 18. If you are in business for yourself, you must take proper precautions to maximize the value of your business and eliminate death and disability problems.

There are specific ways that money can be set up for your children—and for your parents if they are dependent on you for their income.

What is really the best way to utilize life insurance to maximize its benefits for your family? How can one create tax-exempt wealth? And what are some of the specific tax-saving techniques that you can use to reduce your taxes?

Last, to whom do you turn for the proper advice and guidance to help you finalize and implement your plan? The answers to all these questions are contained in the following chapters. Armed with what information they contain, and counseled by the types of advisors recommended in this book, you will have taken a giant step toward future financial independence for your family and yourself.

Put Yourself on Your Own Payroll

Are you having a difficult time saving money? If you feel that all of your money is going out and none of it manages to end up in your savings, then you may have everyone on your payroll. The mortgage company or your landlord is on your payroll. The supermarket is on your payroll. The department store or clothing store is on your payroll. The government that collects your taxes is on your payroll. The utility company is on your payroll. In fact, just about everyone is on your payroll, with the exception of one very important person—yourself. Therefore, why not put yourself on your own payroll? If your plan calls for you to put an extra $25 a week into securities, insurance, or in the bank for a future home or real estate investment, then make certain that you do it. Put yourself at the top of your payroll, so that you don't overlook yourself when it comes time to pay your obligations. If you do, you'll find that there still might not be anything left at the end, but at least you will have provided the funds necessary to protect one of your most valuable assets—your interest in the future of your family and yourself.

How do you arrive at the amount to save each week or each month? The answer is: Save 'til it hurts! If you can easily afford to save $5 a week, save $10 next week—and add $5 each week until you reach what we like to call "the ouch point." Then level out the amount you save each week, *but you must keep the plan in force.*

No one is more important to you than your family (and yourself). So be certain to buy yourself and them a piece of the future each and every month. The day your systematic savings plan starts is the day you formally take your first step on the road to financial independence.

Appendix
YOUR FINANCIAL FIREDRILL follows.

PERSONAL DATA

Name		
Spouse's Name		
Address (Home)		Phone
Address (Business)		Phone

Consultants for Financial and Business Planning	Name	Address	Phone
Attorney			
Accountant			
Trust Officer			
Other Bank Officer			
Life Underwriter			
Insurance Agent			
Stock Broker			
Other			

Name	Date of Birth	Age	Occupation	Health Problems or Special Needs	No. and Age of Grandchildren	Amount of Support by Self/Spouse
Self						
Spouse						
Children and Grandchildren						
Your Family						
Spouse's Family						

Notes:

Citizenship	Husband — United States ☐ Other (Specify) ☐
	Wife — United States ☐ Other (Specify) ☐
Marital Status	Single ☐ Married ☐ Divorced ☐ Widowed ☐
	Date married, divorced, widowed:
	Any former marriages? ☐ Yes ☐ No
	Are you paying alimony? ☐ Yes ☐ No Child support? ☐ Yes ☐ No
Wills & Marital Agreements	Do you have a will? ☐ Yes ☐ No Date of will:
	Does your spouse have a will? ☐ Yes ☐ No Date of last will:
	Have you named guardians for children? ☐ Yes ☐ No Whom?
	Do you have a pre- or post-nuptial agreement? ☐ Yes ☐ No
Trusts	Have you created a living trust? ☐ Yes ☐ No Who is the trustee?
	Who are the beneficiaries?
	Has your spouse created a living trust? ☐ Yes ☐ No Who is the trustee?
	Who are the beneficiaries?

Custodianships	Have you or your spouse ever made a gift under the Uniform Gift to Minors Act?	☐ Yes	☐ No
	Who is the custodian?	Who are the donees?	
Trust Beneficiary	Are you or any members of your immediate family beneficiaries of a trust?	☐ Yes	☐ No
	If so, who?		
Gifts or Inheritances	Do you or your spouse expect to receive gifts or inheritances?	☐ Yes	☐ No
	If so, who? How much?	From whom?	
Social Security Numbers	Your social security number:		
	Your spouse's social security number:		
	Have social security benefits been reviewed lately?	☐ Yes	☐ No
Military Service	Did you serve in the military? ☐ Yes ☐ No	If so, from	to
	Any service-connected benefits? ☐ Yes ☐ No		
	Did your spouse serve in the military? ☐ Yes ☐ No	If so, from	to
	Any service-connected benefits? ☐ Yes ☐ No		

PROPERTY (EXCEPT FOR LIFE INSURANCE OR BUSINESS)

Item No.	Family Property	Fair Market Value and Titled Owner(s)						Present Indebtedness	Cost	When and How Acquired
		Husband	Wife	Children	Joint (survivor-ship rights)	Joint (no survivor-ship rights)	Com-munity Property			
REAL ESTATE										
( )	Residence									
( )	Seasonal Residence									
( )	Other Real Property									
( )										
( )										
SECURITIES (Marketable)										
( )	Corporate Bonds									
( )	Municipal Bonds									
( )	U.S. Govt. Bonds									
( )	Listed Stocks									
( )	Money Market Funds									
( )	Mutual Funds									
MISCELLANEOUS										
( )	Survivor Annuities									
( )										
( )										
( )										
MORTGAGES, ACCOUNTS RECEIVABLE, NOTES (Unpaid Balance Due You)										
( )	Mortgages Owned									
( )	Accounts Receivable									
( )	Notes Receivable									
	Notes:									

Item No.	Family Property	Fair Market Value and Titled Owner(s)						Present Indebtedness	Cost	When and How Acquired
		Husband	Wife	Children	Joint (survivorship rights)	Joint (no survivorship rights)	Community Property			
	PERSONAL PROPERTY									
( )	Household									
( )	Auto(s)									
( )	Boat(s)									
( )	Jewelry-Furs									
( )	Collection-Hobby Equip.									
( )	Interests in Trusts									
( )	Royalties, Patents, Copyrights									
( )	Other									
( )										
	CASH OR EQUIVALENT									
( )	Savings Accounts, Average Balance (Include certificate of deposit and life insurance dividend accumulations)									
( )	Checking Accounts, Average Balance									
( )	Ready Cash									
	MISCELLANEOUS PROPERTY									
( )										
( )										
( )										

LIFE INSURANCE

Item #	( )	( )	( )	( )	( )	( )	( )
Policy Numbers							
Name of Insurance Company							
Issue Age							
Insured							
Owner of Policy							
Type of Policy							
Premium Cost and Mode							
Cash Value							
Extra Benefits (e.g., waiver of premium, accidental death, etc.)							
Amount of Base Policy							
Dividends (Value & Option)							
Term Rider(s)							
Loan Outstanding							
Net Amount Payable at Death							
Beneficiaries and Settlement Option Elected							
1st to							
2nd to							

Item #	( )	( )	( )	( )	( )	( )
Policy Numbers						
Name of Insurance Company						
Issue Age						
Insured						
Owner of Policy						
Type of Policy						
Premium Cost and Mode						
Cash Value						
Extra Benefits (e.g., waiver of premium, accidental death, etc.)						
Amount of Base Policy						
Dividends (Value & Option)						
Term Rider(s)						
Loan Outstanding						
Net Amount Payable at Death						
Beneficiaries and Settlement Option Elected						
1st to						
2nd to						

HEALTH INSURANCE

Disability Income	Policy #1	Policy #2	Policy #3	Policy #4
Disability Income Policy Numbers				
Name of Insurance Company				
Insured				
Owner of Policy Premium Payer				
Premium Cost and Mode				
Type of Continuance or Renewal Provision				
Definition of Disability				
MONTHLY DISABILITY INCOME				
Accident				
Sickness				
PARTIAL DISABILITY				
Accident				
Sickness				
WAITING PERIOD				
Accident				
Sickness				
BENEFIT PERIOD				
Accident				
Sickness				
Supplementary Benefits				

HEALTH INSURANCE (Continued)

Medical Expense	Policy #1	Policy #2	Policy #3	Policy #4
Medical Expense Policy Numbers				
Name of Insurance Company or Service Type Plan				
Insured				
Owner of Policy				
Premium Cost and Mode				
Type of Continuance or Renewal Provision				
Termination Date for Child Coverage				
BASIC HOSPITAL				
Room Rate				
No. of Days				
Hospital Extras				
Other Benefits				
SURGICAL				
Maximum				
Type of Schedule				
MAJOR MEDICAL				
Deductible				
Percentage Participation (Coinsurance)				
Inside Limits				
Overall Maximum				

BUSINESS INTEREST

Full Legal Name _____ Phone No. _____

Address _____

Business now operates as

☐ Proprietorship ☐ Corporation, Fiscal Year Ending _____

☐ Partnership ☐ Subchapter S Corporation

Principal Business activity is:

In what year did this business begin operation?

Date of incorporation, if it began other than as a corporation?

What is your function in the business?

Do you have an employment contract?

PRESENT OWNERS

		Corporation		Other
(A) You _____	Owns ___ % common	___ % preferred	___ % _____
(B) _____	Owns ___ % common	___ % preferred	___ % _____
(C) _____	Owns ___ % common	___ % preferred	___ % _____
(D) _____	Owns ___ % common	___ % preferred	___ % _____
(E) _____	Owns ___ % common	___ % preferred	___ % _____

Do you want your business interest retained or sold if you

Retire? _____ Become Disabled? _____ Die? _____

IF RETAINED

Who will own your interest and how will he (she, or they) acquire it?

_____

Who will replace you in your job?

_____

IF SOLD

Who will buy your interest?

_____

How is purchase price to be determined?

_____

How will the buyer(s) pay for it?

_____

Is this already arranged by legal agreement?

_____

What is your estimate of the lowest price for which the entire business might be sold as a going concern today?

What is the lowest price you would accept for your interest today?

BUSINESS INTEREST (Continued)

If you were not an owner, what is your estimate of the highest price you would pay today for the entire business as a going concern?

What is the highest price you would pay to buy the interest of your co-owners today?

What is the average business indebtedness? _____

Estimate of highest it has ever been? _____

Estimate of lowest it has ever been? _____

Are there any patents or special processes used but not owned by the business?

If yes, who owns what, and under what terms is each used or leased?

What are the prospects for growth, sale, merger, or going public?

SURVIVOR CONTROL (letters in parentheses refer to owners named above):

IF (A) DIES	IF (B) DIES	IF (C) DIES	IF (D) DIES	IF (E) DIES
B wants ___ % control	A wants ___ % control	A wants ___ % control	A wants ___ % control	A wants ___ % control
C wants ___ % control	C wants ___ % control	B wants ___ % control	B wants ___ % control	B wants ___ % control
D wants ___ % control	D wants ___ % control	D wants ___ % control	C wants ___ % control	C wants ___ % control
E wants ___ % control	E wants ___ % control	E wants ___ % control	E wants ___ % control	D wants ___ % control
* wants ___ % control	* wants ___ % control	* wants ___ % control	* wants ___ % control	* wants ___ % control

*New owner to acquire control is:

BUSINESS ATTORNEY

Name _____

Address _____

_____

Phone _____

BUSINESS ACCOUNTANT

Name _____

Address _____

_____

Phone _____

EMPLOYEE CENSUS DATA

Listing below includes: ☐ Key Employees Only ☐ All Employees

	Name			Date of Birth			Date Employed			Earnings		Occupation		Marital Status
Sex	First	Middle	Last	Mo.	Day	Year	Mo.	Day	Year	Amount	Payable	Title	Key Person	
1														
2														
3														
4														
5														
6														
7														
8														
9														
10														
11														
12														
13														
14														

	Sex	Name			Date of Birth			Date Employed			Earnings		Occupation		Marital Status
		First	Middle	Last	Mo.	Day	Year	Mo.	Day	Year	Amount	Payable	Title	Key Person	
15															
16															
17															
18															
19															
20															
21															
22															
23															
24															
25															
26															
27															
28															
29															

BENEFITS ARISING FROM CONTINUED EMPLOYMENT
PART I

You _____

Employer _____

Who could provide specific information that you do not have?

Title: _____

Phone: _____

Department: _____

	Benefit Is Currently Provided	*Complete Description or Contract Is in Possession of Whom?*
EMPLOYEE GROUP INSURANCE		
Life	_____	_____
Survivorship Annuity	_____	_____
Dependent Life	_____	_____
Accidental Death	_____	_____
Travel Accident	_____	_____
Dismemberment	_____	_____
Hospitalization	_____	_____
Surgical Expense Benefits	_____	_____

	Benefit Is Currently Provided	Complete Description or Contract Is in Possession of Whom?
EMPLOYEE GROUP INSURANCE (Continued)		
Major Medical		
Dental Care		
Disability Income		
Legal Services—Prepaid by Employer		
CONTINGENT FUTURE TAX EXCLUDABLE BENEFITS		
Sick Pay		
Employer-paid Health Care		
BARGAIN PURCHASE, USE AND ENJOYMENT		
Split-Dollar Life Insurance		
Company Car Provided		
Club Memberships		
OTHER (specify)		

34

BENEFITS ARISING FROM CONTINUED EMPLOYMENT
PART II

QUALIFIED PLAN ☐ PENSION ☐ PROFIT SHARING ☐ NONE

Amount of Current Death Benefit $ _____ Estimated Pension at Age 65 $ _____

Beneficiary: Primary _____ Contingent _____

Percent Contributed by Employer _____ % by Employee _____ %

Death Benefit Funded by Life Insurance $ _____ Other $ _____

Mode of Settlement _____

HR-10 PLAN ☐ YES _____ ☐ NO

Type of Funding _____

Annual Contribution   Total Contributions   Date Started _____   No. of Employees
(Self) $ _____   (Self) $ _____   Covered _____

Death Benefit $ _____   Primary   Contingent
Beneficiary _____   Beneficiary _____

Mode of Settlement _____

IRA PLAN   YOU ☐ YES ☐ NO   SPOUSE ☐ YES ☐ NO

Death Benefit $ _____   Primary   Contingent
Beneficiary _____   Beneficiary _____

Mode of Settlement _____

SPLIT-DOLLAR PLAN ☐ YES _____ ☐ NO

Describe Plan of Insurance, Death Benefit, Ownership, and Beneficiary _____

_____

TAX-DEFERRED ANNUITY PLAN   □ YES   □ NO

Employer: □ Public School   □ Other _____

Death Benefit $ _____

Primary Beneficiary _____

Contingent Beneficiary _____

DEFERRED COMPENSATION AGREEMENT   □ YES   □ NO

Describe Provisions and Funding _____

_____

_____

STOCK BONUS, STOCK OPTION, STOCK PURCHASE, THRIFT PLANS, SHADOW STOCK   □ YES   □ NO

Describe Provisions _____

_____

_____

DEATH BENEFIT ONLY (salary continuation) PLAN   □ YES   □ NO

Describe Provisions _____

_____

_____

FAMILY INCOME

	You	Spouse	Dependent Children
ANNUAL INCOME			
(1) Salary, Bonus, etc.	$	$	$
(2) Income as Business Owner (self-employment)			
(3) Real Estate (net after taxes, etc.)			
(4) Dividends:			
(a) Closed Corporation Stock			
(b) Investments			
(5) Interest			
(a) Bonds			
(b) Savings Accounts			
(c) Money Market Funds			
(6) Trust Income			
(7) Other Sources			
TOTAL ANNUAL INCOME	$	$	$
INCOME TAX (Federal and State)			
Last Year	$	$	$
Quarterly Estimated Tax This Year	$	$	$
FUTURE INCOME			
Estimated Annual Income Next Year	$	$	$
Five Years	$	$	$

FAMILY FINANCES

Do you live on a monthly budget? ☐ YES ☐ NO How much?			

How much do you
save annually? In what form? Why?

How much do you
invest annually? In what form? Why?

How much do you think you should be able to save and invest annually?

For what?

In order to assist you to accumulate funds would you enter into any of
the following plans:

	YES	NO	Check if Now Using
Allotment from salary	☐	☐	☐
Contractual mutual fund plan	☐	☐	☐
Cash value life insurance plan	☐	☐	☐
Money market fund or certificates	☐	☐	☐

On a scale of from one to five, with one being slight preference and five being
substantial preference, rate, in the order of YOUR preference, the following
methods of saving or investing:

	1	2	3	4	5	Check if Now Using
Savings Account	☐	☐	☐	☐	☐	☐
Cash Value Life Insurance	☐	☐	☐	☐	☐	☐
Government Bonds	☐	☐	☐	☐	☐	☐
Corporate Bonds	☐	☐	☐	☐	☐	☐
Tax-exempt Bonds	☐	☐	☐	☐	☐	☐
Mutual Funds	☐	☐	☐	☐	☐	☐
Money Market Funds	☐	☐	☐	☐	☐	☐
Variable Annuities	☐	☐	☐	☐	☐	☐
Common Stocks	☐	☐	☐	☐	☐	☐
Real Estate	☐	☐	☐	☐	☐	☐
Tax Shelters (oil, cattle, etc.)	☐	☐	☐	☐	☐	☐
Other (specify)	☐	☐	☐	☐	☐	☐

(Continued)

FAMILY FINANCES (Continued)

Compare, in terms of your own priorities, the importance of adequate funds in order to do the following (indicate ranking by first, second, etc.):

Enjoy a comfortable retirement. _____

Take care of yourself and family during a period
of long-term disability. _____

Provide college educations for all children. _____

Take care of your family in the event of your death. _____

Any others that are important to you. _____

_____

_____

OBJECTIVES REQUIRING
ADDITIONAL INCOME OR CAPITAL

Education Fund

Name of Child	Age	Number of Years Required	Estimate of Fund Required
			$
			$
			$
			$
Other (specify)			$
			$

INCOME AND CAPITAL NEEDS FOR
FINANCIAL INDEPENDENCE WITHOUT WORKING

At what age would you like to retire? _____

Estimated Required Monthly Income . . . . $ _____

Expected Sources of Funds (check those now expected) ☐

    Social Security Benefits . . . . ☐

    Other Government Pension . . . . ☐

    Self-Employed Retirement Plan (Keogh) . . . . ☐

    Pension Plan . . . . ☐

    Profit-Sharing Plan . . . . ☐

    Tax-Deferred Annuity . . . . ☐

    Nonqualified Deferred Compensation . . . . ☐

    Nonqualified Annuity . . . . ☐

    Life Insurance Cash Values . . . . ☐

    Independent Income (from p. 314) . . . . ☐

    Other (specify) _____ ☐

Check sources of independent income (see p. 314)

    (1) _____ , (2) _____ , (3) _____ , (4) (a) _____ ,

    (4) (b) _____ , (5) (a) _____ , (5) (b) _____ ,

    (5) (c) _____ , (6) _____ , (7) _____ .

Will income from any of the sources above decrease or terminate in the event

that either you or your spouse dies after it begins? _____

Will basic health care and major medical coverage be continued after

retirement?   ☐ Yes   ☐ No

INCOME AND CAPITAL NEEDS DURING DISABILITY

Estimated Required Monthly Income . . . . $ _____

Expected Sources of Funds (check those now expected)

Social Security Benefits . . . . ☐

Other Government Pension . . . . ☐

Self-Employed Retirement Plan (Keogh) . . . . ☐

Pension Plan . . . . ☐

Profit-Sharing Plan . . . . ☐

Tax-Deferred Annuity . . . . ☐

Nonqualified Deferred Compensation . . . . ☐

Salary Continuation Plan ☐

Disability Insurance ☐

Independent Income (from p. 314) . . . . ☐

Other (specify) _____ ☐

Check sources of independent income (see p. 314)

(1) _____ , (2) _____ , (3) _____ , (4) (a) _____ ,

(4) (b) _____ , (5) (a) _____ , (5) (b) _____ ,

(5) (c) _____ , (6) _____ , (7) _____ .

Estimated Required Monthly Income if Spouse
Were Disabled . . . . $ _____

Expected Sources of Funds (check those now expected)

Disability Insurance . . . . ☐

Other (specify) _____ ☐

Will basic health care and major medical benefits be continued
after disability?　　　☐ Yes　　　☐ No

INCOME AND CAPITAL NEEDS FOLLOWING DEATH

For surviving spouse and dependent children following
your death—

INCOME NEEDS

What is your estimate of the monthly income which
will be needed during the following periods:

(1) Adjustment period (adjustment of standards
of living without you—the breadwinner—
in the transitional period following your
death)   (_____) years . . . . $ _____

(2) Until your youngest child is self-supporting . . $ _____

(3) To provide life income for surviving spouse
after your youngest child is self-supporting . . $ _____

CAPITAL NEEDS

Emergency Fund . . . . $ _____

Mortgage Cancellation Fund (if surviving spouse
will continue to live in family house) . . . . $ _____

Notes and Loans Payable . . . . $ _____

Accrued Taxes (income, real estate, etc.) . . . . $ _____

Education Expense . . . . $ _____

TOTAL . . . . $ ══════════

Will Basic Health Care and Major Medical Coverage
be continued?   ☐ Yes   ☐ No

INCOME AND CAPITAL NEEDS FOLLOWING DEATH (Continued)

Expected Sources of INCOME (check those now expected)

Social Security Benefits . . . . ☐

Other Government Benefits . . . . ☐

Self-Employed Retirement Plan (Keogh) . . . . ☐

Pension Plan . . . . ☐

Profit-Sharing Plan . . . . ☐

Nonqualified Deferred Compensation Plan . . . . ☐

Salary Continuation Plan . . . . ☐

Independent Income (from p. 314) . . . . ☐

Other (specify) _____ ☐

Check sources of independent income (see p. 314)

(1) _____, (2) _____, (3) _____, (4) (a) _____, (4) (b) _____, (5) (a) _____,

(5) (b) _____, (5) (c) _____, (6) _____, (7) _____.

43

Expected Sources of CAPITAL (check those now expected)

Group Life Insurance . . . . ☐

Personal Life Insurance . . . . ☐

Real Estate . . . . ☐

Proceeds of Sale of Business Interests by Agreement . . . ☐

Other (specify) _____ ☐

For You and Children Following Spouse's Death

Additional Income Needs . . . . $_____

Source (specify) _____

Capital Needs . . . . $_____

Source (specify) _____

LIABILITIES

Loans or Other Obligations Outstanding	Creditor	Amount	Insured	Secured

Any other liabilities your estate may be called upon to pay?

Do you foresee any future liabilities (business expansion, new home, etc.)?

ADDITIONAL FACTORS AFFECTING YOUR PLAN

Have you or your spouse ever made substantial gifts to family members, to educational institutions, to tax-exempt beneficiaries? (give details) _____

Special bequests intended, including charity _____

Is your spouse good at handling money? _____

If left on his or her own, would spouse's judgment and emotional stability serve the best interests of the family? _____

What is your estimate of the emotional maturity of your children? _____

What are your feelings about the possible remarriage of your spouse? _____

Tax consideration aside, in what manner would you want your estate to be distributed? _____

WILLS, TRUSTS, LIFE INSURANCE AND TAKING TITLE TO PROPERTY

How to Use These Planning Tools and Techniques to Protect Your Family and Preserve Your Property

6

Do You Really Need a Will?

Do you really need a will? What can a will do for you in your particular circumstances?

A will states what you want to happen to your property when you die. *Without* a will, you *cannot* say:

1. *Who* gets your property,
2. *Who* will be your executor,
3. *Who* will be the guardian of your children,
4. How *much* each beneficiary will receive,
5. *What* asset goes to each person,
6. *When* each person gets his or her share,
7. *How* (outright or in trust) property will be received,
8. How your *executor* is to minimize your taxes,
9. If, or how much, your favorite *charity* is to receive,
10. If, or how much, your sibling or nonrelated friend, or employee is to receive.

With a will, all these objectives are possible.

Let's see what can happen where there is no will. Mark and Cathy were in their early thirties and had two healthy, normal children, Kim (9) and Ted (7). Mark had a good job, and Cathy stayed in their attractive middle-income home and raised the children. Without any advance warning, Cathy contracted a blood disease and died within six months. Four months later, Mark was killed in an automobile accident.

As soon as she heard of Mark's death, Cathy's sister took Ted and Kim home to live with her. Three weeks later, when Mark's brother had the children visiting with him, he and his wife decided the children should remain with them. He, therefore, refused to return them to Cathy's sister. A court fight took place between Cathy's sister and Mark's brother to decide with whom the children would live.

Meanwhile, since neither Cathy nor Mark had a will, the court appointed a friend of Mark's lawyer to serve as executor of Mark's estate. He had a difficult time locating Mark's property. Mark had money scattered in different banks, and only he and Cathy knew where everything was—and nothing was in writing. After considerable time and expense, the court determined that the children should remain with Mark's brother, who was formally named their guardian. But it still was necessary for Mark's brother to appear in court whenever he needed money for the children.

As a result of the conflict and competition between the two families for the children's affections, not to mention the trauma of losing their parents, both children developed serious emotional problems that remained with them for many years. If Mark and Cathy each had made a will, had designated the person or persons whom they wished to act as guardian for their children, and then had informed the guardian(s) where their property was located, many of these unfortunate problems could have been eliminated.

Even where there are no children, it is important to have a will. In Larry's case, his father had left the family business to him, and he was running it quite efficiently. There was more than enough money available to take very good care of Larry and his only sister, Valerie. This was in keeping with his father's wishes, even though his father had left the business entirely to Larry.

However, circumstances change; when Larry was in his late forties, he met someone, married and had a child. When Larry died shortly after the birth of his son, everyone was surprised to learn that a successful businessman like Larry had never made a will. The most surprised person was Larry's sister, Valerie, because under the laws of Larry's state, his wife and son shared equally in his estate while his sister, Valerie, who was not on the friendliest terms with Larry's wife, received nothing. She was now completely cut off from her sole source of income—the business that had been her father's. The business was now being run for the benefit of her brother's new wife and infant son, certainly not the result desired or ever contemplated by Larry or his father.

Disadvantages of Intestacy

Cases similar to these occur every day. The unfortunate results dramatically illustrate the importance of a will. Actually, everyone has a will; if you don't draw one, your state—through its intestacy laws—will draw the will you failed to make. This absence of a valid will is called *intestacy*. The laws of the state in which you live will determine automatically, and regardless of what you may have wanted, the disposition of your property.

Typically, intestacy laws spell out certain preferred classes of survivors. Usually, if you die survived by a spouse, that person will receive the bulk of your estate. Any children and other descendants share what is left. They will divide your estate in the proportions and manner specified by your state's intestacy laws. Other relatives or organizations you care about may receive nothing, as was the case of Valerie.

Generally, if no spouse, children, or other descendants survive you, your parents, brothers, and sisters will receive equal shares of your estate. (One quick and inexpensive way of finding out how your state's intestacy laws work is to visit your local bank's trust department. They generally have free brochures as well as a helpful staff that can explain, in general terms, the intestacy laws of your state.)

Without a will, you cannot direct that any of your property go to a nonrelated individual or a charity. You have lost control not only over who will receive your property at your death but also over how or when they will receive it. You have forfeited the privilege of naming a personal representative to guide the disposition of your estate and make sure things go as you wanted them to. The court-appointed administrator of your estate will have minimum flexibility in dealing with your assets or your loved ones.

Without a will you cannot name guardians for minor or disabled children, and your children will be in the same position as Ted and Kim were when their surviving parent died. If you let the state draw your will, you give up the right to minimize the administrative expenses, and federal, state, and estate death-tax shrinkage through the use of certain deductions, exclusions, and various planning techniques.

A valid will—regardless of how large or how small your estate—allows you, rather than the state, to control the disposition of your personal property.

What Is Probate Property?

Your *probate estate* is the real and personal property you own in your own name. It is property that you personally have the right to transfer according to the terms of the will that you write and which takes effect at your death. Essentially, probate property consists of the assets and interests in property (tangible or intangible) that you own solely in your own name.

There is some property that will not be affected by your will. This is commonly called *nonprobate property*. For example, life insurance is nonprobate property because it passes by contract and not under your will. Regardless of what your will says, life insurance proceeds pass directly to the beneficiary you have named in your policy (unless you have named your estate as beneficiary, a designation that is rarely recommended). Likewise, jointly held property with rights of survivorship and property passing under certain employee benefit plans such as pension, profit-sharing, or 401(k) are nonprobate assets. They will not be probate property because you cannot dispose of those assets by will. They pass according to the terms of the plan and the beneficiary designation signed at work.

Should You Prepare Your Own Will?

Why not prepare your own will? There are many reasons why home-made wills are good examples of the old adage "He who has himself for an attorney has a fool for a client." (Of course, if you are the rare person who can buy a book on how to perform a do-it-yourself kidney transplant, and then do it, be our guest.)

No matter how small your estate or how simple your desire, it's worth the expense to employ a qualified attorney. The complexity and interrelationships of tax, property, domestic relations, and other laws make a homemade will a frivolous, dangerous, and highly expensive way to cut corners. The ultimate cost of such a will can be much greater than one drawn by a qualified attorney, but it will be your heirs, and not you, who pay the price. Consider the case of Roberta who wanted to be certain that she treated her two daughters, Tracy and Joanne, as fairly and equally as possible.

Roberta's husband had died some years before, leaving her with some insurance proceeds, a home, and a life insurance policy on her life on which she continued to pay the premiums. When her daughter Tracy was married, Roberta lent Tracy and her husband, Joe, $20,000. Before the loan to Tracy, both Tracy and Joanne were named as co-beneficiaries of the policy so that each would receive $10,000.

Roberta drafted her own will. Wanting to be fair, she first made a provision in her will that Tracy and Joe did not have to pay back the $20,000 she loaned to them for their home. She then provided in her will that since she had forgiven the $20,000 that Tracy owed on the house, she was now going to leave Joanne the full $20,000 from her life insurance, and not just the $10,000 that the policy presently provided. Roberta, despite her good intentions, could not have made a worse mess of her affairs.

When Roberta died, Tracy and Joe were separated and in the process of getting divorced. By forgiving the $20,000 owed on the house jointly by Tracy and Joe, Roberta handed Joe an instant profit of $10,000, since the laws of their state held that the property being owned jointly by Tracy and Joe was half Joe's. Therefore, when the $20,000 mortgage was marked "satisfied," Joe, the soon to be ex-son-in-law, was $10,000 richer.

As indicated, the life insurance policy was a separate contract between Roberta and the insurance company. The insurance company was bound by law to pay the $20,000 equally to Tracy and Joanne because this was what the beneficiary designation in the policy said. While Roberta had made other provisions in her will, she had neglected to change the beneficiaries on her life insurance policy—the only change that would have had a legal effect on who would receive the insurance proceeds.

The $20,000 owed on the home was still an asset of Roberta's estate and was taxed by the state for inheritance tax purposes, when this might have been avoided had Roberta consulted a qualified attorney.

How Much Should A Will Cost?

What should it cost to have a will drawn by someone who knows how to do it? That depends: The more assets, the more complex your dispositive desires, and the more facts that have to be considered, the more money you have to pay. Quite often, a two- or three-page will may be adequate, and you should be billed approximately $150. In many other cases, the will may be much longer, and the bill higher, because of the time the attorney must spend in drafting it. Don't forget: Your will must not only effectively accomplish the personal objectives you specified with respect to how your assets are to be distributed, but must also take into consideration the federal and state income, estate and gift tax laws, and should be coordinated with your nonprobate assets.

A properly prepared will must provide a plan for distributing your assets at the time and in the manner you want them distributed. It must also consider the needs of your beneficiaries as well as the federal and state laws which impact upon dispositive plans. The document must be unambiguous and completely describe what you want accomplished. Furthermore, the will must be flexible enough to take into consideration any of the many changes in family circumstances which might occur after you sign your will. For instance, what happens if a beneficiary dies before or at the same time you do?

Ask—no, *demand*—that the attorney state his or her hourly charge *before* beginning the work—or agree on a total fee in advance. Just like any other contract for services to be performed, ask the attorney to put the agreement in writing so there will be no misunderstanding.

Changing Your Will

Change is one thing that is certain. Your feelings about your property and the people you want to receive your property will change—and so will they—and their needs. Fortunately, a will is inoperative until you die. Therefore, you can change it any time until then.

Why change your will? Modification should be considered if your health or your beneficiary's health or financial circumstances have changed. A birth, a death, a marriage, or a divorce all significantly change the circumstances that were operative at the time you signed your will. Furthermore, every year the tax law changes in a significant manner, your will should, at the very least, be reexamined.

Using a Codicil

How can you change your will? Changing the will can be as simple as having the attorney draft a *codicil*. A codicil is a legal means of modifying an existing will without rewriting the entire document. It is typically used when the will needs only minor modifications. A codicil is often a single-page document that reaffirms everything you have already stated in your will except the specific provisions that need to be changed. Just like your will, your codicil should be typed, signed, and properly witnessed according to the requirement of your state's laws.

If substantial changes are needed, you should have a new will. You may want to have a new will drafted even though you have not made substantial changes. For example, if you decide not to leave property to someone who is named in your original will, you may want to avoid offending the omitted beneficiary by destroying the old will after a new will is drawn and properly executed.

How to Revoke a Will

You can revoke a will by (1) making a later will which expressly revokes prior wills; (2) making a codicil which expressly revokes any wills; (3) making a later will which is inconsistent with a former will; and (4) physically mutilating, burning, tearing, or defacing the will with the intention of revoking it.

Automatic revocation

Your will may be automatically revoked or modified by state law if certain events occur. The most common such events are: (1) marriage, (2) divorce, (3) birth or adoption of a child, and (4) slaying. For instance, if you legally divorce your spouse, in many states all provisions in your will relating to your spouse become inoperative. Or if you were single when you made your will and then marry, automatically, regardless of what you do or do not say, your spouse has a right to receive that portion of your estate that would have been received had you died without a valid will. Your spouse has a right to his/her intestate share—unless your will actually gives your spouse a larger share.

If you do not provide for a child born or adopted after you wrote your will, in many states, the state "writes" that child into the will for you. Your state may provide that a child born or adopted after you wrote your will will receive that share of your estate not passing to your spouse that would have been given to the child if you did not have a will (unless it appears in the will by specific direction that you intended that child should not benefit under your will).

Almost all states have *slayers' statutes*. These laws forbid anyone who participates in a willful and unlawful killing from acquiring property as a result. In other words, state law automatically writes slayers out of wills.

Right of Election

You may not like it, but many states give a surviving spouse what is known as a "right of election." In other words, your surviving spouse might have a right to "take against your will"—to take a specified portion of your estate regardless of what you did or did not give your spouse in your will. One state, for example, allows a surviving spouse to demand at least that share that would have been allowed had the decedent died without a valid will. For example, if an individual leaves his entire estate to his son, absent a valid pre-or-postnuptial agreement to the contrary, his wife can take the same one-third share of his estate she would have received had her husband died intestate.

Some states even give these "rights of election" to children. There are ways to avoid these rights of election, but they cannot be accomplished by your executor. You must do the planning together with competent counsel.

Letter of Instructions

You may have specific instructions for your executor to comply with, following your death, but that cannot be properly included in your will. We recommend that you prepare a *letter of instructions* to leave with your will. A letter of instructions is a private, informal, nonlegal document, usually left with immediate relatives or the named executor. People frequently have thoughts they want to convey and instructions they wish to have carried out that cannot properly be included in their wills. These suggestions or recommendations should be included in such a *letter of instructions* in the form of an informal memorandum separate from the will. (*Note:* No bequests should be made in this letter of instructions since such documents have no legal standing.) Make several copies of the letter and keep one at home and the others in the hands of the estate's executor or an attorney or an accountant to be mailed or delivered to beneficiaries at the appropriate time.

A letter of instructions might provide directions with respect to (1) location of the will and other documents; (2) funeral and burial instructions (often a will is not opened until after the funeral); (3) suggestions or recommendations as to the continuation, sale, or liquidation of a business (it is easier to freely suggest a course of action in such a letter than it is in a will); (4) personal matters that the testator might prefer not to be made public in a will, such as statements that might sound unkind or inconsiderate but would prove of great value to the executor (for example, comments about a spendthrift spouse or a reckless son); (5) legal and accounting services (executors are free, however, to choose their own counsel—not even testators can bind them in that selection); and (6) an explanation of the actions taken in the will which may help avoid litigation (for instance, "I left only $1000 to my son, John, because . . ." or "I made no provisions for my oldest daughter, Melissa, because . . .").

Anatomical Gifts

Many people desire to make a gift of one or more organs after death, and they should be familiar with the procedures involved. Conversely, anyone who is strongly against a gift of one or more organs after death should be protected from violation of his or her desires by others. The Uniform Anatomical Gifts Act (UAGA) has been enacted in whole or in part in every state and in the District of Columbia. Its purpose is to encourage various types of organ donations and to avoid inconsistency among the various jurisdictions.

The UAGA provides that any person over 18 may donate his or her entire body or any one or more of its parts. The donation can be made to any hospital, surgeon, physician, medical or dental school, or various organ banks or storage facilities. Organ gifts can be made for education, research, therapy, or transplants. These gifts become effective at death and can be made by will. The act also provides that no body or organ gift may be made if there is an objection to such a gift expressed either by will or in some other document.

There are two ways a gift can be made under the UAGA. One is for the donor to designate a specific individual to receive the gift. For instance, a person might specify that one eye be given to a blind sister. A hierarchy of donees can be established, and various body parts can be specified to go to certain donees.

A second way is by granting persons other than the decedent the power to make the gift. In other words, a family member can donate a person's body or organs.

A potential donor or donor's representative should contact the prospective donee with respect to specific requirements for the gift. Form 1 has been prepared by the Real Property, Probate and Trust Law Section of the ABA.*

Tips on Wills

Both you and your spouse should have wills. Those wills should be coordinated. Your attorney should examine documents relating to all your assets, including your life insurance policies, the deeds to jointly held property such as your home and bank accounts, and your certificates for company-sponsored pension and group insurance benefits, before your will is drafted. A will should not be drawn in a vacuum. It must consider and be tied to the values and ownership arrangement of your assets, your overall employee benefit program, and your personal financial plans.

You may have designated a person in your will to take charge of the probate process. That person is called an *executor.*

Don't name your attorney as your executor merely because he or she is an attorney. In fact, there are a number of reasons why the attorney who drafts your will should *not* be named as your executor: (1) if you do,

---

*For more information on anatomical gifts, see *The Executor's Manual,* Doubleday and Company, Inc., Garden City, New York 1986.

Form 1

I, _____ of _____, _____
make the following statement regarding anatomical gifts which I have checked
and initialed:

SPECIFIC GIFTS

ENTIRE BODY

☐ I give my entire body, for purposes of anatomical study, to _____
_____ . If, for any reason, _____ does not accept this gift, I
give my body to _____, for purposes of anatomical study.

GIFTS TO INDIVIDUALS

☐ I give my ___(part or parts)___ to _____, if needed by him or her for
purposes of transplantation or therapy.
☐ I give my ___(part or parts)___ to _____, if needed by him or her for
purposes of transplantation or therapy.

GIFTS TO INSTITUTIONS AND PHYSICIANS

☐ I give my ___(part or parts)___ to ___(name of hospital, bank, storage facility, or physician)___ , for purposes of
research, advancement of science, therapy, or transplantation.
☐ I give my ___(part or parts)___ to ___(name of hospital, bank, storage facility, or physician)___ , for purposes of
research, advancement of science, therapy, or transplantation.

PROSTHETIC DEVICES

☐ I give my ___(type of prosthetic device)___ to ___(name of hospital)___ for critical evaluation,
study, and research.

INTENTION

☐ If any anatomical gift cannot be effectuated because of the donee's non-exis-
tence, inability, or unwillingness to accept it, I request that one of the authorized persons make anatomical donations in a manner consistent with my
desires expressed in this statement.

☐ I express my desire not to make anatomical gifts under any circumstances. It
is my wish that no part be used for transplantation, therapy, study, or research.
I request that my personal representative and next of kin respect my wishes.

THIS STATEMENT INCORPORATES ALL OF THE PROVISIONS ON THE REVERSE OF IT.

Signed this _____ day of _____ , 19_____ , at _____ .

_____   _____
Witness   Witness

Form 1 *(continued)*

PRIORITY OF DONATION

A gift of any part to an individual recipient for therapy or transplantation shall take precedence over a gift of that part to any other donee.

INSTRUCTIONS

If I have made any written instructions regarding the burial, cremation or other disposition of my body, I direct that any donee take possession of my body subject to those instructions, if that donee has actual knowledge of those instructions. If there is any conflict between the statements made in this document and any of those instructions, my wishes regarding anatomical gifts shall be given preference over my instructions regarding the disposition of my body.

COUNTERPARTS

I may be signing more than one statement regarding anatomical gifts. I intend that only signed documents be effective and that no person shall give any effect to any photocopy or other reproduction of a signed document.

DEFINITIONS

The terms "bank or storage facility," "hospital," "part," and "physician" have the same meaning which the Uniform Anatomical Gifts Act accords to them. The term "authorized persons" means the persons authorized to make donations under the Uniform Anatomical Gifts Act in the order or priority provided in that Act.

WARNING

This form is designed to be used with the advice of an attorney. It has been drafted in accordance with the provisions of the Uniform Anatomical Gifts Act. Because the law regarding anatomical gifts may vary in each state, attorneys advising on use of this form should be familiar with the law of the relevant jurisdiction.

[This form has been adapted from that of the Real Property, Probate and Trust Law Section of the American Bar Association.]

your beneficiary can't fire him; (2) there can't be armslength bargaining with regard to legal fees if he hires himself or his law partner as the estate's attorney; and (3) you will have no one to look over his shoulder to make certain that his duties are being properly performed. (There may be circumstances under which your attorney might be the only logical choice, but never let the attorney make that decision.) We feel that it is unethical for an attorney to name himself or herself without your knowledge and full understanding of the implications of that action.

Keep your will where it can be found quickly. The person you have named as executor should know where it can be found. Make sure your attorney, or perhaps some other advisor, has a copy.

We recommend that *you* keep the original of your will. A bank safe deposit box is the best place (but be sure local law and custom will not unduly delay access to your executor). If your will (the original) is retained by the attorney who drafted it, it will be awkward for your executor to exercise the right to select another attorney.

Flexibility and control are two of the most important attributes of a good estate plan, and *you*—rather than those you hire to accomplish your objectives—should keep them.

Don't name anyone as guardian or executor without conferring with them first. Both jobs involve awesome responsibilities, are highly time consuming, can be extremely complicated, and, if handled improperly, can be personally costly to your executor. Typically, the best person to name as executor is your primary beneficiary. That person has the most to lose if things are not done right and the most to gain from efficient and creative estate administration.

If you do not have a close friend or relative who is able and willing to handle that responsibility, choose a bank or trust company to act as executor. A professional executor will give your family the benefit of a competent and impartial personal representative to handle the estate's affairs.

Consider that an individual named as executor can hire a bank or trust company to help with the administrative, investment, and other managerial and record-keeping functions of an executor—and fire that bank if services are not satisfactory.

In every case, you should name a back-up executor, guardian, and trustee, in case the party you have named for some reason will not or cannot serve or, having agreed to serve, is unable to continue to serve.

Don't make any changes to your will—even minor changes—without consulting your attorney. You could inadvertently modify or nullify all or a significant portion of your will.

How Your Executor Handles Probate

Unless you are different from most people, you probably will own property and owe debts when you die. Your estate may have claims against other persons, such as accounts receivable, or lawsuits in progress. Your executor has the duty of collecting the money that is owed to you.

The executor then must satisfy any debts to your creditors (including the federal and state governments to whom you or your estate owe taxes).

The next major duty of your executor is to distribute what is left to the appropriate individuals or organizations. The process of proving that the will was *your* will—and that it was your *last* will—is called *probate* and is generally supervised by a local court known as the Probate Court, the Surrogate's Court, or Orphan's Court.

If you die intestate, that is, without a valid will, the court will appoint someone to do the executor's job. That person will be called an *administrator* and has essentially the same duties and legal privileges as an executor. (Executor and administrator are the male terms; executrix and administratrix are the female counterparts. We will use executor and administrator to simplify the discussion, including males and females in the terms.) Your executor or administrator acts on behalf of your estate. Your executor must complete any transactions begun by you during your lifetime, as well as handle tasks that are directly caused by or related to your death. The duties of your executor (collecting your property; paying your debts, expenses, and taxes; and distributing your assets to your beneficiaries) must be accomplished with care and with the best interest of your family (your beneficiaries). For example, your executor may have to bring suit on your estate's behalf or release someone from liability. Without the probate process, there would be no one legally entitled to do these things. Titles to real estate could not be made marketable because no one would be legally empowered to act on behalf of your estate. Probate is, therefore, a very important process in which your executor carries out his/her tasks under court supervision and scrutiny. In fact, your personal representative will not be discharged from his or her duties by the court until an accounting of all assets, liabilities, and dispositions has been made. For a thorough understanding of the duties and responsibilities of an executor, and a review of the entire probate process, see *The Executor's Manual,* Doubleday & Company, Inc., Garden City, New York.

Checklist of Executor's Primary Duties*

1. Probate of will.
2. Advertise Grant of Letters.
3. Inventory of safe deposit box.
4. Claim for life insurance benefits—obtain Form 712
   a. Consider mode of payment.

Source: The Tools and Techniques of Estate Planning, 6th Edition, The National Underwriter Co., Cincinnati, Ohio.

5. Claim for pension and profit-sharing benefits.
   a. Consider mode of payment.
   b. Obtain copies of plan, IRS approval, and beneficiary designation.
6. Apply for Social Security and VA benefits.
7. File Form 56—Notice of Fiduciary Relationship.
8. Open estate checking and savings accounts.
9. Write to banks for date of death value.
10. Value securities.
11. Appraisal of real property and personal property.
12. Obtain 3 years of U.S. individual income tax returns and 3 years of cancelled checks.
13. Obtain 5 years financials on business interest plus all relevant agreements.
14. Obtain copies of all U.S. gift-tax returns filed by decedent.
15. Obtain evidence of all debts of decedent and costs of administering estate.
16. Were any of decedent's medical expenses unpaid at death?
17. Has the estate received after-death income taxable under Section 691 of the IRC?
18. Prepayment of state inheritance tax—check state law to determine if permissible and advantages, and, if so, the applicable deadlines.
19. Consider requesting prompt assessment of decedent's U.S. income taxes.
20. File personal property tax returns—due February 15 of each year estate is in administration.
21. File final U.S. and state individual income tax return (IRS Form 1040)—due April 15 of the year after the year in which death occurs, and gift tax returns—due (a) April 15th of the following year or (b) by time estate tax return is due, whichever is earlier.
22. Is the estate subject to ancillary administration?
23. Are administration expenses and losses to be claimed as an income or estate tax deduction?
24. Obtain alternate valuation date values for U.S. estate tax.
25. Payment of U.S. estate tax with flower bonds—must be tendered to Federal Reserve with Form within 9 months of death.
26. Consider election of extension of time to pay U.S. estate tax—must be filed on or before due date of U.S. estate tax return.
27. Consider election to defer payment of inheritance tax on remainder interests—where permitted, determine deadline for election.
28. Consider election for special valuation of farm or business real estate under IRC Section 2032A—must be made with timely filed U.S. estate tax return.

29. File form notice to IRS required by Section 6039A of IRC—due with final U.S. individual income tax return or U.S. estate tax return.
30. File inheritance and federal estate tax return—federal due within 9 months of death—extensions may be requested—check local state law for due date and possible extension.
31. File inventory—check local state law for requirements and due date.
32. Consider requesting prompt assessment of U.S. estate tax return.
33. Apply for U.S. I.D. number if estate will file U.S. income tax return.
34. File U.S. Fiduciary Income Tax Return (Form 1041)—choice of fiscal year.
35. Consider redemption under IRC Section 303.
36. Apply for tax waivers.
37. File account or prepare informal receipt and release or family agreement.
38. Prepare audit notices and statement of proposed distribution.
39. File schedule of distribution if applicable.

Avoiding Probate

You hear so much about avoiding probate because, at one time, courts charged high probate fees, lawyers based their fee on the size of your probate estate, and because it has proven to be a "panic and panacea" for selling books on the subject. You are first panicked by the prospect of a complex and overly expensive process and then told, "If you buy my book, you've solved your problems and have no worries."

In most states, probate is now a relatively inexpensive process (call your local probate court for a list of the charges). Attorneys are more commonly billing clients by the hours they actually spend rather than a percentage of the probate estate. *You have an absolute right to demand hourly billing and an accounting of the time spent.* We suggest you negotiate for hourly billing or a flat fee with a "cap" on the maximum charge *before* you allow work to begin. Insist that the attorney put his or her fee arrangement in writing. Although you should not deal with an attorney merely because he or she has the biggest reputation in town or charges the highest fee, keep in mind that the lowest fee is also not necessarily the best. The person charging a higher fee may do the work in less time or avoid errors or seize opportunities overlooked by a less experienced lawyer. (See Chapter 24 for a discussion of how to select advisors.)

There are still good reasons, however, for avoiding probate with respect to certain assets. For example, if you own property in more than one state, multiple probates called *ancillary administrations* will be required. Property will have to be probated in each state where property is owned.

Another reason for avoiding probate with respect to assets such as the family home or checking accounts is that the probate procedure can be time consuming. Typically, the entire procedure takes from a minimum of nine months to as long as two or three years in some cases. Your attorney will point out those assets which should be held in a manner that will not pass through probate.

Avoiding probate is essential if privacy is important (once the will is probated, it becomes a public document).

Although there are many advantages to passing property outside of probate (for example, cash passing through a life insurance contract is less likely to become subject to contest than cash or property passing under the provisions of a will), probate equates to court supervision. That means the state court, a disinterested party, will be safeguarding the interests of your beneficiaries. This "watchful" objective control over the executor often outweighs the relatively minor costs involved in probate.

Keep in mind that many expenses and taxes will be incurred whether or not you avoid probate. Cash will still be needed to pay these expenses.

If too much property passes automatically to your spouse, your estate will be set up for the "2d death-tax wallop." (See the discussion on overqualification of the marital deduction in the next chapter.)

Avoiding probate often equates to loss of control. If your surviving spouse receives property outright, he or she can do anything he or she wants to do with it, including leaving it all to a second wife or husband or their children. In fact, even if your spouse attempts to leave all your assets to your children, his or her second spouse may be able to elect against your spouse's will and may end up with as much as one-third or even one-half of your estate.

Whatever you decide about avoiding probate, don't buy *any* book (including this one), fill it out, sign and pull out the forms and then expect that you have really beat the system. No forms fit everyone's situation, and no forms conform to every state's laws. Simplistic reliance on a form book can be as dangerous as the indiscriminate use of an over-the-counter drug to cure a ruptured appendix—and your whole life's efforts may ride on the results. A blind avoidance of probate may save hundreds of dollars of legal fees, but at the cost of thousands of dollars of unnecessary death taxes.

If you want to avoid probate, do it wisely as part of an overall plan that considers:

1. Federal and state death taxes.
2. Federal and state income taxes.
3. Federal and state gift taxes.
4. Your personal objectives.

5. Your beneficiaries' needs and circumstances.
6. Your cash flow.
7. Your peace of mind.

How to Remove Assets from Your Probate Estate

If you still want to avoid probate, here are 7 ways to do it:

1. Title your property jointly with your spouse or other heir (read Chapter 9 and beware of unintended gift-tax costs).
2. Buy life insurance and name someone other than your estate as beneficiary.
3. Set up or participate in a pension plan, profit-sharing plan, IRA, or HR-10 (Chapter 17), and name someone other than your estate as beneficiary.
4. Sell property to a relative in return for a private annuity or sell property in return for installment payments (Chapter 14).
5. Participate in a Death Benefit Only Plan and have your employer name your spouse or children as beneficiaries (Chapter 15).
6. Make gifts while you are alive (Chapter 12).
7. Set up a living trust (Chapter 7).

Here's a bonus: The best way to avoid probate of assets is to never own the right to pass the asset on in the first place. Be sure to read Chapter 20 on GRITS, SPLITS, and RITS, three techniques for bypassing both probate and death taxes.

We want to emphasize the importance of working with an attorney, a chartered life underwriter (CLU), chartered financial consultant (ChFC), certified financial planner (CFP), certified public accountant (CPA), and a trust officer who will be able to ask—and answer—each of the following questions about the probate avoidance technique you have selected. Will it:

1. Avoid probate in *both* spouses' estates?
2. Save or eliminate federal estate taxes?
3. Save or eliminate federal generation-skipping taxes?
4. Save or eliminate federal income taxes?
5. Save or eliminate state income taxes?
6. Save or eliminate state death taxes?
7. Accomplish your "people planning" objectives?
8. Give your family the investment guidance and flexibility you want them to have?
9. Be coordinated with the dispositive provisions of your employee benefit plans?

7

What You Should Know about Trusts

Just what is a trust? How does a trust work? What are its advantages and disadvantages?

A trust is a *relationship*. It's the relationship that exists when one party (called a grantor, settlor, trustor, or donor) transfers money or other property (called the trust *corpus* or *principal*) to a second party (a trustee), who must use that money or property solely for the benefit of a third party (the beneficiary). The essential concept is that the trustee (which can be one or more persons and/or a corporate financial institution) holds (for administration, management, and investment purposes) the legal title to the property you place in the trust but may use the property and the income it produces only for the benefit of the beneficiaries you have selected (which may include you and your spouse).

How to Set Up a Trust

How is a trust established? Let's take the case of Bob and Nancy as an example. Their attorney, Mark, prepared a written document called a *trust agreement*. The attorney spelled out in the trust agreement Bob's and Nancy's wishes as to how the assets of the trust were to be managed and invested, who was to receive the assets and income, how that money or property was to be paid out, and at what ages (and upon what events) each of their beneficiaries was to receive his or her share. The trust also indicated the names of the trustees.

How to Select a Trustee

Mark pointed out several important points to Bob and Nancy before he drafted their trust. First, he told them that they could have more than one trustee. If they selected several parties (such as more than one person or a person and a bank), each party would be a co-trustee, and they would make decisions jointly (but be jointly liable for any mistakes).

Nancy wanted to know what characteristics a good trustee should have. Mark suggested that their trustee or trustees should have (a) sound

65

business and financial judgment; (b) a knowledge of the principles of asset investment and management; (c) an intimate knowledge of the needs of each beneficiary; and (d) be able to survive through the term of the trust, regardless of how long that might be (some trusts last for two or three generations).

Mark suggested that a trust company, or bank authorized to perform trust duties, is often the best choice to meet these requirements. When Bob asked why Mark felt a bank would make a good trustee, he replied that most trust companies and banks have investment experience and would not be incapacitated by death or disability, or become unavailable (banks take holidays but never vacations).

More important, Mark added, unlike a family member, a corporate trustee can carry out the directions of the trust instrument objectively and impartially. The value of this objectivity is particularly important in avoiding intrafamily conflicts of interest that often occur where the trustee and one or more beneficiaries are members of the same family. A corporate trustee can say "no," where appropriate, without starting a family feud.

Bob asked if a corporate trustee, acting alone, might be impersonal and lack a familiarity and understanding of family needs. The attorney's reply was that, if Bob and Nancy felt that was a problem, the solution was to name both a corporate trustee and one or more individuals as co-trustees. He also suggested that they or their beneficiaries could reserve or be given the power to change to another corporate trustee. Note that, if co-trustees are used, you must consider such issues as (a) must trustees act unanimously or does the majority rule? (obviously, this is a problem with only two trustees); (b) who succeeds and what happens if either a corporate or individual trustee resigns, dies, becomes disabled, or becomes incompetent? and (c) under what circumstances, if any, could a co-trustee delegate responsibility?

Factors to consider in selecting a trustee

Advantages of corporate trustees such as banks and trust companies

1. Perpetual existence (Unlike an individual trustee, banks don't die, become disabled, or retire.)
2. Experience (The job of a trustee entails investment expertise, bookkeeping, tax, and knowledge of state law which few individuals have.)
3. Objectivity (Impartiality is extremely important to minimize conflicts of interest in decision making and allocating assets and income among beneficiaries.)
4. Safety (Banks and trust companies are audited both internally and externally and have substantial physical safeguards for financial assets.)

Disadvantages of corporate trustees such as banks and trust companies

1. Conservative investment policy (Some individuals feel the conservative policies of banks result in less favorable investment returns than might otherwise be obtained.)
2. Disinclination to handle certain assets (For instance, banks typically will not want the responsibility of running family businesses and tend to sell or liquidate them as quickly as possible.)
3. Employee turnover (Beneficiaries may actually deal with a number of people over the course of time.)
4. Inflexibility (Out of concern for potential surcharge by beneficiaries and because of governmental oversight, corporate trustees may at times be inflexible or lack compassion in their dealings with beneficiaries.)
5. Fees (An annual fee is charged, typically based on a percentage of both the principal and income of the trust. Some banks charge a distribution fee based on a percentage of any principal paid out from the trust.)

Advantages of spouse or adult child of grantor (the person establishing the trust) as trustee

1. Knowledge and interest (Typically, the spouse or adult child will know the beneficiaries' circumstances and needs and is interested in their welfare.)
2. No fees (Although an individual could—and in some cases should—charge fees, often a personal trustee will not.)

Disadvantages of a spouse or adult child as trustee

1. Nonperpetual existence (An individual trustee can die, become disabled or incompetent, resign, or lose interest.)
2. Lack of expertise (The spouse or child may not have the knowledge or experience to do fiduciary accounting. Few professional accountants are competent in this area.)
3. Lack of time or inclination (Investment and management of assets is time consuming, and the costs of malfeasance are high. Most individuals will not want this responsibility.)
4. Conflict of interest (If the trustee is a beneficiary and has the power to use income or principal for the benefit of one family member over another, the possibility of using that right for the trustee's benefit—or bending backwards to avoid the problem to the trustee's detriment—is likely. The trustee may be unduly influenced or pressured by certain family members to make decisions in their interest. The potential for family discord is high. A family member trustee may use trustee's powers to control, punish, or reward family members.)

5. Marriage (A relative trustee who marries or remarries can be a problem if influenced by a new spouse who was not originally a family member.)
6. Tax traps (Where individuals are given broad powers over trust property which they may use to benefit themselves, unwanted estate tax, income tax, or generation-skipping taxes may result.)

Nontax Advantages of a Trust

Why set up a trust? What are the advantages of a trust, and how could you benefit from one? Bob and Nancy, like most people who set up a trust, wanted to accomplish a number of objectives.

There are many reasons other than tax savings for making gifts in trust, rather than giving property outright to your beneficiaries. These "people oriented" objectives can be divided into three categories: (1) management of assets, (2) conservation of assets, and (3) disposition of assets. Some common situations indicating the desirability of a trust are:

1. Quite often, a property owner will feel that the beneficiary is unwilling or unable to invest, manage, or handle the responsibility of an outright gift. For example, Bob and Nancy don't want to give outright gifts to their minor children, but they do want to provide for their financial security. Another good example where trusts should be considered is in the case of recipients who are legally adults but who lack the emotional or intellectual maturity, physical capacity, or technical training to handle large sums of money. Many individuals can't or don't want to handle assets (such as a business) that require constant and high-level decision-making capacity. A trust is often used to postpone full ownership until the donees are in a position to handle the property properly.

2. You may want to achieve the income and estate tax advantages of gifts but are reluctant to place all the ownership rights in the hands of a donee. You could utilize a trust as the solution to the ambivalent position of wanting to institute a program of gifting but fearing the possible results of an outright ("no strings attached") transfer, which might lessen the donees' dependence on you.

3. A trust is also indicated where the proposed gift property does not lend itself to fragmentation, but the donor desires to spread beneficial ownership among a number of people. For example, a large life insurance policy (and the ultimate proceeds it generates when the donor dies) is often better held by a single trustee than jointly by several individuals. Another example of such property is real estate. Often, land is more valuable if it is not divided. A ten-acre tract of land may be worth substantially more than ten one-acre tracts. If a trust is used as a receptacle for the gift, ten beneficiaries could share in the growth and income from the

land without necessitating an actual division of the property itself. An apartment house is still another example of an asset that is much more efficiently and profitably handled through a single unified management. Of course, at a specified given event, the trustee could be directed to sell the property and divide the proceeds or split up the property itself.

4. In lieu of an outright gift, you may want to use a trust if conservation of assets and particular dispositive plans are important. For instance, where control is essential, a donor will often want to limit the class of beneficiaries and prevent the donee from disposing of property to persons outside the family. In fact, one of the reasons Bob and Nancy are setting up their trust is to prevent their daughter's spouse from acquiring rights to Bob and Nancy's chain of flower shops. A gift in trust for their daughter, Barbara, or for the benefit of "Barbara and her children" (or even for "Barbara and her husband as long as they are married") provides protection against an unsuccessful marriage.

5. If your major asset is a closely held business, a trust provides a vehicle for you to make gifts of the corporation's stock with minimal loss of control.

6. A trust is often used instead of an outright gift because a gift in trust can provide protection against creditors of both the donor and donee.

7. Trusts are often used to familiarize a trustee (who eventually will be managing assets "poured-over" from the donor's will or paid by contract to the trust from life insurance and pension proceeds) with the donor's assets, his family, his plans, and his relationship of each to the other. Smaller gifts in trust can be made immediately. If the trustee invests and manages the property wisely, more property can be placed into the trust at later times or at the estate owner's death. In other words, lifetime gifts to the trust give the donor an opportunity to watch the trustee (and the beneficiaries) in action and make suggestions as to property investment, management, and income and capital payments.

8. Consider a trust as a means of providing income for a child (and principal at the trustee's discretion for emergencies) without making that child a fortune hunter's target.

9. If you own several pieces of property of equal value, you could make outright gifts of parcel A to your son and parcel B to your daughter. However, you may be treating the children unequally since one property could increase in value while the value of the other could fall, or the properties could increase (or decrease) in value at different rates. But by placing both properties in trust and giving both children equal shares in trust property, you could equalize benefits between the children.

10. Property that requires management should not be placed directly into a minor's hands because major decisions cannot be made and the property cannot be sold, exchanged, or mortgaged without the appointment of a guardian. This is often an expensive, inflexible, and troublesome procedure. Once an outright distribution is made, a child is free to spend or use it upon reaching majority but often doesn't have the financial maturity to invest, manage, or spend it wisely.

11. An outright gift will often return to the child's parents (or to the child's spouse) should the minor child predecease the parents. This would defeat many of the donor-parent's tax and personal objectives. This can be avoided in a properly drafted trust.

12. Finally, when compared with an outright gift, which is subject to the probate process (explained in Chapter 6), a trust can provide privacy and relative security from a will contest.

In summary, a trust is one of the best ways the donor can give a gift and, at the same time, achieve flexibility to meet future contingencies and attain his or her personal objectives with respect to the beneficiaries.

Income Tax Savings Potential

What are the tax reasons for setting up a trust? The answer is that significant income and tax savings can be realized through trusts. In an *irrevocable* trust (you can't change the terms or get the property back once it is set up), you can actually shift the burden of income taxes from you—at your income tax rates—to the trust itself and/or its beneficiaries, both of whom typically are in lower income tax brackets than you are. The difference in income tax rates could amount to substantial annual savings.

Income retained by a trust will generally be taxed to the trust. The first $5000 of income will be taxed at a 15 percent rate. The next $8000 is taxed at a 28 percent rate. Taxable income between $13,001 and $26,000 is taxed at a 33 percent rate. Taxable income in excess of $26,000 is taxed at a 28 percent rate.

If a trust had taxable income of $6000 in a taxable year beginning after 1987, the tax would be $1030 ($750 plus 28 percent of $1000). If taxable income was $15,000, the tax would be $3650 ($2990 plus 33 percent of $2000).

Taxable Income	Schedule for 1988 Tax Payable	Rate on Excess
$0–5000	15% of taxable income	
$5001–13,000	$750 plus	28% of taxable income over $5000
$13,000–26,000	$2990	33% of taxable income over $13,000
over $26,000	28% of all taxable income	

A Special Schedule Is Used for 1987

Taxable Income	Tax Payable	Rate on Excess
$0–$500	11% of taxable income	
$501–4,700	$55 plus	15% of taxable income over $500
$4701–7550	$685 plus	28% of taxable income over $4700
$7551–15,150	$1483 plus	35% of taxable income over $7550
Over $15,150	$4143 plus	38% of taxable income over $15,150

If the beneficiary of a trust is age 14 or older, the following illustrations show that significant savings can be realized over time. It assumes a $100,000 investment that is earning 5 percent interest each year for 10 years. The parent is in a 33 percent tax bracket. The trust beneficiary is in a 15 percent bracket. If no trust were established, each year the parent would receive $5000 and would net $3350 after taxes.

But if the asset was placed in a trust and its income was paid out to the beneficiary each year, the after tax yield would increase to $4325—a $975 a year gain. (The child's taxable income is reduced from $5000 to $4500 because of the $500 standard deduction explained below.) Over 10 years, the total tax savings would be $12,877. In 20 years, the tax savings (together with interest) grows to $33,851. If the income were accumulated at interest in the trust, the annual advantage is slightly less—$915. (The trust's taxable income is reduced from $5000 to $4900 because of a $100 exemption allowed to such trusts.) But the savings over no gift of income-producing property is considerable:

Post TRA 1986 Income Shifting: Child 14 or Over

Amount of investment	$100,000
Rate of return on investment	0.050
Years investment lasts	10
Parent's combined (federal and state) tax bracket	0.33
Child's combined (federal and state) tax bracket	0.15
Trust's combined (federal and state) tax bracket	0.15

	Parent	Child	Trust
Interest income	$5000	$5000	$5000
Tax	1650	675	735
After-tax income	3350	4325	4265
Annual advantage		975	915
Total savings over	10 years	$12,877	$12,084
Total savings over	15 years	$22,091	$21,632
Total savings over	20 years	$33,851	$32,663

The 1986 Tax Reform Act (TRA '86) provided that unearned income paid to children *under* age 14 will be taxed to the child. Essentially, the so-called "kiddie tax" works like this:

1. The first $500 of unearned income is not taxable because of the child's standard deduction;
2. The next $500 of unearned income is taxed to the child at the *child's* 15 percent tax bracket;
3. Unearned income in excess of $1000 is taxed to the child but at the child's parent's bracket.

So, if a 13-year-old received $1300 of income from a trust, the child would pay no tax on the first $500, tax at the child's bracket on $500 ($75), and tax at the parent's rate on the remaining $300. TRA '86 provided that once a child reaches age 14 in any day during the year, all unearned income will be taxed to the child—at the child's tax bracket.

Note that if you (or your spouse) retain certain powers over the assets you place in the trust or over the income produced by those assets, you will be taxed on trust income just as if you were still the owner of the trust's property. These powers include the right to:

1. Control beneficial enjoyment (say who gets what);
2. Exercise certain managerial powers;
3. Receive income from the trust;
4. Use trust income to pay for your legal obligations;
5. Revoke the trust;
6. Receive trust property back.

But if you haven't kept these powers, a well-drafted trust can save your family thousands of dollars. That's because income accumulated by such a trust is taxed to the trust at its tax bracket—regardless of the age of the child who is its beneficiary. Even greater savings can be realized by splitting income between a trust and a child age 14 or over since income remains in the 15 percent and 28 percent bracket longer that way. That income tax savings alone over a period of years could fund a year or two of a child's college education if the trust was established soon enough.

Estate Tax Savings Potential

You can avoid significant federal estate taxes and state death taxes when you place property into a trust. That is because, if you arrange the trust properly and the trust is irrevocable, the property (and the income it produces) is no longer in your estate. (There may, however, be gift tax implications when you put the property into the trust. The transfer of property to the trust is really an absolute gift to the beneficiaries of the trust. If the gift is large enough—over $600,000—you will have to pay gift taxes.)

Trusts That Protect You

You may be capable of investing or managing assets but can't—or don't want to—take the time to do so. Many people relieve themselves of property management through trusts. A trustee can assume the responsibility of investing, managing, and conserving the property on behalf of your beneficiaries (including you, if that's what you want). Furthermore, a trust may be a great way for you to protect yourself in the event you are unexpectedly disabled due to a sickness or injury and become unable to manage your assets.

Types of Trusts

What are the various types of trusts that you can use to meet your objectives? There are a number of types of trusts. The terms of those trusts can be as wide and varied as the imagination of your tax counsel and the needs and desires of the parties you want to benefit.

The two most common types of trusts are *living* (often called *inter vivos*) trust and the *testamentary* (created under your will and taking effect at your death) trust. A third type is a combination of the two. It's called a *life insurance trust/pour-over will* combination (LIT/POW).

We will look at each of these types of trusts and see how they work.

Revocable living trust defined

A *revocable* trust is one that allows you to change your mind and regain property that you have put into the trust at any time or change the terms of the trust. If you have made a trust revocable, you can also specify who is to receive income or principal at any time. Because you have complete control of the property and the income it produces, for federal income and estate tax purposes, when you establish a revocable trust you are treated just as if you never gave up the property you have placed in the trust. Therefore, if Bob establishes a revocable trust, and Bob puts property in the trust, and that property earns income, Bob will be taxed on it. Even if his children actually receive the income, Bob would still be subject to income tax since he is treated as if he never gave the property away. This same result would apply for federal estate tax purposes. The property in the trust at Bob's death would be taxed in Bob's estate.

But note the effect of what is happening in this example. Bob's children are receiving the income. The IRS would treat Bob as if he had received the income and then gave it away to his children. So Bob may not only be taxed on the income produced by the assets in his trust, but he also may be liable for gift taxes on the income he "received" and "gave away."

Advantages of a living trust

Why then would Bob and his wife Nancy set up a revocable living trust? One reason is that a living trust makes it possible to provide management continuity and income flow even after Bob and Nancy die. No probate of the assets in the trust would be necessary since the trust would continue to operate after they die in the same way it did while they were alive.

Bob and Nancy will obtain a second advantage from a living revocable trust. The burdens of investment decisions and management responsibilities can—when they want them to—be shifted from their shoulders and assumed by their trustees. Bob and Nancy could still control investment decisions and management policy as long as they were alive and healthy. But they could use the trust as a "backup" in case they become unwilling or unable to manage their own assets. Often, this type of revocable living trust is called a *step-up* trust. That's because the trustee would step-up to take Bob and Nancy's place in decision making and in day-to-day management if they want to be relieved of the burden of managing trust property. A step-up trust would also be of considerable help if Bob and Nancy became incapable of acting on their own behalf in later years because of sickness or accident and could not manage or invest their property.

Another advantage of a revocable living trust is that, unlike the terms of the wills they signed, the terms of the trust and the amount of assets that Bob and Nancy place into it will never become public knowledge at their death. The public has no right to know the terms and conditions of a revocable living trust. Only their trustees and beneficiaries will have access to the trust instrument.

Disadvantages of living trusts

There are disadvantages to a revocable living trust: Typically, the trustee will charge fees to manage and invest property placed into the trust. Since such a trust should be drawn by a competent tax attorney, legal fees are involved in drafting a revocable living trust. We repeat the axiom, "The person who acts as his or her own attorney has a fool for a client." Nowhere is this more applicable than in the drafting of wills and revocable trusts. Homemade wills and trusts torn out of form books have caused incredible amounts of litigation and court costs. It's almost impossible for a lay person to understand all the intricacies of both federal and state law and the other procedural state law requirements for drafting and executing trusts. It's impossible for "do it yourself trust" texts to encompass or keep up with the changing laws in all states or customize the documents to the particular needs and circumstances of the thousands of individuals who may buy the books. More often than not, the legal fees involved in straightening out homemade trusts will greatly exceed the small fee an attorney would have charged to prepare the proper documents.

The irrevocable living trust

Many individuals have established *irrevocable* living trusts. Once you put property into an irrevocable trust, you relinquish the right to receive the property back, terminate the trust, or change its terms.

Another drawback is that you may be making taxable gifts. For example, if Bob and Nancy had set up such a trust, each time they put property into the trust, they would really be making a gift to each of the trust beneficiaries. If the gifts were large enough, they could even be liable for gift taxes.

Furthermore, a trustee would charge fees for asset management.

Worse yet, Bob and Nancy would lose the use of trust property and any income that property may produce.

Why then would anyone ever establish an irrevocable living trust?

The answer is that only an irrevocable trust can reduce income taxes, possibly save massive amounts of federal estate and generation-skipping transfer tax and significant amounts of state income and death tax as well. That's because when property is placed into such a trust, the property and income it produces no longer belong to the grantor. After the transfer of the property to such a trust, if the trust is properly arranged, the assets in it and the income produced by it will no longer be in the grantor's estate for federal (and often state) death or generation skipping tax purposes.

Testamentary trusts

As their names imply, both the revocable and irrevocable trusts are trusts established when you are living. The *testamentary* trust is established at death through the terms of your will.

The major advantage of a testamentary trust is that fewer documents are needed to put this type of trust into effect. For example, if Bob and Nancy had their attorney draw an irrevocable living trust or a revocable living trust, an attorney would have to draw two sets of documents, the trust and their wills. With a testamentary trust, the will and the trust are all in one document. So there may be a slight savings in legal fees. (Although in this case, the savings will be minimal, and you'd have to take the risk that the testamentary trust may never come into existence if the will is not probated or if it is successfully attacked). Neither income nor estate taxes are saved through a testamentary trust because you own the assets and the income until you die.

Life Insurance Trust with a Pour-Over Will (LIT-POW)

A life insurance trust and pour-over will combination can be the cornerstone of your estate plan. Here's how it works.

A living trust is established immediately. It can be either revocable or irrevocable. You can "fund" it by putting cash or other income-producing property into it immediately. You can choose to leave it "unfunded," that is, not put any significant amount of cash or other income-producing property into the trust. Many states allow a trust to come into existence with no funds, merely naming the trust as beneficiary of certain specified life insurance policies.

When you die, your will provides that assets passing under your will, *probate assets*—after payment of debts, expenses, taxes, and specific bequests—are to go—*pour-over*—into the life insurance trust. Probate assets are poured, together with the proceeds (death benefits from the policies) of the insurance that has the trustee named as the beneficiary, into the trust.

Why a life insurance trust? The trust contains provisions as to how your life insurance and all your other assets will be administered and distributed. The big advantage of the life insurance trust/pour-over will combination is that all your assets are easily coordinated and administered in a unified manner according to your wishes. Although the trust is called a life insurance trust, other assets, such as pension or profit-sharing proceeds, can be paid to the trust. The trust will be effective after your death even if your will is held to be invalid.

Other types of trusts

There are other types of trusts. In fact, the number of trusts that can be designed is limited only by the creativity and imagination of the attorney. One of the more popular types of trusts is the *marital* trust, commonly referred to as the "A" trust since it is often formed under Clause A of the trust. This marital or A trust is designed to qualify for the estate tax marital deduction.

The marital/family (A–B) trust combination is an arrangement to give your surviving spouse full use of the family's economic wealth, while at the same time minimizing, to the greatest extent possible, the federal estate tax payable at the death of both spouses. It's actually two separate trusts created under one document.

The first trust, or the marital trust, is designed to qualify for the estate tax marital deduction. This is the deduction allowed for the net value of gifts passing at death from one spouse to a surviving spouse in a qualifying manner. Property in the marital trust will generally be taxable at the surviving spouse's death for federal estate tax purposes.

The second trust is called the *family, nonmarital,* or *bypass* trust. Lawyers may refer to it as the B trust since it is often formed under Clause B of the trust. This trust bypasses taxation in the estate of the surviving spouse. It is designed to hold assets for the economic well-being of both the surviving spouse and other family members. The property in this family (bypass) trust will pass free of federal estate taxes at the death of the surviving spouse. In fact, it is this family or bypass trust that is primarily responsible for minimizing the overall impact of death taxes upon the death of both spouses and, therefore, maximizing the amount passing to your children.

Because of a formula provision, just enough (and no more) assets are placed into this trust to fully utilize your *credit equivalent.* In other words, up to $600,000 (the amount everyone can pass estate-tax free to anyone they want) goes into this trust. Some attorneys call this the CEBT (Credit Equivalent Bypass Trust).

Even though assets in the family trust (CEBT) will not be taxed when the surviving spouse dies, creative drafting on the part of your attorney can provide a substantial amount of economic security (without estate taxation) for your surviving spouse. For example, the surviving spouse can be given the right to receive all the income annually or more frequently from this family trust without causing its assets to be includable in his or her estate. Likewise, the trustee can be given discretion to give additional amounts of capital to your surviving spouse. The surviving spouse can even be given certain discretion as to the amount and form of payment to the next trust beneficiaries (the children). This family-bypass trust can be made quite flexible and is one that should be given careful consideration if the size of the estate warrants its use.

Another type of commonly used trust is known as the *Section 2503(c)* trust. This is a gift tax tool that enables an individual to make a gift to a minor in trust and still obtain the $10,000 annual gift tax exclusion. The use of the irrevocable funded trust for gifts to minors eliminates many of the practical objections to outright gifts to minors and, at the same time, makes it possible to obtain gift tax savings.

Questions to Ask Yourself

Each of these trusts is covered more extensively in other chapters. But before we leave the topic of trusts, here is a checklist of questions you should ask yourself if you've already set up a trust:

1. Have we/I retained for beneficiaries the right to change corporate trustees because of a geographical move or personality conflict or given them power to appoint additional trustees?
2. Have we/I selected a person who:
   a. has little or no business, investment, or money management experience or financial responsibility;
   b. may have an interest adverse to my beneficiaries or who can't make impartial decisions;
   c. hasn't got the time or inclination to devote to proper estate administration;
   d. may not get along with one or more of the beneficiaries;
   e. may be forced to choose between personal interests and the interests of other beneficiaries;
   f. doesn't know the beneficiary selected?
3. Should we/I consider *sprinkle* powers (giving the trustee the right to distribute income or principal to the beneficiaries who need it the most)?
4. Should we/I require documented accounting on a quarterly basis to beneficiaries?

Trusts—A Summary*

Type of Trust	Chapter for More Information	Who Gets the Income?	Who Is Taxable on Trust Income?	Who Gets the Assets?	Are Trust Assets Excludable from or Deductible by Your Estate?	Can You Get Trust Assets Back?
Revocable	7	You do	You	You choose	No	Yes
Irrevocable	7	Terms of trust determine	Trust if income retained, beneficiary if paid out. Taxed at beneficiary's bracket if 14 or over, otherwise taxed to beneficiary at parent's bracket	Terms of trust determine	Yes	No
2503 (c) minor's	19	Held in trust or paid to minor	Trust if held, minor if paid out. Taxed to minor at parent's bracket if minor under 14, otherwise to minor at minor's bracket	Minor at age 21	Yes	No
Charitable remainder	23	You do	You	Charity	Yes	No
Marital (power of appointment)	13	Surviving spouse	Surviving spouse	Surviving spouse or person he/she appoints	Yes	N/A
Marital Q.T.I.P.	13	Surviving spouse	Surviving spouse	Parties you select	Yes	N/A
Credit equivalent bypass (C.E.B.T.)	13	Surviving spouse for life, then children	Surviving spouse for life, then children	Children	Yes	N/A
Grantor retained income (G.R.I.T.)	20	You do	You	Parties you select	Yes, if you survive specified term	No

*As is the case with any chart, the consequences shown above are only overviews. There are many exceptions covered in the chapters indicated.

8

Life Insurance—A Key Estate Planning Tool

Life insurance is one of the most important tools available to provide financial security after your death to those persons and organizations you love. This chapter defines what life insurance is, how it works, and how you can make it work for you.

Life Insurance Defined

Life insurance is a legal contract. In return for a stipulated consideration (a premium), one party (the insurer) agrees to pay to the other (the insured), or his/her beneficiary, a specified amount upon the occurrence of death or some other designated event. It's a contract that buys "time" in terms of dollars. In other words, it's an agreement under which economic protection is provided for your family against the risk that your income will stop at your death.

The term *life insurance* includes accidental death benefits under health insurance policies, whole life, and term insurance. Life insurance is owned for both personal and business uses and includes the group coverage you have from your employer as well as individually purchased plans.

How Financial Planners Use Life Insurance

We don't believe in life insurance—we believe in what it *does!* Sometimes when a client asks us: Do I need life insurance? Can't I do without it? We reply *you* don't need life insurance at all! But others may—desperately.

Here's how life insurance can be used:

1. Life insurance is purchased to provide an income for family expenses such as food, clothing, and shelter—family needs that continue long after the head of a household dies.
2. Life insurance can provide cash to pay college expenses, mortgage balances, or other large capital needs.

3. Estate planners recommend life insurance to provide cash for the payment of estate and inheritance taxes, debts, administrative costs, and other estate settlement expenses. Life insurance provides a way to pay federal estate taxes at a "discount." For example, if you were to purchase a $100,000 policy and die within the first year (say you've paid $2000 in premiums), $100,000 worth of estate taxes and other expenses can be paid at a cost of only $2000. The $98,000 difference can be considered a discount. Another way to look at it is that you obtain an "instant estate" of $100,000. If dividends are arranged properly (using dividends to purchase 1-year term insurance with the balance purchasing paid up additional insurance), the discount will continue even if the cost of money is factored into the equation. The following illustration is based on a 41-year-old client, $300,000 of whole life insurance, and a 6 percent after-tax "cost of money."

Cost to Provide Liquidity with Discounted Dollars

Amount of liquidity to be provided	$300,000
Individual's current age	41
Premium	$6,224
After-tax cost of money (net interest rate)	0.06

	If Death Occurs at End of:				
	5 Years	10 Years	15 Years	20 Years	Life Expectancy
Proceeds	$323,606	$375,729	$471,570	$639,895	$1,562,083
Outlay	31,120	62,240	93,360	124,480	258,296
Cost of	6,070	13,573	45,286	98,250	796,172
Proceeds	323,606	375,729	471,570	639,895	1,562,083
Total Cost	37,190	75,813	138,646	222,730	1,054,468
Net Gain	286,416	299,916	332,924	417,165	507,615

This table illustrates the discount in terms of both death benefit and cash value as a percentage of premiums.

Discounting the Federal Estate Tax

End Year	Amount Payable ($)	Cumulative Premiums ($)	Cost per $	Tax-Free Proceeds Above Prems	Cash Value	Cash Value As % of Premium
1	303,832	6,224	0.02	$297,608	$ 855	13.7
5	323,606	31,120	0.10	$292,486	$ 31,577	101.5
10	375,729	62,240	0.17	$313,489	$ 92,343	148.4
20	639,895	124,480	0.19	$515,415	$313,331	251.7

4. Life insurance can be thought of as an incredibly effective and inexpensive way to transfer capital—a means of transferring assets from your estate to your children or grandchildren in the most efficient manner possible. For example, properly arranged life insurance (owned by a third party who is also your beneficiary) can shift assets from you to that individual (or individuals) without probate costs, without inheritance or other state death taxes, without income taxes, without transfer fees, without federal estate tax and without the generation-skipping transfer tax.

5. Life insurance is used in businesses to indemnify the business for the loss of a key individual. This is called *keyman* or *key employee* life insurance. The proceeds of such coverage have protected the profits and sometimes the very existence of thousands of partnerships and corporations. Banks look favorably on a firm that has insured its most valuable assets, its key personnel.

6. Life insurance is also used to fund a "buy-sell." In other words, it serves as a mechanism for providing the cash for a corporation or surviving shareholder to purchase the stock of a deceased co-shareholder.

Financial planners consider life insurance the foundation upon which your financial house should be built. Don't leave home without it!

What Type Should You Buy?

What are the various types of life insurance and which type is right for you? The answer is, it depends. It depends on your need and ability to pay. We caution against self-styled experts who are sure their type is best before they even know your needs or circumstances.

Term insurance

Term insurance is die-to-collect insurance. Under this type of coverage, your beneficiaries collect only if you die before the term expires. At the end of the term, the coverage runs out. Because the insurance company's liability is limited and typically of short duration, the cash outlay for term insurance protection is relatively low. For instance, Chet is 35 years old. Chet is interested in providing dollars to his wife, Cathy, and his children if he should die. At Chet's age the premium for $100,000 of insurance is less than $300 the first year (but, of course, this goes up every year). So term insurance is the coverage to buy if you're looking for maximum short-term protection for a minimum cash outlay. Please notice we *did not* say term insurance is the cheapest or the best type of coverage—only that it produces the most short-term coverage for the least outlay.

Chet and Cathy asked their insurance agent, Ric, if there was more than one type of term insurance. Ric replied that there are basically four types of term insurance. The first type of term insurance is *annual renewable* term (also called *yearly renewable* term or YRT). This type of policy is renewable each year regardless of the insured's physical condition. However, premiums increase year by year (because the risk of death increases year by year) and are often quite expensive at ages greater than 50 or 55.

If you have group insurance at work, yearly renewable term is the type of insurance policy used. If you are young and paying for some of the group coverage, you may be able to save money. The difference between the group plan you have at work and the YRT you purchase on your own is that, if you are young and in good health, you may be better off purchasing insurance on your own. If you are older or in poor health, you are probably better off with the group coverage. That's because, with group insurance, young and healthy employees, in essence, subsidize older and less healthy members of the group. (If your employer is paying for the entire coverage, it pays in come cases to see if it would be less expensive for your employer to "bonus out" cash to covered employees and purchase term insurance individually.)

No matter what type of term policy you buy, demand the *guaranteed renewable* feature. On almost any term policy, you can add this right to renew the policy for another year without passing an exam. It will boost the premium slightly, but if you come to the end of your term and you are seriously ill, wouldn't it be nice to be able to continue the term insurance? (The premium rate you will pay when you renew will be based on the age you are at that time—not on your age when you bought the original policy.)

Convertible term is a contractural right to exchange your term policy for a whole life type of policy without evidence of insurability. This means that you do not have to prove you are physically (or otherwise) in a "standard" class of risks in order to stop the term from running out. You have until a specified age—such as 65—to convert your term into whole life coverage at standard premium rates even if you have cancer or some other terminal illness.

The contractural right to convert, which you should demand no matter what type of term you purchase, can be extremely important even if you don't become ill. Sooner or later, as you grow older, the rates for renewing your term policy will become prohibitive. (Ask your agent for the rates you'd have to pay to renew a policy when you reach ages 55, 60, 65, and 70. And check out the tables below showing—in five-year intervals— what happens to premium rates.)

In many policies, at age 60, 65, or 70 you cannot renew your policy— for any amount of money.

You may be asking yourself, why will I need life insurance when I reach that age? The answer is, you may need life insurance no matter how your life turns out. If your other financial ventures haven't been

Renewable Term Insurance Premiums

Age	Annual Premium for $100,000 of Protection
55	$ 1,200
60	$ 1,800
65	$ 2,800
70	$ 5,000
75	$ 8,100
80	$14,200
85	$23,300
90	$36,900
95	$56,800
99	$77,200

successful, your life insurance may be the only significant financial asset to provide security for your family and pay the bills you have left behind. Conversely, let's say you have been successful, very successful, in real estate or stocks or in a business. Even if things have gone well financially, your assets may be *nonliquid;* they may not be available to pay death taxes or other estate settlement expenses (which must be paid in cash and generally within 9 months of your death). If you have it, life insurance can satisfy that need.

The third type of term insurance coverage is called *decreasing term.* You've probably heard of *mortgage* insurance. This is nothing more than decreasing term coverage that is used to pay off a mortgage. The death benefit decreases over the specified period of time (essentially at the same rate as your mortgage). The premium for decreasing term coverage generally remains level.

It is important that you name a member of your family and not a bank as the beneficiary of this coverage. If a bank is named as beneficiary, the mortgage will be paid off, but your family may lose the right to a very favorable mortgage interest rate. You've protected the bank at your family's expense. On the other hand, if a family member is the recipient of the insurance proceeds at your death, that individual can choose to pay off the mortgage or decide to continue it at favorable rates and invest the insurance proceeds at a substantially higher interest rate.

Level term is the fourth type of term insurance coverage. Death benefits under a level term remain the same for the entire term of the policy. Generally, the premium also stays level. Level term policies are sold in one-year, five-year, ten-year, or twenty-year terms. Some companies express the duration in terms of the age you'll be when the policy runs out—such as "term to age 65."

Whole life

Chet asked his agent, Ric, if there is a term insurance policy that will never run out and in which premiums remain level for as long as Chet lives. Ric responded that *whole life* (permanent) insurance is "term to age 100." Ric explained that one of the major characteristics of whole life insurance is that the premium remains level throughout the life of the contract and that it can be kept for as long as Chet lives, no matter how long he lives. The insurance company can never cancel the policy no matter how old Chet becomes and regardless of what his health or hobbies.

A whole life contract is, in essence, a "term for life" policy. To maintain a level premium as you grow older, the insurance company builds up a *reserve*. It is the amount of money, together with the future premiums you'll pay and the interest that will be earned, that in later years will be used to keep the contract going when the level premiums you actually pay become insufficient.

This reserve that builds up in early years and is used up in later years can also serve another purpose: If you need money for an emergency or opportunity, you can borrow a guaranteed portion of this reserve (the "cash value") from the insurer. This policy loan can be made at extremely favorable rates. Alternatively, if you surrender the contract, since the company no longer has a potential liability, you can cash in (*surrender*) the policy for its "cash value."

Obviously, to build a reserve requires that the premium for whole life be higher than the premium for term insurance (just as the premium for twenty-year term is higher than that for ten-year term). A $100,000 policy for a man Chet's age, for instance, is about $1800 a year. (The rates for whole life, like term insurance, can vary significantly from company to company, so when purchasing *any* life insurance policy, insist that your agent shop . . . shop . . . shop!)

We recommend that you buy term and invest the difference. Establish a reasonable after-tax rate of return the "difference" should earn. Buy a lot of term—all the term insurance you honestly think your widow and surviving children will need. Then try, for one year, to invest the difference between the whole life premium and the term premium. If you did—and didn't touch the money you invested for the entire year *and* your investment equals or exceeds your after-tax objective, do it again and again until the year you find that (a) you've forgotten to invest the difference, or (b) the difference didn't grow as it was supposed to grow. (Many of us find that one of these two things happens more quickly than we expect.) We recommend as strongly that you be honest with yourself—and self disciplined. If you feel you cannot or would not meet your "invest the difference" goals (and most people don't), you are better off starting with whole life, universal life, or variable life. You will be amazed at the high rates of return that build up inside some of the policies being currently issued.

Keep one other thought in mind: If the "difference" you invest does grow and compound beyond your wildest dreams in the form of stocks or real estate or a business, how will your executor pay the estate and inheritance taxes? Probably your CPA or attorney will recommend that you help your executor to pay these costs by purchasing life insurance to pay estate settlement costs at a discount. So, eventually, you'll probably end up converting your term to some form of whole life.

How to Keep Your Insurance Going *without* Paying Premiums

What if you find after a few years that you can't afford to pay premiums but still need insurance protection? Should you cancel your policy? Before you do, remember you have "settlement options." These are guaranteed choices built right into your policy that can't be denied to you. For example, if you have a whole life policy, you can elect either "reduced paid-up" life insurance or "extended term" life insurance instead of cashing in your policy.

When you elect "reduced paid-up" life insurance, the cash value that is in your contract will be used by the insurance company to buy as much permanent life insurance as possible on your life. It will be the same type as the original policy, but it will be "paid-up." In other words, you will never have to put another nickel of premium into the contract, and you'll be insured for as long as you live.

For example, if Chet purchases a $100,000 whole life policy at age 35 and keeps it for 15 years, you'll see in the table on the next page the cash values at this time can be used to purchase a fully paid-up whole life policy with a face amount (death benefit) of $51,400. Although the death benefit payable to Chet's beneficiaries is smaller than if he'd continued to pay premiums, it still has a cash value as well as the continuing protection.

A paid-up option would be the right one to use where your need for insurance has decreased, but there is still some need and it can be expected to continue for quite some time or is indefinite.

If you can no longer afford to pay premiums and your life insurance needs have either stayed the same or actually increased, the right choice may be *extended term* life insurance. In this case, the cash value would be used to buy an amount of level term insurance equal to the face amount of the original policy. However, it would not purchase a policy for as long as you live. Instead, it would purchase a policy that would last for a term of time. How long a term? Again, looking at the guaranteed value schedule, you'll see that if Chet purchased a $100,000 policy at age 35 and stopped payment premiums 15 years later, at that time he could have the insurance company purchase a term insurance policy with a face amount of $100,000 that would last for a term of 20 years and 65 days.

This is a particularly good buy, since the premium rates that are applicable under these nonforfeiture options are lower than they would be if Chet purchased a new policy of the same type on his own. That's because the insurance company doesn't charge you any underwriting or administrative expenses, and there is no agent's commission to be paid.

Plan and Additional Benefits	Amount	Premium	Years Payable
Whole Life (Premiums payable to age 90)	$100,000	$2,000	55
Waiver of Premium (to age 65)		43	30
Accidental Death (to age 70)	100,000	78	35

(A premium is payable on the policy date and every 12 policy months thereafter. The first premium is $2,000.)

TABLE OF GUARANTEED VALUES

End of Policy Year	Cash or Loan Value	Paid-up Insurance	Extended Term Insurance Years	Days
1	$ 140	$ 300	0	152
2	1,740	4,500	4	182
3	3,380	8,600	8	65
4	5,060	12,500	10	344
5	6,760	16,400	12	360
6	8,790	20,700	14	335
7	10,840	25,000	16	147
8	12,930	29,100	17	207
9	15,040	33,000	18	177
10	17,190	36,900	19	78
11	19,080	40,000	19	209
12	20,990	43,000	19	306
13	22,940	45,900	20	8
14	24,900	48,700	20	47
15	26,900	51,400	20	65
16	28,910	54,100	20	66
17	30,950	56,600	20	52
18	33,010	59,100	20	27
19	35,080	61,500	19	358
20	37,180	63,900	19	317
Age 60	46,200	72,000	18	111
Age 65	55,040	78,600	16	147

(Paid-up additions and dividend accumulations increase the cash values; indebtedness decreases them.)

Direct Beneficiary: Cathy Horst, wife of the insured
Owner: Chet Horst, the insured
Insured: Chet Horst

Policy Date: May 1, 1981
Date of Issue: May 1, 1981

Age and Sex: 35 Male
Policy Number: 000/00

Borrowing from Your Policy

Earlier, we referred to policy loans. There are several differences between a loan you take out from a life insurance policy and a loan from a bank.

One advantage of a policy loan is the lower interest rates (possibly 5 to 8 percent lower) than what you'd have to pay at a bank.

A second advantage is that you know in advance exactly how much you can borrow from your insurance policy. You can be sure the insurance company will make the loan, regardless of the condition of the economy or your own financial situation. The only collateral for the loan is the policy itself, so you don't tie up other assets.

Third, you never really have to pay off a policy loan. Your loan will be subtracted from the death benefit if you do not pay off the principal before you die.

The reason you pay any interest at all is that the insurance company, in determining its premium rates and making its promises, has assumed that it would have the use of that money. So when you borrow it, you pay (a modest rate of) interest to the insurance company to make up for its loss of investment income.

If you look at your contract, you will see that the insurance company has guaranteed a specific rate of interest. Most new policies provide for an 8 percent policy loan interest rate.

In some states you'll pay a floating interest rate based on the prime if your policy is relatively new. This is one advantage of holding on to older policies. Another reason to keep the policy you have is that many older policies contain an astounding 5 or 6 percent policy loan interest rate.

Deductibility of Interest

Interest paid on personally owned life insurance will, in most cases, be considered *consumer* interest. This means that, if certain requirements are met, a partial interest deduction will be allowed as follows:

Year	Interest Deductible
1987	65%
1988	40%
1989	20%
1990	10%
1991 (and later years)	0%

Interest paid on business-owned (corporations, partnerships, and sole proprietorships) life insurance policies will be deductible in full and without limit if (a) certain requirements are met and (b) the policy was purchased on or before June 20, 1986.

Interest paid on business-owned life insurance policies purchased after June 20, 1986, is not fully deductible. The deduction is limited to the interest payable on up to $50,000 of loans from all policies owned on the life of the insured by the business. Interest in excess of the amount owed on $50,000 is nondeductible.

A strong note of caution: Many individuals who can no longer deduct interest will be tempted to surrender older policies that have been heavily borrowed against. These people—especially those who have been borrowing policy cash values to pay premiums ("minimum depositing" their contracts)—may be heading toward a form of tax suicide. The surrender of a life insurance policy is a taxable event. For example, assume Jane purchased a policy 20 years ago. Each year she had the insurance company automatically take her cash value buildup and use it to reduce her premium outlay. Assume total loans have been $40,000. Assume total premiums have been $20,000, and the cash value at surrender is $2000. Her gain—taxable all in the year of surrender—at ordinary income rates is $22,000. That's $42,000 ($2000 she *actually* receives plus $40,000 she is deemed to have received) less her cost ($20,000). In many cases, dividends will reduce cost further and significantly increase taxable gain. We recommend that you contact a CLU, ChFC, CFP, CPA, or a tax attorney before surrendering such a policy.

Types of Whole Life

Whole life insurance comes in two varieties. The first is known as *straight* life. The second is known as *limited payment* life. In a straight life policy, you pay a level premium each year from the time you take the policy out until the time you either die or surrender it (cash it in). But you can use policy dividends to pay up the policy much more quickly.

With a limited payment life policy, premiums are payable over a shorter period of time (compressed). For example, Chet is 35 years old. If he purchased a $100,000 straight life policy, the face amount would be $100,000. If he purchased a $100,000, 20-payment life policy at the same age, the death benefit would still be $100,000, and the protection would still be provided for as long as Chet wanted to keep the policy in force. But because premiums would be compressed into a much smaller period of time (20 annual payments), they would be considerably higher than under the straight life plan.

You may have heard about several other types of whole-life plans, such as *modified* life and *preferred risk* life. A modified life insurance policy typically provides a given amount of insurance at unusually low premium rates for an initial period (for example, the first three years) after issue, and then the premium is correspondingly higher for the remainder of the premium paying period. Modified plans generally have lower initial cash value than a corresponding face amount of typical straight life would have.

Preferred risk is the type of policy that generally requires that you be in above average health. Typically, preferred risk plans are sold only to professionals or to others who are in a low-risk occupation, are in above average health, or are nonsmokers. Also, preferred risk policies are generally sold only in higher amounts, such as $50,000 or $100,000.

But in return for being a preferred risk, the premiums you pay under such a plan could be substantially less per $1000 of protection than you would pay on a standard policy. It is definitely worth your while to qualify for a preferred risk plan if you can.

Interest-sensitive whole life

Many individuals express a desire for a traditional whole life product—one with (a) a level death benefit and (b) minimum assured cash values—but which was specifically designed to take advantage of high interest rates and improved mortality. Interest sensitive life does just that. The death benefit is level. The premium may change based on the insurer's experience. Cash values may change based on the insurer's experience, but a policy owner is assured a minimum cash value. Current interest (earnings based on current investments rather than on all investments in the insurer's portfolio) is applied to both cash values and dividends.

If interest rates are high, this type of policy will counteract inflation and capitalize on current economic conditions. But if current economic conditions are poor, premiums can increase to a point in excess of what would have been paid under the traditional whole life plan. The cash value could be lower than under a traditional whole life product.

Interest-sensitive whole life is similar to universal, variable, and single-premium whole life in one very important respect. Great "investment" rewards are available only at the price of increased investment risks. It is this cost a policy owner must be willing to pay in order to achieve greater returns than the solid guarantees inherent in the traditional whole-life product. Ask yourself to what extent you are willing to accept greater risks in return for the potential of greater reward.

Universal life

A number of insurance companies are now offering a policy known as *Universal Life*. Universal life was designed as a means of providing a better rate of return than is provided by the typical cash value permanent life insurance policy by taking advantage of high interest rates and improved mortality (and by shifting more of the investment risk to the policy holder).

Universal life permits the policy holder to change the amount and timing of premiums and the size of the death benefit automatically as needs change. A universal-life policy is, generally speaking, one in which the investment, expense, and mortality elements are separately and specifically defined. It works like this:

1. Policy owner selects a death benefit level.
2. The premium is paid periodically or intermittently.

3. The insurer takes out enough to pay for expenses and mortality (death risk) charges.
4. The remaining premium is then credited toward the contract owner's cash values.

Interest earned on the remaining cash is then credited at rates based on current investment earnings. (Specific features will vary from company to company depending on marketing policies and product objectives.)

Pay close attention to how the interest rate is determined. We prefer policies which base interest rates on an objective source outside the insurer's control (such as crediting cash values with a rate of return equal to the federal government's Treasury Bill rate). Under this configuration, increased interest rates result in higher cash value levels; increased expense loads and increased mortality charges result in lower cash values. Since these vary *considerably* from company to company, we repeat our admonition: Shop! shop! shop!

There is no such thing as a "standard" universal-life plan. Each owner selects the level of premium and death benefit desired as well as the length of the premium paying period.

Significant flexibility in premium payments is possible. Usually a stated minimum premium must be paid the first policy year. But after that, the contract owner can vary the amount, the payment date, or frequency of subsequent premiums. (Depending on the amount of the initial premium, additional premiums or premium increases may be limited to stated minimum or maximum levels.) "Stop and go" features allow the discontinuance as well as subsequent resumption of premium payments at any time. (It is not necessary to reinstate the policy to do this.) In other words, you can skip premiums, pay lump sums (within given limits), or change the timing of your premium payments.

As long as there is enough cash value to pay the expense ("loading") charges and mortality costs, the policy will remain in force. If the cash value falls below that level, the policy will terminate. However, there is a "grace period" (which we'll explain below).

Inflation seems to make universal life, with its relatively high rates of return, a very viable and appealing product. It is an important alternative to low-outlay term insurance as well as competitively priced whole life insurance.

When you purchase a universal life contract, you are accepting certain downside risks. Poor investment performance will result in lower cash values. If the "investment" (cash value) portion of the contract is too high relative to the amount of life insurance protection, the plan may not be considered a life insurance product for tax purposes. The results would be tax disaster. We suggest you insist on a home office letter stating that the policy will meet the tax law definition of life insurance.

Have your insurance agent give you a list of the advantages and disadvantages of universal life in your personal situation.

Adjustable life insurance

As our needs change, the amount and type of insurance we own should probably change, too. In recognition of that fact, a number of companies have created *adjustable* life insurance.

An adjustable life insurance policy, as its name implies, allows you to start with term and change to permanent, or start with permanent and change to term, or apportion your premium dollars periodically between the two types of coverage in accordance with your needs. Not only can you change the type of coverage, you can also change the amount of coverage. You can decrease the amount of insurance coverage you have without cancelling your policy. (You can do this with a typical life insurance policy by splitting the policy into two or more smaller ones and then cancelling one of the smaller contracts.)

Here is how adjustable life insurance works. You tell your agent how much you can afford each year for insurance premiums and together you determine how much life insurance protection you need. This information is given to the insurance company's computer, which then tells you whether the amount of money you have committed will purchase all the protection you need using the lowest cost premium plan available. If the premium you have committed is not sufficient, the computer program will illustrate an insurance package with less protection, and the lowest premium policy available will be purchased.

But if the amount of money you are willing to pay each year is greater than the cost of the protection you want using the lowest premium policy, your coverage will be adjusted automatically to a combination of term insurance and permanent insurance. As long as you continue to pay an amount at least equal to the premium needed to buy your desired insurance coverage using the lowest premium policy, you will be fully protected. If more money than the lowest efficient amount is needed, some or all of your protection will be in the form of permanent insurance.

There is an alternative approach: You can change the amount of the premium you are willing to pay and thereby purchase a different amount of term and permanent combination.

What are the drawbacks of adjustable life? Basically, the net cost under these contracts may not be as favorable as it would under a similar nonadjustable contract (assuming no change in coverage). Furthermore, the adjustable life contract cannot match certain "pure" type policies such as the annual renewable term life policy. This is an extremely low-outlay type of coverage (at least in early policy years), but it cannot be selected under the adjustable life type contract.

The adjustable life contract is most popular for relatively young individuals who currently need substantial amounts of insurance protection but who have minimal ability to pay. The flexibility of adjustable life is extremely important because of the changing needs and changing circumstances of such individuals.

Variable life

Variable life is another new insurance product. Unlike universal life, the premium is fixed. The death benefit is guaranteed to be not less than the face amount but can increase considerably if investment earnings exceed the assumed rate of interest.

The underlying investment nature of a variable life policy is security based, and (unlike universal life) you—the policy owner—get to choose the investment. You can select among the insurer's portfolio of stocks, bonds, or money market funds. The portion of the premium allocated to policy reserves is credited with the investment results of the funds you selected.

Variable life works like this:

1. You pay a premium to the insurer.
2. The insurer deducts certain charges. These include:
   (a) The cost of insurance.
   (b) A sales charge (the "load").
   (c) State premium taxes.
   (d) Annual administrative expenses.
   (e) A risk charge which insures the death benefit will not fall below a certain amount.
   (f) Policy issuance expenses (this is a first year only charge).
   (g) Investment advisory services and brokerage fees.
3. The balance is invested at your direction. Most companies give you a choice among 3 or more separate accounts.
4. The policy death benefits increase or decrease according to investment performance. (There is a guaranteed minimum amount.)
5. The cash value increases or decreases depending on investment performance of the separated account.

Single premium whole life

Life insurance with its tax-deferred appreciating cash values became extremely popular at the demise of most tax shelters in 1987. Single premium whole life is an *attempt* to satisfy the statutory guidelines for tax-advantaged life insurance while maximizing an investment orientation.

Unlike the traditional policy, in single premium whole life, the entire single premium paid at purchase is credited immediately with the declared rate of interest. The insurer recovers the cost of insurance and expenses from the difference between the declared interest rate and the rate the insurer actually earns. When the policy is surrendered, the insurer deducts any unrecovered costs from the policy's value.

Cash values can be obtained by surrendering the policy (any gain would be taxable). Policy loans are also available. Companies at this time are crediting all policy values—even those actually borrowed—with a rate of interest set at or close to the rate charged on money borrowed. The attempt is to allow the policy owner to enjoy interest income free of current taxation without jeopardizing the tax-advantaged status of the policy. But since the effect is as if the insurer neither charged or credited interest on borrowed sums, is this really a loan (tax free) or is it a withdrawal (taxable currently)? The stakes are high. We recommend you demand a "comfort letter" from the home office of the insurance company stating that they guarantee their arrangement meets current life insurance federal and state tax guidelines and that "loans" will be treated as loans rather than withdrawals.

Computing Your Life Insurance Needs

How much insurance do I need? That is a very difficult question. You need information on your personal financial status, your company's employee benefits, and social security benefits. There are literally dozens of different charts, formulas, and computer programs to answer that question. Here's a quick way to "guesstimate" your *minimum* needs:

First, list your current expenses (go through your cancelled checks for the amounts). Use Table A as a guide.

Table A

		Could Be Reduced to
a. Rent or mortgage (include taxes and insurance	$	$
b. Food		
c. Utilities		
d. Transportation (car payments, maintenance, repairs, insurance, gasoline)		
e. Education		
f. Insurance premiums		
g. Clothing		
h. Household items (appliances, furnishings, tools		
i. Recreation (dues, hobbies, entertainment)		
j. Medical and dental expenses		
k. Installment payments		$
l. Pocket money		
m. Savings		
n. Other		
TOTAL MONTHLY NEEDS	$	$

Second, opposite each expense, write the amount it could be reduced to if the family breadwinner were to die. Total the monthly needs and multiply by 12 to arrive at a *minimum* annual need. It takes 60 to 75 percent of your family's current gross income *to maintain your living standard* after one spouse dies.

Third, use the formula in Table B to determine how much *new* insurance—if any—you need (or how much surplus you can drop).

There are a couple of easier ways. One is to have two or three insurance agents analyze your situation. You can pick the analysis that gives you the lowest insurance need. Alternatively, you can take the average of the insurance needs projected by the agents. If you choose to be conservative, you could use the highest amount. (You are probably best off picking the figure used by the agent who seems most competent.)

Or, you can forget that approach altogether and allocate a given number of dollars (such as 3 to 5 percent of your after-tax income) to life insurance and buy as much insurance as that amount of money will buy.

Consider hiring an agent. Pay the agent for the time spent in making an analysis, with the stipulation that you wouldn't buy insurance from him/her in any event.

Regardless of what amount you finally settle on, or how you decide the amount of insurance to buy, remember this: No survivor ever complained that the family breadwinner carried too much insurance.

Exercising Your Policy Rights

There are many legal rights that you have in an insurance policy, and the more you know about them, the easier it is to exercise them. Let's look at some of the ownership provisions, dividend provisions, and various additional benefits (called *riders*) such as the accidental death benefit, disability waiver of premiums, and guaranteed insurability (often called insurance of insurability) option.

Table B

	Example	Your Numbers
a. Income I need	$ 20,000	$ _____
b. Interest rate I can earn	.10	$ _____
c. Capital I need (divide #1 by #2)	$200,000	$ _____
d. Capital I *already* have	$130,000	$ _____
e. New life insurance needed (subtract #4 from #3)	$ 70,000	$ _____

When Chet purchases his life insurance policy, regardless of whether it is term, whole life, universal, or variable life, he will have the right to name and change the beneficiary. This is the first and most important right you have in a life insurance policy. It is extremely important that you always name a secondary beneficiary. That way, if the primary beneficiary you have named dies before you do or "disclaims" (refuses to take) his or her share, your estate won't inadvertently become your beneficiary.

What's wrong with naming your estate as beneficiary? A lot! Typically, if your estate becomes your beneficiary, the proceeds become subject to the claims of your creditors. Policy proceeds may also become subject to a disgruntled heir who attacks the validity of your will. In most states, paying life insurance to any beneficiary *other* than your estate will make the proceeds eligible for special exclusions, exemptions, or tax rates. But, if your estate is your beneficiary, the proceeds may be exposed to state death taxes. So with life insurance what is important is not only what you have, and how much you have, but what you do with what you have! (That's one reason a caring and knowledgeable agent is essential!)

We have already described the major distinction between term insurance and permanent insurance. Permanent insurance contains guaranteed cash values. These cash values are an outgrowth of the fact that in the early years of the contract, the annual premium you were charged is higher than the actual cost needed to provide you with insurance protection in the early years. As noted previously, that excess money (the "reserve") is necessary for the insurance company to make up the deficiency of the level premium in later years when the annual cost of providing you with insurance protection actually exceeds the level premium you are paying.

The cash values are the portion of the insurance company's reserve that is available to you. You can borrow this money from the insurance company at a favorable rate of interest (in some cases as little as 6 to 8 percent), or if you cash the policy in, since you are releasing the insurance company from its potential liability (the death benefit), you may keep all the cash value and have no liability to the insurance company.

The policy cash value increases year by year. In fact, if you will look at your policy, you will find that there is a schedule that contains a guaranteed year-by-year increase in the cash values. (See the chart on p. 86.) The amount of this guaranteed annual increase in cash value will differ from company to company.

Most policies have relatively small annual cash value increases during the first year or two, but the increases will become greater as you keep the policy for a longer period of time. The small cash value in the early years of the policy protects the insurance company from the substantial loss it would incur if you cashed the policy in during the first year or two after it was purchased.

The right to borrow on your policy or cash it in is called a *nonforfeiture* option. You could take the guaranteed value in cash (see the table on p. 86), or elect to have it applied under one of the nonforfeiture options.

Policy Riders

Riders are provisions you can add on to your basic policy as options. One rider we strongly recommend is called *disability waiver of premium*. It provides that if you are totally and permanently disabled for a period of six months or longer, the insurance company not only takes over future premium payments to keep the policy in force but also repays all the premiums you may have paid during that six-month period. Disability waiver of premium is a "must buy" for whole life insurance.

What is the advantage of adding a waiver of premium rider to term insurance? One obvious advantage of this rider is that if you become disabled the premium for the term insurance will be waived. But another advantage is the effect of disability on your right to convert to a permanent policy and keep the term coverage from running out.

Some term insurance policies with waiver of premium will not allow *conversion* (a contractural right to change) to a permanent policy if you have become totally disabled. Other contracts do allow conversion. When you are comparing term insurance policies, be sure to check which provision you'll have. If you become disabled, it's advantageous to have a contract that automatically converts your term to a permanent contract, since the policy will not only stay in force and have its future premiums waived but also build cash values and dividends.

Some insurance agents recommend that instead of purchasing waiver of premium on your whole-life policy you buy additional amounts of disability income insurance. Why buy the waiver of premiums through a totally separate disability income policy rather than through a life insurance policy?

First, the additional costs under your personally owned disability income insurance may be lower than the disability waiver of premiums under your basic life insurance policy.

Second, and probably more important, the definition of "total disability" is typically more liberal in a disability income policy than the definition in your life insurance policy. For instance, under a disability income policy you'll receive income benefits if you are unable to perform *your present* occupation. Only after two years will you have to demonstrate that you are unable to perform in *any* occupation for which you are reasonably fit by virtue of education, training, or experience in order to continue to receive benefits. The point is that it is possible to be classified as disabled under the disability income policy long before you will be considered disabled under the life insurance policy definition. (Be sure to read about disability insurance in Chapter 19.)

Guaranteed Insurability (G.I.)

Another benefit that can be added to your basic policy and may be advisable when you are young is known as *guaranteed insurability* or *insurance of insurability*. This benefit allows you to purchase additional life insurance at certain specified future dates without proving you are insurable. This new insurance can be obtained at standard rates. When a given option date arrives, you have the right to purchase additional life insurance without proving you are insurable. On that option date, you can exercise all, part, or none of the option to purchase additional insurance.

Guaranteed insurability options are *noncumulative*. You use them or you lose them. The rights when you exercise a guaranteed insurability option are those applicable to the age and the year in which you exercise the option. In other words, if you wait until you are 35 to exercise an option to purchase more insurance, you will pay standard rates for a 35-year-old individual of your sex.

A typical guaranteed insurability rider allows you to purchase additional insurance three years after the date of your original insurance purchase and every three years thereafter until you reach age 40.

If you marry or have (or adopt) a child, some companies will allow you to move up a purchase date, and others will allow additional purchase dates, over and above those you already have.

Typically, these guaranteed insurability riders will allow you to purchase up to an amount equal to the face amount of the original policy (or some lower specified dollar amount). For example, if you purchased a $100,000 policy, the company may issue a guaranteed insurability rider enabling you to buy $25,000 of additional insurance every three years until your 40th birthday.

The guaranteed insurability rider is a good deal if your family has a history of serious illness (such as high blood pressure or kidney problems) prior to age 40. Since you will probably need more insurance in the future if you are below age 40, the guaranteed insurability guarantees that you will be able to buy additional insurance at standard rates regardless of your physical condition or the hobbies you may acquire (such as sky diving or scuba diving) in the future.

Another extremely important advantage—with some companies—is that, if you become disabled and you have waiver of premium under your original policy, not only will premiums be waived under that policy, but also the guaranteed insurability option will automatically be exercised to purchase new insurance. Premiums under the new insurance will automatically be waived. Obviously, when comparing policies, this feature is extremely important.

How to Avoid Estate Tax

If avoiding federal estate taxes is a major goal, many attorneys advise keeping insurance out of your estate. What is the best way to get life insurance out of your estate and keep it out? The easiest answer to that question is *never to have it there* in the first place. If at all possible, your beneficiary (such as your spouse) should own the policy right from the beginning. If your spouse (or adult child or trust for your spouse/minor child's benefit) purchases the policy and your spouse or child pays the premium personally, nothing will be includable in your estate. If that party cannot afford to pay premiums, the next best thing is to place money in an unrestricted bank account in that person's name. The money can then be used at that person's discretion to purchase insurance on your life. If you should die within three years of your gift of cash, neither the cash nor the proceeds of the policy should be included in your estate.

Alternately, if you are assigning a policy to someone to get it out of your estate, make an absolute transfer—don't keep any right to the policy, or the IRS will attempt to bring it back into your estate.

He or she who hesitates is lost. If you are going to give a policy on your life to someone else or to a trust to remove it from your estate, do it now. If you die within three years of a policy transfer, for tax purposes, it is in your estate. (The 1986 Tax Reform Act didn't change this.)

Beware of this tax trap: If your spouse purchases a policy on your life, he/she should be the beneficiary of the policy. If your wife names your children as the beneficiaries of a policy she owns on your life, at your death the IRS will claim that she is making a gift in the entire amount of the proceeds to your children. For instance, assume your wife buys a $100,000 policy on your life and names your children as beneficiaries. If you predecease her, at your death she will be deemed to be making a gift of $100,000 to your children.

What should be done? She should name herself the beneficiary. Then she should have your attorney provide in her will that, at her death prior to yours, the policy should go to you (if that is what you want to happen), or it should go directly to your children. Alternately, your life insurance agent can provide for a *contingent* owner, an individual who'll become owner of the policy in the event your wife predeceases you. You can be that contingent owner, or it can be your children or a guardian or trustee for your children's benefit.

The Best Policy Owner May Be You

Insurance proceeds from a policy you own on your own life payable to your spouse are in your gross estate. At best, until 1982 only a portion of these proceeds was deductible under the "marital deduction" allowed for property left outright (or in a manner tantamount to outright) to a spouse. No deduction at all was allowed if your wife received only the income from the proceeds, with the balance going to your children.

Current federal estate tax law is very different. You can now name your spouse as beneficiary of an unlimited amount of life insurance. Because of the unlimited marital deduction, not one dime of it will generate federal estate tax in your estate. You can even provide that your spouse is to receive only the income and that the balance is to go to your children. Your estate will still receive a martial deduction, and no tax will be generated even if the proceeds total $10,000,000 or more. The cost of this right to pick your children (or anyone else you want) as the ultimate recipient of the principal is that your executor must agree that when your spouse dies the principal remaining at that time becomes taxable in your spouse's estate.

Formerly, an estate planner would almost always advise successful clients to divest themselves of life insurance and have their spouses, or a trust for their spouses' benefit, own the insurance. But under current law, getting insurance out may not be "in" if the same tax result can be accomplished without giving up control of the policy and its valuable contractural rights. Before you make any decisions, talk to both your agent and your attorney about the best way to set up policy ownership.

The Transfer for Value Tax Trap

Another tax trap to avoid is the *transfer for value* problem. Here's how it works: Typically, the proceeds of a life insurance policy will be federal income tax free. So if you die and your beneficiaries receive $100,000, the entire amount is income (but not federal estate) tax free. This income tax exclusion is available even if you name your estate as beneficiary. (Estate planners generally recommend against naming your estate as beneficiary because of federal estate and state death tax and creditor implications.)

The general rule exempting life insurance proceeds from income taxation is an extremely valuable one. The federal income tax on $100,000— if the proceeds of the policy *did* become taxable—could be as much as $33,000.

The problem is the insidious "transfer for value" rule. The best way to explain how this rule works is through an example. Let's assume you sold a policy on your life to your spouse or child. The transfer of that policy in return for valuable consideration (the money you received) would "taint" the insurance proceeds. The death benefit would lose its income tax free status. The entire amount received by your spouse or child when you die would be subject to ordinary income tax (with the exception of the consideration paid for the policy plus any premiums the new owner pays after transfer). If you sold a $100,000 policy for $5000 and the new owner paid two $2500 premiums shortly before your death, $90,000 of the proceeds would be subject to ordinary income tax. That's tax disaster!

The transfer for value rule is highly technical. The important thing is to know that, if you transfer any interest in a policy and receive any kind of valuable consideration (other than love and affection), you may be setting the transfer for value trap. The solution is not to make *any* transfers of insurance on your life to any family member or trust for *any* reason without first checking with your agent and counsel.

Using the Grace Period Effectively—the 60-Day Umbrella

Every insurance policy must, by law, contain a *grace period*. This is a limited time during which a policy will remain in force even if you don't pay the premium when it is due. The grace period is one month. If you pay the premium at any time before the end of that grace period, the policy will not be cancelled. If you die during the grace period, the company will pay your beneficiaries just as if you had kept the insurance in full force. If you don't pay the premium by the end of the grace period, the policy will be cancelled. Of course, if it is a permanent policy and has a cash value, one of the nonforfeiture options described above can be selected.

The grace period makes it possible to shop for life insurance using the *60-day umbrella*. Many times you're not sure if the policy you are looking at is the best buy, but you know you need insurance and you know you need it immediately. What should you do? *Do not* take a chance! Purchase the insurance even if you feel there may be another policy that you could purchase at a lower cost. This gives you not 30 days but (together with the one month grace period) over 60 days to "look around." During that time, you are fully insured. If you decide the policy you have selected is the best available, pay off the premium that you should have paid during the grace period. But if you find a policy with a lower net cost (and its other features are comparable) have the new coverage begin on the 59th day (a little overlap is better than a lapse of even a few minutes). By using this method, you have the option of keeping or refusing the first policy, and your family has been protected meanwhile.

Automatic Premium Loan (APL)

Automatic premium loan. This is a provision that is in every whole life policy. It is designed to prevent a permanent policy from being cancelled if the premium has not been paid within the grace period. Under the APL provision, if you don't pay a premium by the time the grace period expires (31 days after the due date of the premium), the insurance company will pay the premium for you out of any policy loan value. This automatic loan is treated the same as any other policy loan. In other words, you are not required to pay the insurance company any money, but if you die, the loan can be taken by the insurance company from the death proceeds.

What's the advantage of APL? APL prevents a policy from "lapsing" (terminating) unintentionally. The nicest thing is that this provision is available at no additional cost. That means there is almost no reason why it shouldn't be elected in every policy that develops cash value. (Call your agent and make sure all your permanent policies have APL.)

Your Reinstatement Rights

Reinstatement is another privilege you have with every policy. If you allow a policy to lapse (either inadvertently or purposely) and your coverage is cancelled, you can still reinstate the policy if you meet certain conditions.

First, most policies contain a time limit within which you must choose to reinstate the policy. Typically, this is three to five years from the date the policy is cancelled. Second, if you decide to reinstate a policy, you will usually have to present new evidence of insurability. That means that you may have to take a new physical exam or answer certain questions about your health, occupation, and avocations. Furthermore, you have to pay any premiums (together with interest) that you would have paid had you not allowed the policy to lapse.

But why would anybody choose to pay back premiums (plus interest) to reinstate an old policy rather than simply buying a new one? One reason is that, in the old policy you have already paid off high first-year costs that are involved in putting a new life insurance policy into force. That means that you are building up cash values and dividends (explained below) more quickly than if you started a brand-new policy.

Second, many older life insurance policies have a lower policy loan interest rate than policies currently being used. In the long run, this can save you hundreds or even thousands of dollars.

Third, because you are older, a new policy would require you to pay a higher annual premium.

Be sure, before you do anything, to have your insurance agent show you—*in writing*—the pros and cons of reinstating the insurance you have allowed to lapse.

Protection under Your Reinstatement Clause

Life insurance is unique among all legal contracts. Life insurance is the only contract that has an incontestable clause in it. (This may be another reason for reinstating a lapsed life insurance policy rather than purchasing a new one.)

An incontestable clause provides that after a life insurance contract has been in force for a stated period of time (typically, two years), the insurance company legally *cannot* deny a claim because of any error, concealment, or misstatement that you have made. Once the contestable period has expired, there are very few grounds on which an insurance company could challenge a death claim. Obviously, this clause has substantial value to a beneficiary after your death.

Another extremely important provision in a life insurance policy is a suicide clause. A suicide clause provides that, if you commit suicide *within* a specified period of time after the purchase of a contract (generally one or two years), the insurance company will pay your beneficiary an amount equal to the premiums you have paid (some companies also pay interest). Once your policy has been in effect for the stated period of time, the insurance company must pay the full face amount even if your death is the result of suicide.

Policy Dividends Defined

Knowing how to use policy dividends can make your life insurance much more effective and financially more profitable.

Life insurance, either term or permanent, may be *participating* or *nonparticipating.* Participating means that your policy shares in the favorable investment, expense, and underwriting experience of the company. In other words, if the company earns more than it expected, the favorable position of the company will be shared with its policy owners. These refunds are called *policy dividends.*

Technically, premiums from participating policies are set at a slightly higher rate than would normally be required in order to provide funds that might be needed by the insurance company in the event it has an unexpected emergency. But at the end of every year, the insurance company will refund (in the form of a policy dividend) a portion of the premium you paid that it doesn't need, i.e., an amount that reflects its favorable experience in investment income, operating expenses, and death claims.

It is important to note that the insurance company does not guarantee the amount of such policy dividends. This is particularly important in comparing or selecting an insurer. Ask your agent to show you not only what the company projects but how well dividends in the past have matched its dividend projections. The amount of dividend you receive will be determined by the actual year-to-year experience of the insurance company.

The insurance companies you should consider typically tend to be conservative in their estimates of future policy dividends. In many cases, actual dividends are substantially higher than their projections. If actual dividends have equaled or exceeded the estimated dividends in the past, you have some indication that the company's estimates of potential future performance are not highly inflated. (Check *Best's Reports* or

Flitcraft, two statistical sources on insurance company performance, in the business section of your public library.)

Using Your Dividends Most Effectively

What you do with your dividends is particularly important if your estate is small or medium sized. As the policy owner, you can elect to:

1. take dividends in the form of cash;
2. use your dividends to reduce the premiums you would otherwise pay;
3. buy paid-up additional insurance (see explanation that follows);
4. leave the dividend with the insurance company to earn (taxable) interest (the dividend is not taxable but the interest is);
5. purchase one-year term insurance equal to the cash value of the policy;
6. use dividends to pay off the policy at an earlier date than expected; or
7. use some combination of these.

The first option needs no explanation. The insurance company will send you a check each year (typically, starting at the end of the first or second year), and you cash the check.

The second option is that the insurance company automatically uses your dividend to reduce your next premium due on the policy. This is very much the same as if you had received the dividend and endorsed your check directly to the insurance company. Using this option lowers your outlay.

The third option involves using your dividend to purchase more life insurance. If you elect to buy *paid-up adds,* as insurance agents call it, your dividend will be used as a single premium. It will buy an additional amount of completely paid-up life insurance. The new coverage you buy with your dividend will be the same type as the policy you already own. This single premium purchases insurance based on your attained age, but it is a better deal than if you bought a new policy on your own. That is because there is no charge for underwriting expenses or commissions, and it requires no physical examination. We highly recommend this option.

The fourth option is to leave your dividend with the insurance company to earn (taxable) interest. Here, the insurance company is more or less acting like a bank or savings and loan institution. Although the dividend you receive is not taxable (because it is treated as a partial return of your premium), the interest you earn on your dividend accumulations will be taxable as income to you in the year you earn it even if you choose not to take it in that year. Typically, the interest rate paid on dividend accumulations will be comparable to (or in many cases better than) the rate you could earn in a local savings institution. However, be sure to check.

The fifth option is often called the *fifth dividend* option. Your dividend, whatever its amount, can be used to purchase one-year term insurance. The premium will be based on your attained age. But the rates again are very low because you are not charged for underwriting expenses, and you pay no commissions. This is such a good deal that the insurance company puts a limit on how much term insurance you can buy using your policy dividends. Typically, the maximum amount of one-year term insurance that your dividends will buy cannot exceed the cash value of the policy at the end of the prior year. But what happens if you have more dividends than you need? You have a right to select one of the other options for the balance of your dividend.

Vanishing Premiums

Because of the high rates of return enjoyed by insurers in the last few years, coupled with decreased mortality costs and reduced business expenses, policy dividends have been higher than ever. What does this have to do with the premiums? Actuaries figured out that, if you purchased a new policy this year, within 6 to 8 years, you could stop paying premiums and be insured for life.

How is this *vanished premium* possible? In participating policies, each year's new dividends (at a point in time typically 6 to 8 years after the policy is purchased), when added to the surrender value of paid-up additional insurance acquired from dividends until that point, are enough to pay the full premium forever. In nonparticipating policies (see the next section), the insurer uses each year's excess interest (interest earned over and above the amount guaranteed in the policy) to vanish premiums. The insurance company withdraws, automatically, a portion of that excess interest. When current excess interest, together with a withdrawal of accumulated excess interest, is enough to pay the full premium each year, the premium vanishes.

Nonparticipating Policies

Some policies do not participate in the favorable underwriting, investment, or experience of the company. If you have purchased a nonparticipating policy (*non-par policy*), regardless of how well the company has done, you won't receive any policy dividend. But premiums you will have paid for a non-par policy will be less than the gross premium for a participating policy of the same type and amount.

Should you buy a par or non-par policy? No one knows for sure which will be a better buy. It appears that inflation will continue, life expectancies will increase, and mortality costs will reduce. That should mean that future policy dividends on participating contracts purchased today will increase each year. But the question is, how long will your policy stay in force? With a participating policy, the longer you keep your policy, the lower your costs (because you receive more dividends). But you've also got to factor in the time value of money and the advantage of buying the same amount of insurance with less premium dollars when you purchase a non-par policy.

Term Insurance Riders—What to Get—What to Avoid

We have already discussed some riders or benefits you can add to your life insurance policy. Term insurance riders are popular on whole life plans, but there are other features you can add to your basic policy. For example, for a small extra premium, you can add an accidental death benefit to your basic plan. Should you die by accident before a specified age, a large additional benefit will be paid to your beneficiaries.

The most popular form of accidental death benefit is known as *double indemnity* since the accidental death benefit is based on a multiple of the face amount of the underlying policy. If you purchased a $500,000 policy, the accidental death benefit would be equal to (or a multiple of) the face amount. Typically insurance companies issue double or triple indemnity.

Should you have an accidental death benefit rider? Death by accident is statistically infrequent. However, if you are between 25 and 45, the odds are that your death within that period of time will occur because of an accident. If you are over age 45, the likelihood is that your death will occur through some kind of illness.

The key point to remember is that whatever amount of money your family needs is not increased because you die by accident. As a matter of fact, just the reverse is often the case. If you die by accident, the financial impact is sudden but often short. Conversely, death through illness is often long and drawn-out and, therefore, extremely expensive.

Your family needs adequate coverage regardless of when or how you die, and that should be your major concern. When you purchase insurance, to get peace of mind—no questions asked—buy *full-time, no restrictions* coverage. This should also answer your questions about "airport insurance." Why purchase insurance that covers you only for a few hours and has an "annual cost" per hour that's sky high? If your family needs the coverage, your insurance should be in force around the clock, 365 days a year.

How Is Life Insurance Taxed?

Premiums you pay for life insurance are not deductible. Premiums are considered nondeductible personal expenses. There are two special cases where the outlay for premiums is deductible. The first is where the premium payment is considered alimony. The second is the premiums you pay on a policy you have assigned (transferred absolutely) to a charity. The rules to gain deductibility in either of these two cases are highly technical, and the tests are easily flunked. Be sure to talk to both your insurance agent and your tax advisor before taking action in this area.

As mentioned earlier, dividends you receive on participating policies are not taxable income because life insurance policy dividends are considered to be a partial return of your premiums rather than payments of profits from the insurance company.

If you leave your dividends on deposit with the insurance company to accumulate interest, any *interest* on that accumulated dividend *is taxable* just as if you had earned the interest in a bank. But dividends that are used to purchase paid-up additional insurance or one-year term insurance create no income tax liability. The IRS treats such dividends as if you have received them in cash (a tax-free return of your capital) and then used them to buy single premium insurance.

How are you taxed when you cash in (surrender) a policy? If you receive more back than you paid, the difference will be considered ordinary income. It is taxable in the year you surrender the policy. What you paid (your cost) is measured by the total premiums you paid (excluding premiums paid for accidental death benefits or waiver of premium). If you have received your dividends in cash or used them to reduce your premiums, it is only your net premiums (gross premiums less dividends received in cash or applied to reduce policy premiums) that determine your costs on the contract. For instance, if you paid in $10,000 but received $2000 in dividends back, the cost would be $8000. If you cashed the policy in for $12,000, you would have a $4000 ($12,000 [amount realized] less $8000 basis) gain taxable at ordinary income tax rates. Remember, since TRA '86, income averaging of a large gain is no longer available.

How are you taxed if you take the money over a period of years rather than in a lump sum? Many people choose to take living benefits of a life insurance policy under a *settlement* option. A settlement option is a way you can take money other than in a lump sum. Proceeds that an insurance company places under a settlement option are taxed under the annuity rules. Basically, annuity rules are designed so that a portion of each payment you receive will be a nontaxable return of your cost. The other portion of each payment will be taxable income.

Your insurance agent can work with you and your tax advisor to determine what portion of each payment will be taxable and what portion will be income tax free.

At the insured's death, the proceeds of a life insurance policy are income tax free. Any interest earned on the proceeds is taxable.

How You Should Pay Premiums

How you pay insurance premiums can make all the difference. Insurance companies will calculate premium rates on the assumption that you will pay the entire premium at the beginning of the policy year.

Under that assumption, the insurance company will be able to invest your premium dollars for the entire year.

But if you pay premiums semi-annually, quarterly, or monthly instead of annually at the beginning of each year, the insurance company has less use of the money. To make up for that loss, there is an additional charge. Furthermore, it has the extra administrative expense involved with collecting premiums more often than once a year. How can you beat these surcharges?

One way is through a bank authorization. Many companies will allow you to make premium payments directly from your bank account. You authorize your bank to pay the insurance company monthly with funds from your account. Because of the savings involved in computer-to-computer transactions, the surcharge is reduced to approximately what it would be if you paid premiums semi-annually. Another way of accomplishing the same objective is through a payroll deduction plan. Many insurance companies will allow you to pay the same surcharge that would be levied on a semi-annual basis even though you are actually having salary withdrawals on a monthly basis. Of course, your employer has to be willing to assist the insurance company, and typically there must be at least ten employees participating in the payroll deduction plan.

How to Fight the Unfightable (Inflation)

Inflation is an enemy that every financial planner is struggling to defeat. Inflation has a particularly significant effect on the death benefit payable from your life insurance policy. If we assume a 10 percent annual inflation rate and death occurs 20 years from the time the policy is purchased, the purchasing power of the dollars paid will be substantially less than those same dollars at today's prices. For instance, assuming a 10 percent annual inflation rate and a $50,000 policy, the $50,000 would purchase only $7430 worth of goods twenty years from now—compared to $50,000 worth of goods and services if death occurs immediately. Stated in a different way, it will take $350,000 of life insurance 20 years from now to provide you with the purchasing power $50,000 will give you today.

Fortunately, inflation is a two-edged sword. Since the premiums you pay are level, the cost of paying premiums reduces year by year. For instance, if you assume the $50,000 policy requires an annual premium of $1250, you will have paid approximately $25,000 in premiums. But the "buying power," that is, the cost of these premiums, is only a little bit greater than $10,000.

Another factor that should be considered is what you do with policy dividends. If you receive them in cash or use them to reduce your premium payments, they will, of course, reduce your cost substantially. If you use them to purchase additional one-year term insurance, you'll have much more than $50,000 of coverage.

Many insurance companies have developed other tools to fight inflation. One of these is known as the *adjustable premium* policy. Under this arrangement, the initial premium is guaranteed for the first two policy years. After that time, the premium can increase but only to a specified maximum. The premium can be reduced, perhaps even below the initial premium, if the actual experience of the company is better than that upon which the guaranteed maximum is based. Savings that result from better-than-expected experience under this contract automatically reduce the premium you would pay.

Another type of contract to fight inflation is the *automatically increasing* whole life insurance policy. Under this arrangement, the face amount of the policy automatically increases at a given rate each year. One whole life policy grows at a compound rate of 3.5 percent annually for the first 20 years. Naturally, the premium must increase as well. Every five years the premium increases in an amount equal to 25 percent of the original premium. The last increase would occur after the fifteenth year, and the premium would remain level from then on. Obviously, to the extent inflation exceeds 3.5 percent compounded annually (which it has done with a vengeance in several of the last ten years), this policy will only partially offset inflation.

Perhaps the best way to fight inflation is to use policy dividends to purchase as much term insurance as possible. Dividends on a whole life policy, as described above, can be used to purchase one-year term insurance at extremely low cost.

9

How to Title Your Property

How you title property is extremely important. Should your car be in your name alone? Why does almost every married couple who owns a home have title in both names? When should property be in one name alone, and what are the advantages of one method over the other? Most important, what's the best way for you to take title to your assets?

Jack and Donna recently purchased a new home. The title to their home reads, "Jack and Donna Pursel, tenants by the entireties." What does a *tenancy by the entirety* mean, and what are the tax implications? How does a tenancy by the entirety differ from a *joint tenancy with the right of survivorship* or *tenancy in common?*

Different Forms of Joint Ownership

Let's start by examining the similarities and distinctions among (1) tenancy by the entirety, (2) a joint tenancy with the right of survivorship, and (3) a tenancy in common.

In the first two cases, if either Jack or Donna (the joint tenants) should die, the interest of the decedent passes by law directly to the survivor. So if Jack dies first, Donna automatically owns both her interest and the interest Jack had owned. In either case, the property she'll own will be free from the claims of Jack's personal creditors.

These first two forms of property ownership either implicitly or directly give the co-owners *rights of survivorship.* This means the survivor doesn't have to worry about what the decedent's will says—or does not say. Because Jack's interest passes by law and not under his will, Donna will not have to worry that Jack's other heirs may attack his will. She takes her interest in these first two forms of jointly held property automatically and immediately at his death.

Another similarity between these two forms of joint tenancy is that in both cases the property passes outside of probate, the legal process under which a will is proved to be the decedent's last will and under which the estate is administered (discussed in detail in Chapter 6). Avoiding probate may save costs in some cases and avoid delays. Joint tenancy may also save state inheritance and federal estate taxes.

109

A distinction between a tenancy by the entirety and a joint tenancy with a right of survivorship is that the latter may consist of any number of persons and can exist whether or not those persons are related by marriage. Jacks' two brothers and three cousins could join Jack and purchase property jointly, and each co-tenant could have rights of survivorship. But a tenancy by the entirety can exist only between a husband and wife. A spouse who owns a property interest as tenant by entirety cannot unilaterally sever (sell or give away) his/her interest. Severance can only occur by mutual agreement, termination by divorce, or conveyance by both spouses to a third party. For example, Donna could not sell or give away her share of the house unless Jack agreed to the sale in writing.

Each joint tenant of a *rights of survivorship* tenancy can, without anyone else's approval or signature, sever (*partition*) the tenancy. In the example above, one of Jack's cousins could unilaterally decide to sell her interest—or give it away—say to her friend, Sadie. Sadie, the purchaser (or donee), would then be a *tenant-in-common* with all the other co-tenants. That means, if Sadie dies, her interest does not go automatically to the survivors. Instead, it would go to her beneficiaries under her will or, if she didn't have a valid will, to her heirs under her state's intestacy laws. If Jack (or any of the other tenants with rights of survivorship) died, his property interest would be redistributed among the survivors—except for Sadie, who didn't have survivorship rights.

In those situations in which title is held as tenants-in-common, upon the death of one co-tenant, his/her share passes to the heirs designated in a valid will or, if there is no valid will, the share passes under state intestacy laws. The surviving tenant-in-common doesn't receive anything (unless he or she also happened to be an heir under the deceased tenant's will or under state intestacy laws). This means that if one co-tenant dies, his/her interest passes under the deceased co-owner's will and, therefore, becomes subject to probate. It will not pass to the survivor tenant-in-common (unless it does so under the decedent-tenant's will or by the laws of intestacy).

Advantages of joint tenancies with rights of survivorship

What is good about tenancies by the entirety or joint tenancies with rights of survivorship? Why do so many people own property in one of these ways?

First, you can be certain if your co-tenant dies that the property will be quickly, easily, and (in most states) automatically and immediately transferred to you. So you have the psychological sense of family unity and security. That is why most financial advisors recommend that the family home and small checking and savings accounts be held in this manner.

Second, as was mentioned, in many states the personal creditors of a co-owner cannot make claims against jointly owned property. Donna can be sure that her home and other jointly held property is safe from Jack's business and personal creditors.

A third advantage of jointly owned property pertains to state death tax savings. Some states exempt jointly owned property from state death taxes. This can be significant and become particularly important if there is no state limit to the amount of jointly held property that is exempt. For instance, Jack and Donna live in Lancaster, Pennsylvania. Pennsylvania's inheritance tax for property owned by one spouse and left to the other spouse is 6 percent. But if the same property is jointly held, when one spouse dies, there is no inheritance tax. So if their home, purchased solely with Donna's earnings, is worth $200,000, the state inheritance tax savings is $12,000. In other words, if Donna owned the same house solely in her name, at her death Jack could have been subjected to a $12,000 state death tax. But because it is jointly held between spouses, it is totally exempt (as is all the other property Jack and Donna own jointly with each other) from Pennsylvania inheritance taxes. Inheritance taxes could also be saved even if the joint owners were not husband and wife. If Jack had a $10,000 Certificate of Deposit in his name, and left it to his daughter Amy in his will, inheritance taxes would have to be paid on the entire $10,000 (at 6 percent it would be $600). However, if Jack had titled the account in his name and Amy's name as joint tenants with right of survivorship, at Jack's death, Amy only pays tax on one-half of the amount, or $300. The tax is paid only on the fractional portion of the property that Jack owned at the time of his death.

Freedom from probate is a fourth advantage. Since jointly owned property with right of survivorship does not pass through probate, there is no possibility that the change of ownership will be delayed in estate administration or be subjected to the additional costs of probate.

A fifth advantage is a by-product of the fourth—property that passes by survivorship is not subject to the same public scrutiny or publicity that accompanies the probate of a will which then becomes a public document. This aspect is particularly important if you don't want well-meaning (and sometimes not so well-meaning) and often misguided friends, relatives, and other "advisors" telling your survivor how to handle his or her assets.

Disadvantages of joint ownership

One big disadvantage of joint ownership is loss of control. Property held in joint ownership with survivorship rights can't be disposed of in your will or through a trust you have established. So regardless of what Jack says—or does not say—in his will, if he was a joint tenant with right of survivorship in land in Wildwood with his brother and cousins, at his death the property would pass to them—and not to Jack's wife, Donna. (Many people have elaborate wills and trusts that will be totally useless at the death of the first of two co-tenants to die, since the decedent's will does not operate on joint tenancy property.) The bitter irony is, even though the property will go to Jack's cousins rather than his wife, Jack's estate might have to pay estate taxes on the property.

Second, neither Donna nor Jack could unilaterally rent their home, sell it, or give it away (this disadvantage, of course, serves to protect the other joint owner, and from that viewpoint is advantageous).

Title to jointly held property passes immediately and automatically to the surviving co-tenant. Although this sounds good, Jack can't provide for any management of the property (in other words, he cannot have it go to a trust to assure that it will be handled wisely). This may force Donna to make investment and management decisions she may not want to make (or be capable of making).

Hidden state gift tax costs (not all states have gift taxes) can be an unpleasant surprise at both the creation and the severance of a joint tenancy or tenancy by the entirety. (Federal law provides for an unlimited "marital deduction" for gifts one spouse makes to another—you can literally give your entire estate to your spouse and pay no gift tax.) Say Donna calls her stockbroker and has him purchase one hundred shares of Z Steel Company stock "in my name and my husband Jack's name as joint tenants with the right of survivorship." Jack is being given an interest he did not have before. Donna is making a gift of about half the value of the property. If it is large enough, in many states this gift may generate state gift taxes.

Now assume the stock appreciates substantially, and Jack and Donna decide to sell it. If Jack tells Donna to put the proceeds in her bank account, he may be making a gift of his interest to her. So it is possible that your state's tax authority will claim that two taxable gifts have been made: One when the property was titled jointly and Donna gave Jack his interest, and another when Jack gave his interest back to Donna.

Still another problem inherent in too much jointly held property is what estate planners call "overqualification" of the marital deduction. It means you have needlessly subjected too much property to taxation at your surviving spouse's death. How? By passing more property than is necessary to maximize the use of the "marital deduction."

For example, assume Jack's estate, at the time of his death in 1987, was worth $900,000. Deductible debts and expenses total $100,000. What would happen if Jack's entire $800,000 "adjusted gross" estate were held jointly with Donna? Everything would pass to Donna at his death. The federal estate tax law allows Jack to leave Donna (through will or otherwise) an unlimited amount of property estate tax free. The catch is, when Donna dies, the property she's received from Jack (as-suming she hasn't given it away or used it up) is added to her own assets and taxed. Worse yet, Jack's estate was allowed—and could have taken—a "unified credit" that would shelter up to $600,000 from tax; Jack could have passed $600,000 to his children that wouldn't have later been taxed when Donna died. But he did not. By *overqualifying the marital*, that is, by passing too much to Donna, he *underutilized his unified credit*. That's all legal jargon for saying that $600,000, that didn't have to be subject to tax when Donna dies, will now have to be subjected to tax.

How could this overqualification have been avoided? If the property was owned only in Jack's name, Jack could have given Donna an amount equal to his estate after adjustment for debts and expenses ($800,000), less the amount he could pass tax free under the unified credit to anyone he wanted ($600,000). She could have received $200,000 outright or in a "marital" trust. This trust would have provided management protection and investment advice for the $200,000, but would have made the funds available to Donna at her request. Alternatively, Jack could have given $200,000 to Donna outright.

The other $600,000 could have been left by Jack to a "family" (estate planners call this a *nonmarital* or by-pass) trust. That family trust would provide further security for Donna during her lifetime. She would receive all income from the trust as well as certain other rights and privileges. But at her death, property in that trust would go directly to their children. Because of the way the trust was arranged—it would bypass federal estate tax at her death, i.e., not be taxed again in Donna's estate.

It is possible, therefore, through a *zero tax marital deduction formula clause* in a will or trust, to pass just the right amount of property (no more and no less) to a surviving spouse. This zero tax marital deduction maximizes the utility of both the estate owner's unified credit and the marital deduction. The surviving spouse does not receive more than the amount of property that will maximize tax savings at the first spouse's death. At the same time, assets have been kept away from the surviving spouse's estate property and can pass free to children or other heirs at the death of the surviving spouse. This zero tax technique can save—literally—tens (and in some cases hundreds) of thousands of dollars from federal estate taxes. See the discussion of the marital trust in Chapters 7 and 13, and ask your attorney to check to see if too much of your property is jointly held or if you ought to be taking advantage of the zero tax marital formula concept.

Community Property System

There are presently eight states that use the community property system of determining the interests of a husband and wife in property acquired during the marriage and a number of other states (such as Wisconsin) with marital property laws that have an effect similar to community property. All other states and the District of Columbia apply common law principles of marital property ownership.

The community property states are Arizona, California, Idaho, Louisiana, Nevada, New Mexico, Texas, and Washington. Although the underlying theory of the marital community is the same in each of these jurisdictions, there are distinct variations and differences among the eight states. Accordingly, the statutes and case law of a particular state must be consulted to determine the precise rules that will apply to your marital property.

By definition, community property ownership can exist only between husband and wife. The marriage is viewed as a form of partnership between the husband and wife. There is an operative presumption that property acquired during the marriage is community property. Each spouse is permitted, however, to acquire and own his or her "separate property" in addition to community property.

During the marriage, special rules govern the management, control, and disposition of community property. When the marriage is dissolved by divorce or death, the community ceases its existence; the property is divided or partitioned between the spouses or between the surviving spouse and the decedent spouse's estate.

Community property, once acquired, will generally retain community status even upon removal to a common law jurisdiction. Conversely, separate property will remain separate when brought from a common law state to a community property state.

Community property defined

Most community-property statutes define community property by first defining separate property and then defining all other property as community property. Generally, separate property is property owned by either spouse before marriage, as well as any property acquired after marriage by gift, bequest, devise, or descent, together with rents and profits from such property. All other property acquired by either spouse after marriage is considered community property.

Quasi-community property

Generally speaking, the community-property system does not provide for typical common law interests such as dower, curtesy, or statutory rights of election of a share of a spouse's estate. Thus in the typical community-property state, a decedent cannot elect against a spouse's will.

Altering Community Rights

In general, husband and wife may agree either before or after marriage to alter community-property rights. For example, they may agree that listed common stock that was acquired after marriage will be divided equally between them so that half belongs to each spouse as separate property. They could also agree that all stock owned as community property—or a major portion of it—would become one spouse's separate property. Furthermore, they could agree that all future earned income of one spouse would be the separate property of the spouse who earned it. A division of the property in other than equal shares, however, could cause one spouse to have made a taxable gift to the other.

Management of community property

In most community-property states, the husband and wife jointly manage real property, and both must join in the execution of any deed. On the other hand, the husband is traditionally the manager of the personal property, and his discretion is absolute, although he cannot defraud his wife of her rights. The wife controls the personal property to the extent that she can validly contract for necessities.

Estate taxation of community property

Only one-half of the value of community property is included in the estate of the first spouse to die. Similarly, if community property has been converted either to a tenancy-in-common or a joint tenancy with the right of survivorship, only one-half of the value of the property is includible in the gross estate of the first to die.

Effect of New Domicile on Property Rights

The move from a community-property state to a common-law state should not, of itself, alter the rights of the parties or the nature of their interests in the property. As a matter of fact, the attempt on the part of one spouse to alter substantially the rights of the other spouse in community property would be in violation of due process under the Fourteenth Amendment of the United States Constitution.

PART THREE

ESTATE PLANNING TAX STRATEGY

How to Avoid, Reduce, and Defer Estate, Gift, Inheritance, and Income Taxes

10

The Tax Strategy Estate Planning Alphabet

This book covers literally hundreds of tools or techniques available to more efficiently and effectively help you accumulate, conserve, and distribute your estate. But before deciding on which technique to use, consider the tax strategy that makes them work. In fact, tax strategy is often the key to achieving your desired objective.

We start the planning of our clients' estates with the *Estate Planning Alphabet*—a nmumonic device that helps remind us of the various tax-oriented strategies available under the new law. The Estate Planning Alphabet consists of:

C, D, D, D, D, E, F, and G

which stand for: Create, Divide, Deduct, Defer, Discount, Eliminate, Freeze, and Gelt. Here's how the Estate Planning Alphabet can spell tax savings for you:

C **Create.** In Chapters 13 and 15, you'll read how to create assets that will not be subject to federal (and in many cases state) death taxes by setting up a *Supertrust* or by implementing a SIBP, a survivor's income benefit plan.

D **Divide and conquer.** Estate and gift tax rates are similar to the income tax rates in that they are all *progressive*. (That doesn't mean things get better.) Progressive means the more you earn, the greater your wealth—or the more you give away, the more income or estate or gift tax you must pay. But by dividing you can conquer. You can turn the progressive nature of these tax rates against themselves. Through a form of "tax judo," you can cut down or cut out the tax bite. In Chapters 16 and 19, you will learn many ways to create new taxpayers or more effectively use family members to reduce the tax burden.

D Deduct. Deductions are an important part of tax planning. But we often overlook or underutilize or inadvertently fail to qualify for devices such as the estate and gift tax marital deduction described in Chapter 13, IRAs, HR-10s, 401(k) plans, or SEPS, or qualified pension and profit-sharing plans described in Chapter 17.

D Defer. When you can defer the payment of tax, you achieve several advantages. First, if there is less income in a given year to tax, you may avoid surcharges that push you out of lower brackets and into higher ones. Likewise, personal exemptions that might otherwise have been phased out are retained to shelter income that otherwise would have been taxed.

Second, you may be able to move the income from a high to a lower bracket year. For example, you may shift income from your peak earning years to lower income (and, therefore, lower bracket) retirement years. You may be able to shift income from low or no deduction years to years when high deductions shield more income from tax.

Third, you can earn money with the tax you otherwise would have paid, using *the time value of money.* If you can stretch out the deferral long enough, you'll have years to invest money that otherwise would have been paid in taxes. In some cases, the unpaid tax may never have to be paid. You'll learn more about deferral devices in Chapter 14.

D Discount. If you plan ahead, your federal estate taxes can be paid for at a discount of pennies on the dollar. In fact, you'll be surprised and pleased to know that state taxes and other estate settlement costs can be paid at just pennies on the dollar with assets that aren't themselves included in your estate. Two estate cost discount devices are described in Chapter 14.

E Eliminate. "The federal estate tax is a voluntary tax; you can pay it if you want to but if you don't want to, you don't have to." It's true. You can significantly reduce or even eliminate the tax on hundreds of thousands—even millions—of dollars of wealth. Although there is no free lunch in the tax law, and every planning move has its cost, if you are willing to pay the price (often a surrender of control or possession of an asset), you can significantly reduce or even eliminate income, estate, or gift taxes. Read how in Chapters 12 and 13.

F Freeze. You can *freeze* the growth of wealth, avoid needless exposure to higher and higher estate tax rates, and shift growth (and therefore the tax on wealth) to lower bracket family members. You'll keep more of your family's wealth by reading and implementing the ideas in Chapter 16.

G Gelt trip through time. *Gelt* is the Yiddish word for money. During the last few years, sophisticated planners have developed a number of devices to save vast sums of money. These devices are based on the concept of the time value of money and a judicious use of IRS time/money valuation tables. You'll find a thorough discussion of GRITS, SPLITS, and RITS in Chapter 20.

In Summary

Once you've learned how to use the tax strategy estate planning alphabet, you'll want to combine it with the dozens of nontax tools and techniques described in this book. These nontax devices include a properly drafted will, adequate amounts of the right type of life insurance, and the creation of a comprehensive record-keeping and goal-tracking system.

11

How to Protect Your Family from Confiscatory Death Taxes

Part 1:
The Federal Estate Tax and the
Generation-Skipping Transfer Tax

One word that appropriately characterizes both the federal estate and generation-skipping transfer tax is "confiscatory." If you don't plan, the federal government—rather than your family—will be the "beneficiary" of a large part of your estate.

Understanding how the federal estate tax works is the key to beating the system. We'll examine what to do—and what not to do—as we look at the case of Jim and his wife, Grace. Jim is 42. Grace is 38. Jim is a senior executive in a small but highly profitable investment company. Jim and Grace have three children—Ted, Jeff, and Jonathan. We'll do a quick overview of the computation process and then come back and look at how each tax provision works. As we proceed you may want to substitute your own figures. You may be surprised!

Computing the Tax

Here is how the federal estate tax would be computed (we'll follow the form on page 132:

1. First, Jim's executors would have to compute his "gross estate." This is the total of all property Jim owned when he died. It also includes some property that Jim didn't own technically but which the tax law requires his executor to include in his estate. (This will be discussed in greater detail later.)
2. After Jim's executor computes his gross estate, deductions can be taken for funeral and administrative expenses as well as for certain debts and taxes. The result is Jim's *adjusted gross estate.*

3. Then (one or more) deductions may be allowed for (1) property passing to a surviving spouse (the *marital* deduction), and (2) property passing to a charity (the *charitable* deduction). The result, after taking these deductions, is the *taxable estate*.

4. The term *taxable estate* is slightly misleading because certain gifts Jim made during lifetime (so-called "adjusted taxable gifts"—the taxable portion of gifts you make after 1976) must be added back at this point. The federal estate tax rates are applied to the total.

5. Jim's executor may reduce the tax otherwise payable by one or more credits. The credits, which provide for a dollar-for-dollar reduction of the tax, are:

   (a) The unified credit (a credit in 1987 and later years equivalent to the tax on roughly $600,000 worth of assets. The credit is allowed to every taxpayer regardless of how that property is left or to whom. The $600,000 unified credit may be used during lifetime to offset gift taxes for lifetime gifts or at death to offset estate taxes or used partially during lifetime and then the credit remaining can be used at death);

   (b) The credit for state death taxes (Jim's estate will be allowed a federal credit for the state death taxes his estate actually pays—up to specified limits);

   (c) The credit for foreign death taxes (if Jim owned property subject to tax in another country); and

   (d) A credit for estate taxes paid by the estates of other decedents for assets included in Jim's estate. (This is called the credit for tax on prior transfers and is allowed only if the two deaths occur within a short time of each other.)

6. After the estate tax is reduced by the sum of these credits, another tax must be considered. This is a 15 percent excise tax (essentially an estate tax) levied only on certain pension or profit-sharing accumulations paid at death, so called *excess accumulations*. This tax is added to any estate tax remaining. The net is the total federal estate tax.

Note that total liquidity costs (demands for cash) include the following:

a. Funeral and administration costs (line 2 on page 132)
b. Debts and unpaid taxes (line 3 on page 132)
c. The state death tax payable (line 14 B-1 on page 132)
d. The net federal estate tax payable (line 16 on page 133)
e. Total cash bequests (line 17 on page 133)

How to Reduce Your Estate Taxes

Jim could save estate taxes if he knew what was includable in his estate and why. Then with the advice of his advisors, he could remove the appropriate assets. Let's go back to the beginning of the computation process and see what would be includable and how we could prevent or minimize estate tax inclusion.

As we go, make a list of the property you own that would be includable under each category and state the approximate value. We'll run what estate planners call a *hypothetical probate*, a financial x-ray of how much tax and other expense your estate would have to pay if you died today. When you finish, you'll have a good idea of how much liquidity your executor must have to avoid a forced sale of assets to raise cash.

Category 1   Property titled solely in your name

Jim's executor must include all the property he owned in his own name at the time of his death. Any cash, stocks, bonds, notes, real estate, or mortgages payable to Jim, as well as any *tangible* personal property (touchable, movable property) Jim owns, such as watches, rings, and other personal effects, must be included. Bank accounts Jim keeps in his own name (both checking and savings) are includable. Even the right to future income is includable. (If Jim had the right to partnership profits, dividends, interest payments, or bonuses that he hadn't actually received when he died, the value of these amounts must be included in Jim's estate.)

How could Jim avoid taxation on property he owns in his name? One way is to get it out of his name and have someone else own it. Jim could make small gifts each year to his wife, Grace, and to his three children. A better way is to purchase assets in their names right from the start. That way the appreciation grows in their hands. That's another way of saying that Jim wouldn't have to pay a gift tax on any future growth since he's given away cash and, therefore, removed the asset it is used to purchase at the lowest possible cost. For example, instead of buying stock at $10 a share and then giving it away when it's worth $100 (and paying gift tax based on the $100 date-of-gift value), Jim should give cash now to a custodian or trustee for his children. Then the stock could be bought in their names so that if it grows from $10 a share to $100 over the next five years, neither the initial value nor the growth would occur in Jim's estate.

- **List approximate value of assets you own in category 1 $_____**

Category 2   Gifts in which you retain the income or control over the property or income

The best way to explain this category is to say: You can't give away your cake and expect to continue to eat it—and still avoid the estate tax. If Jim gives away property but keeps the right to the income it produces or the right to determine who will receive the income or the right to use or possess or enjoy the property itself, that retained right will cause the entire value of the property—measured on the date of Jim's death—to be includable in his estate.

The logic for this seemingly harsh rule is that the right to enjoy or control property or determine who will receive the property or its income is a key characteristic of property ownership. To an important degree, giving away property but keeping the income is an incomplete disposition; your donee's full and complete possession or enjoyment of the property doesn't start (and, therefore, your ownership does not end) until you die.

How can you avoid inclusion under this category? The answer is to make each gift absolute and with no strings attached. For example, according to a number of cases, you could give your home to your spouse and continue to live in it as long as you make her absolute owner of the property. You could give your home to your children, but it's very important that you either move out or pay them a reasonable rent and have all documents changed to indicate that they are, in fact, the new owners (it also helps if they pay real estate taxes and the other expenses of running the home).

- **Approximate value of assets you own in category 2 $_____**

Category 3   Gifts made conditional on surviving you

Jim gives an asset to one of his sons in trust but conditions the son's right to it on surviving him. For instance, Jim might put real estate worth $100,000 in trust for his son, Jonathan. Assume the trust provides that "the property is to go to my son, Jonathan, if he survives me, *but if* he does not survive me, the property is *to go back to* my estate or to the person I name in my will to receive it." If there is a meaningful probability that the property will return to Jim (or a beneficiary of Jim's estate), the value of the property transferred will be includable in Jim's estate.

Jim's right to regain the property (or the right to say who will receive it) if his son does not survive him is called a *reversionary interest*. This type of transfer is includable in Jim's estate because it is considered to be—in substance—a substitute for disposing of the property by will.

How do you defeat this section of the tax law? Very simple. Your attorney should specify that the property will go to some party other than you or your estate if the condition you've established isn't met. For instance, you might say, "If my daughter is not alive at the time of my death, my land in Wildwood is to go to my nephew, Farnsworth."

- **Approximate value of assets you own in category 3 $_____**

Category 4   Gifts you made but retained the right to alter, amend, revoke, or terminate.

Most gifts are outright. We give our children or relatives presents on their birthdays or holidays. We give them cash or stocks or bonds or set up bank accounts for them.

But sometimes because of the size of the gift, the lack of maturity, or the financial management or investment ability of our recipients, we want to tie up the gift or place certain limitations or restrictions on it. Usually such gifts are made through a custodial account (like the Uniform Gifts to Minors Account) or in trust.

Jim, for example, might set up gifts in trust for his minor children. So far so good. He's been wise to provide management protection and investment advice for them. But if Jim retains a right to change the gift he's made, or to alter it, amend it, revoke, or terminate it, the value of the property subject to that power will be in his estate. Worse yet, it will be in his estate at its value when he dies—not when he made the gift. For instance, if Jim put $10,000 into a trust for his children and it grew to $80,000 by the date of his death, the entire $80,000 would be in Jim's estate if he held one of the prohibited powers.

What are the forbidden rights that will cause estate tax inclusion? The mere power to control the date a beneficiary will receive his interest will cause inclusion. So if Jim, in the trust instrument, retains the right to accelerate one son's interest so that he receives it sooner than another son, the property will be in Jim's estate (even if Jim can't personally benefit in any way).

Worse yet, the IRS construes this rule broadly. That means that even if Jim held an alter, amend, revoke, or terminate right as trustee or co-trustee, the property would still be in his estate.

How do we avoid inclusion under this law? Be sure you are not trustee or co-trustee or custodian for a gift you make or a trust you establish. Also, provide in the trust or custodial instrument a substitute (other than yourself) in case the *fiduciary* (the person with the responsibility of safeguarding your beneficiary's interests) you named cannot or will not serve.

- **Approximate value of gifts you own in category 4** $_____

Category 5   Annuities or similar arrangements you purchase (or that are purchased on your behalf) that are payable to you while living, and then to your designated survivor

If you are receiving an *annuity* (a systematic liquidation of principal and interest) that will last as long as you live and payments are to continue for the lifetime of a survivor you have selected, at your death the *present value* of your survivor's interest will be in your estate.

Say Jim purchased an annuity (or Jim's employer buys one or creates one for him as an employee benefit) that would pay $30,000 a year for 10 years at either retirement or death. The value of the income stream Grace is expected to receive is discounted to its present value as of the date of Jim's death (there are IRS tables used to make this present value calculation) and included in Jim's estate.

Fortunately, there are two qualifications: First, if you purchase an annuity (or your employer provides one for you as an employee benefit) and it ends at your death, nothing will be in your estate. This is because the federal estate tax is a levy on the transfer of property. If there is no transfer or shifting of rights when you die, nothing is includable in your estate—and so there is no federal estate tax.

Second, to the extent that your survivor furnished part of the original cost of the annuity, that portion of the value of the survivor's annuity will not be in your estate. So if Grace paid for 25 percent of the annuity, only 75 percent of the present value payable to her at your death will be in your estate. (If your employer paid part of the price, that contribution, however, is treated as if made by you.)

Here are some suggestions:

1. Don't make your estate the beneficiary of your pension proceeds.
2. Be sure you've named a person or trust you set up while you are living as beneficiary.
3. Be sure to name a secondary beneficiary in case the one you've named dies before you do.
4. Typically, your beneficiary should be your spouse if you are married. In fact, federal law prohibits you from naming any other beneficiary without your spouse's written and informed consent.

- **Approximate value of benefits that fall into category 5 $_____**

Category 6   Jointly held property where someone else automatically receives your interest by surviving you

Many of us own property "jointly with the right of survivorship" or as "tenants by the entireties" (basically the same thing except that this form of ownership exists only between husband and wife). Most of us own our houses this way. It means that upon the death of either joint owner, the survivor automatically (regardless of what our wills say) becomes owner.

There are two rules that affect this category of property. The first is the *50-50 rule*. It provides that only half of jointly held property with right of survivorship will be in your estate—regardless of who contributed what to the purchase price. For instance, even if Jim and Grace had purchased their $130,000 home entirely from Jim's income, under the 50-50 rule, only $65,000, 50 percent, will be includable in Jim's estate. If Grace died first, 50 percent of the $130,000 value of the home would be in her estate even though she made no contribution. But since it would qualify for the estate tax marital deduction, the includable amount would not create any estate tax.

This 50-50 rule can only be used if the property is owned by you and your spouse (and no one else). So it wouldn't work for property that is owned by you and your brother as joint tenants.

The 50-50 rule will work for personal as well as real property. For instance, if Jim calls his stockbroker, Ed Sigmond, and purchases 100 shares of stock as joint tenants with the right of survivorship with Grace, the property qualifies under the 50-50 rule.

How then is property that isn't taxed under the 50-50 rule treated? The answer is: Under the *percentage of contribution* (also called the *consideration furnished*) rule. This rule is simple—but sometimes harsh. In a nutshell, it taxes jointly held property entirely in the estate of the first joint tenant to die—except to the extent the survivor can prove contribution (out of funds other than those acquired by gift from the decedent).

Say Jim and his brother, John, bought property worth $30,000. John used $10,000 he inherited as his share of the contribution to this property, which was titled jointly with Jim. Since John could prove contribution—from his own funds—of one-third of the purchase price of the property, then only two-thirds of the value would be in Jim's estate. If John died first and Jim could prove he paid for two-thirds of the purchase price for the original property, only one-third would be in John's estate under this rule.

The percentage of contribution rule is used in every case where the 50-50 rule does not apply. This makes it extremely important that joint tenants, other than spouses, keep meticulous records—and separate bank accounts—and a financial diary as to whose funds purchased what.

Picture a brother and sister working an entire lifetime, side by side. The brother dies and the government wants to tax all their jointly held property in his estate. Without records (we suggest a "partnership" or corporate agreement that "splits" profits and assets where the joint tenants are in business together or making investments jointly), the survivor may have little chance of success in proving contribution. Often a farm or small business is lost because the decedent's estate cannot afford the federal estate tax on the entire property.

- **Approximate value of assets you own in the 50-50 part of category 6 (list only the value of the includable one-half)** $_____

- **Approximate value of assets you own that would be taxed under the percentage of contribution rule (multiply your original percentage contribution times today's fair market value) of category 6** $_____

Category 7   General powers of appointment—an unlimited right to specify who receives someone else's property

When Jim's grandfather died, his will established a trust and placed $400,000 of stocks and other securities into it. Jim's father, Marty, was given a *general power of appointment* over the assets in the trust. That means that even though Marty didn't technically own the property, Marty could specify who was to receive it. This *power to appoint* (choose the recipient of someone else's property) was so broad that it was considered "general." Under this general power of appointment, Marty could have named anyone, even himself or his estate or his creditors, as the recipient(s) of his father's property.

If Marty's father had provided that Marty could only choose between his children (Jim and his sister, Martha) or some other preselected class of beneficiaries and could not appoint the property to himself or his estate, the power would be *limited* or *special*.

The distinction between a general and a limited (special) power is important: If you have a *general* power over the assets in someone else's trust as Marty did, the value of those assets are includable in your own estate. But if your power is *limited* and you can't withdraw the assets yourself or name the recipients in your will, the assets will not be in your estate.

Jim plans to set up two trusts for Grace in his will. One trust will give her a general power of appointment over trust assets. So she can demand everything in the trust for herself or anyone else immediately and without limitation. This will be called the *marital* trust since it is designed to qualify for the marital deduction described below. Any assets remaining in this trust when Grace dies will be in her estate, since her rights to the property in it are tantamount to outright survivorship.

The second trust Jim will create is a *nonmarital* (often called a *family* trust). Although it provides additional income and security for Grace (who will receive all of the trust's income for as long as she lives), its assets will *not* be includable in her estate. That's because she will be given a limited power of appointment. Jim has given Grace the right to *appoint* trust income or principal to any one of their children. She can pick the child she thinks needs or deserves it most (or is in the lowest tax bracket). In this way, the limited power adds additional financial flexibility without causing these assets to be subject to a second estate tax when Grace dies (they will be taxed once when Jim dies).

Both general and special powers of appointment are important estate planning tools that your attorney can build into your estate plan with little trouble.

- **Approximate value of category 7 assets, property subject to a general power of appointment that I control** $_____

Category 8   Life insurance that you own or have important rights over or that is payable to or for the benefit of your estate

Incidents of ownership test.   If, at the time of your death, you own life insurance on your life (or you gave it away within three years of your death), it will be included in your estate regardless of whom you have named as beneficiary.

In fact, if you merely have the right to benefit in any meaningful way—or determine who will enjoy that benefit in an economic sense—the policy will be in your estate. For instance, even if Jim had given away a policy on his life but kept the right to name the policy beneficiary or surrender the policy or borrow its cash value or almost any other so-called "incident of ownership," the entire death proceeds (and not just the value of the right he retained) would be in his estate. Inclusion of the entire death benefit would be required even if Jim couldn't exercise the power for his own benefit.

Life insurance is includable in your estate if you:

1. Own it.
2. Have the right to cash it in or surrender the policy.
3. Retain the right to change the beneficiaries (or retain the right to veto the owner's attempt to change the beneficiary).
4. Retain the right to borrow on the policy or use it as collateral for a loan.

Life insurance is also includable in your estate if it is owned by a corporation you control (*control* is defined as the ownership of *more* than 50 percent of the corporation's voting stock) to the extent it is payable to someone other than the corporation or its creditors. For example, if the XYZ corporation owns a policy on the life of X, its 62 percent shareholder, and the proceeds are paid to his son when X dies, the policy proceeds will be in the shareholder's estate. Note that the *entire* proceeds—not merely 62 percent—will be includable under this rule. To add insult to injury, the IRS will probably claim that the proceeds are 100 percent taxable as a dividend. This results in two taxes on the same payments.

Payable to estate test: The second rule that applies to life insurance is, no matter who owned the policy or held *incidents of ownership* in it, it will be includable in your estate if it is payable to your estate or benefits your estate. So if Grace purchased a policy on Jim's life but named Jim's estate as beneficiary, the entire proceeds would become subject to federal estate tax.

How to Remove Life Insurance from Your Estate

Life insurance can be removed from your estate in two ways. The first is by assigning it (transferring it irrevocably) by gift (love and affection). Remember, this is another way of saying you are giving up control of the policy and can't get it back unless it is gifted back to you.

The second way to transfer life insurance out of your estate is by sale. You can sell it for cash or accept some other consideration in exchange for the policy or the right to receive the proceeds. But there is an insidious tax trap to be avoided in transfers where the new owner pays *any* amount of valuable consideration. The problem is called the *transfer for value* rule. The result if a life insurance policy or an interest in a policy is transferred for valuable consideration is this: All or a substantial portion of the insurance which is normally income tax free becomes subject to ordinary income tax. For instance, if Jim or Jim's employer sold a $100,000 policy on his life to Jim's wife, Grace, or to a trust for her benefit, the proceeds would be subject to ordinary income tax when Jim died. If the trust purchased the policy, the federal income tax on $100,000 could be almost $33,000.

Never make a transfer of life insurance without first consulting both your insurance agent and tax counsel and considering both the nontax and tax implications.

- **Approximate value of category 8 assets, life insurance you own, or that is payable to your estate $_____**

Now total up all the approximate values you have entered on the bulleted lines above. The sum is roughly your "gross estate." Don't worry that the figures are not exact or precise. We're just trying to "guesstimate" your estate's probable "liquidity" need—its need for cash.

Adjusting the gross estate

Your estate tax is not based on your gross estate. That's only the starting point for computing the tax.

Stage 2 is an artificial point called the *adjusted gross estate*. In other words, your executor makes an adjustment to the gross estate.

Funeral expenses (subject to reasonable limits) are deductible. These expenses include interment, burial lot, or vault, grave marker and perpetual care costs.

Administrative costs are deductible. Administrative costs include expenses incurred in administering property in your estate. This means your executor can deduct (a) expenses incurred in the collection and preservation of assets that will pass under your will, (b) costs incurred in paying off your debts and (c) the expenses incurred in distributing what's left to your beneficiaries.

These administrative expenses include court costs, accounting fees, appraiser's fees, brokerage costs, executor's commissions and attorney's fees. How much will they be? That depends.

Estate settlement costs will vary widely from location to location. They'll also be affected by both the size of your estate and the complexity of the administrative problems. For instance, if all your assets were liquid, that is, if everything you owned was cash or could be converted into cash quickly and without cost or trouble, your attorney would have an easy job and the costs would be low. Bank accounts, money market certificates, and life insurance are good examples of "low cost," highly liquid assets. But if there's little cash and many assets and properties, all of which have to be valued or appraised, your estate expenses will be higher. Check with a local bank or a CLU, ChFC, or CFP. They can give you an idea of what percentage of your estate will probably be used to meet these expenses.

Determination of Cash Requirements

(1) Gross estate		$_____
Minus:		
(2) Funeral and administration expenses (estimated as ____% of ____)	_____ ✓	
(3) Debts and taxes	_____ ✓	
(4) Losses	_____	
Total deductions	$_____	_____
Equals:		
(5) Adjusted gross estate		_____
Minus:		
(6) Marital deduction	_____	
(7) Charitable deduction	_____	
Total deductions	$_____	_____
Equals:		
(8) Taxable estate		_____
Plus:		
(9) Adjusted taxable gifts (taxable portion of post-1976 lifetime taxable transfers not included in gross estate)		_____
Equals:		
(10) Tentative tax base (total of taxable estate and adjusted taxable gifts)		_____
Compute:		
(11) Tentative tax (apply rates from page 150 to line 10)	_____	
Minus:		
(12) Gift taxes paid on post-1976 gifts	_____	
Equals:		
(13) Tax payable before credits		_____
Minus:		
(14) Tax credits		
(a) Unified credit	____	
*(b) State death tax credit	____ (b-1)_____ ✓	
	(State death payable)	
(c) Credit for foreign death taxes	____	
(d) Credit for tax on prior transfers	____	
Total Reduction	____	_____

Determination of Cash Requirements *(continued)*

Plus:
  (15) 15% Tax on excess accumulations
      from pension plan   _____

Equals:
  (16) Net federal estate tax payable   _____ ✓

Plus:
  (17) Total cash bequests   _____ ✓

Equals:
  (18) Total cash requirements
      (sum of 2, 3, state death tax
      payable, 16, and 17) $_____

See maximum credit table for state death taxes, p. 140. Apply rates to line 8 taxable estate.

Determination of Cash Requirements
(Community Property States)

  (1) Gross estate $_____

Minus:
  (2) Funeral and administration expenses
      (estimated as _____ % of _____)   _____ ✓
  (3) Debts and taxes   _____ ✓
  (4) Losses   _____
    Total deductions $_____   _____

Equals:
  (5) Adjusted gross estate   _____

Minus:
  (6) Marital deduction   _____
  (7) Charitable deduction   _____
    Total deductions $_____   _____

Equals:
  (8) Taxable estate   _____

Plus:
  (9) Adjusted taxable gifts (taxable portion
      of post-1976 lifetime taxable transfers
      not included in gross estate)   _____

Equals:
  (10) Tentative tax base (total of
      taxable estate and adjusted
      taxable gifts   _____

Compute:
  (11) Tentative tax (apply rates from
      page _____ to line 10)   _____

Minus:
  (12) Gift taxes paid on post-1976
      gifts   _____

Equals:
  (13) Federal estate tax payable
      before credits $_____   _____

Determination of Cash Requirements
(Community Property States) *(continued)*

Minus:
  (14) Tax credits
      (a) Unified credit   _____
      *(b) State death tax credit   _____   (b-1) _____   ✓
                                                    (State death payable)
      (c) Credit for foreign death taxes   _____
      (d) Credit for tax on prior transfers   _____
      Total Reduction   _____   _____

Plus:
  (15) 15% Tax on excess accumulations from pension plans   _____
Equals:
  (16) Net federal estate tax payable   _____   ✓
Plus (in states where appropriate):
  (17) Total cash bequests   _____   ✓
  (18) Spouse's share of community expenses
      (a) Administration expense
          (estimated as _____%
          of _____)   _____   ✓
      (b) Debts and taxes   _____   ✓
      Total costs   _____

Equals:
  (19) Total cash requirements
      (sum of 2, 3, state death tax
      payable, 16, 17 and 18) $_____

See maximum credit table for state death taxes, p. 140. Apply rates to line 8 taxable estate.

About Attorney's Fees

One hint for the person you've named as your executor. Shop around! We suggest you shop around for an attorney the same way you shop for any other service. It's extremely important that your executor(s) demand (and be satisfied with) a written *hourly* fee structure and a rough estimate of the number of hours involved or a cap on the maximum fee that can be charged. The laws of most states allow the executor to choose the estate's attorney—regardless of who drew the will or who was specified in the will to be the estate's attorney.*

*Read *The Executor's Manual* (Doubleday and Company) for step-by-step guidance.

- **A guesstimate of these two categories of costs is** $_____

(A minimum of $10,000 for this category is suggested.) If you multiply category 1 assets by 5 percent, you'll have a rough idea of the minimum funeral and administrative costs you can expect.

A third category of deduction is allowed for debts and taxes. Your executor can deduct all your bona fide debts—including mortgages and liens that you owe when you die. So if you own a $100,000 home in your own name but your outstanding mortgage is $60,000, your executor will enter $100,000 in category 1 but will be allowed a $60,000 deduction here.

Deductible taxes include income, gift, and property taxes you owe at the date of your death.

- **A guesstimate of this third category of costs is** $_____

The fourth category of deduction is casualty losses incurred while your estate is being administered. Few estates receive any deduction for this category, but from time to time an uninsured fire, theft, or other loss creates a deduction. (For planning purposes you can ignore this category, but if you are probating an actual estate it must be considered.)

- **Now total up all your estate's deductions** $_____

Then subtract that amount from the figure you have guesstimated to be your gross estate. The result is your *adjusted gross* estate.

As you will see from the estate tax computation form on page 232, we're now at Stage 2 (line 5). From the amount we've arrived at, we can subtract a marital deduction, for certain transfers to a surviving spouse, a charitable deduction for certain transfers to charities, and perhaps take a deduction of 50 percent for sales of employer securities to an employee stock ownership plan (ESOP).

The most important deduction in most estates is the marital deduction. (Look at line 6.) That's because it's the largest deduction most estates of married couples receive. It's typically allowed for property that's in your estate and will go to your surviving spouse either outright or in a manner that's equivalent to outright.

This deduction is (virtually) unlimited. You could actually leave your spouse your entire estate and, regardless of the size of your estate, the deduction could wipe out the federal estate tax entirely. Of course, it can't be more than the net value of what you leave your spouse. And you have to remember that if your spouse dies before you—even one minute before you—there will be no marital deduction in your estate.

- **My marital deduction will be roughly** $_____

Your estate will be entitled to a charitable deduction for anything you leave to charity at your death (line 7). Like the marital deduction, the charitable deduction is virtually unlimited. Conceivably, you could leave your entire estate to charity and no matter how large your bequest, your estate would receive a deduction for the entire amount.

- **A guesstimate of my charitable deduction is** $_____
- **Total deductions** $_____
- **Subtracting the total deductions from the adjusted
  gross estate results in my taxable estate** $_____

This brings us to Stage 3, the taxable estate. Actually, this is a misnomer because the taxable portion of certain lifetime gifts you made, post-1976 taxable gifts that have not been included already in the computation, are added in here. List the taxable portion of any post-1976 taxable gifts (so-called *adjusted taxable gifts*) you didn't include in your gross estate by this point.

- **A guesstimate of adjusted taxable gifts** $_____

The sum of your taxable estate and adjusted taxable gifts is the amount upon which the federal estate tax is based. It's called the *tentative* tax base.

- **A guesstimate of my tentative tax base is** $_____

The table shown on page 137 is the rate schedule you apply to the tentative tax base. For example, if your tentative tax base is $250,000, your tax would be $70,800.

Note that the rates are progressive. The tax on a tentative base of $1000 is $180. But the tax on 100 times that much, $100,000 is $23,800, much more than 100 times $180. The tax on $1,000,000 is much more than 1000 times $180—it's $345,800. You are up to at least a 50 percent rate once your estate exceeds $2,500,000. That's another way of saying without planning, 50 cents of every additional dollar you earn and keep from that point on will not go to your heirs—it goes to the federal government.

- **A guesstimate of the tentative federal estate tax payable by my executor** $_____

As you can see by the form on page 132, there are reductions allowed even from this tentative tax. If any gift taxes had been paid during your lifetime, they can be subtracted from the tentative tax (line 12).

Unified Rate Schedule for Estate and Gift Taxes

If the amount with which the tentative tax to be computed is:	*The tentative tax is:*
Not over $10,000	18% of such amount
Over $10,000 but not over $20,000	$1,800 plus 20% of the excess over $10,000
Over $20,000 but not over $40,000	$3,800 plus 22% of the excess over $20,000
Over $40,000 but not over $60,000	$8,200 plus 24% of the excess over $40,000
Over $60,000 but not over $80,000	$13,000 plus 26% of the excess over $60,000
Over $80,000 but not over $100,000	$18,200 plus 28% of the excess over $80,000
Over $100,000 but not over $150,000	$23,800 plus 30% of the excess over $100,000
Over $150,000 but not over $250,000	$38,800 plus 32% of the excess over $150,000
Over $250,000 but not over $500,000	$70,800 plus 34% of the excess over $250,000
Over $500,000 but not over $750,000	$155,800 plus 37% of the excess over $500,000
Over $750,000 but not over $1,000,000	$248,300 plus 39% of the excess over $750,000
Over $1,000,000 but not over $1,250,000	$345,800 plus 41% of the excess over $1,000,000
Over $1,250,000 but not over $1,500,000	$448,300 plus 43% of the excess over $1,250,000
Over $1,500,000 but not over $2,000,000	$555,800 plus 45% of the excess over $1,500,000
Over $2,000,000 but not over $2,500,000	$780,800 plus 49% of the excess over $2,000,000

For 1984-1987—*In the case of decedents dying and gifts made in 1984, 1985, 1986, and 1987:*

Over $2,500,000 but not over $3,000,000	$1,025,800 plus 53% of the excess over $2,500,000
Over $3,000,000	$1,290,800 plus 55% of the excess over $3,000,000

For 1988 and Later Years

Over $2,500,000	50%

The most important of the remaining reductions are the tax credits (line 14). The key credits are the *unified* credit and the *state death tax* credit.

The unified credit (line 14a) is a dollar for dollar reduction against the federal estate tax otherwise payable by your executor. It's called a *unified* credit because it can be used as an offset against gift as well as estate taxes (or both but to the extent you use it while you are alive it's used up. It wouldn't be available again when you die.)

Fortunately, the credit is large. It's so large that your tentative tax base has to exceed $600,000 before you pay one dime in federal estate tax.

The unified credit was phased in as follows:

	Year			
	1984	*1985*	*1986*	*1987 and Later*
Estate protected by the credit	325,000	400,000	500,000	600,000
Actual credit	96,300	121,800	155,800	192,800

- **The tax figure calculated above can be reduced by** $_____
  (Insert the actual *credit* for this year)

The second major credit is the one allowed for state death taxes. There's a table on page 140 that gives you the upper limit on this credit.

To figure your state death tax credit (put your answer on line 14 of the form on page 132), find your taxable estate (line 8) and apply that amount to the table below. For instance, the credit for an individual who had a taxable estate of $200,000 is $1200. That means your federal tax burden would be reduced by $1200—if your executor paid at least that much in state death taxes.

- **The federal estate tax payable can be further
  reduced by a credit of** $_____

Tax on excess accumulations

The Tax Reform Act of 1986 imposed a 15 percent tax on "excess accumulations" from qualified retirement plans. An excess accumulation is the excess of:

a. the value of a participant's interest in a qualified plan over
b. the present value of an annuity paying $112,500 a year for the participant's actuarial life expectancy—measured as of the day of the participant's death.

Essentially, the 15 percent tax is imposed upon that amount that Congress felt was too much to allow. For example, suppose a person retired, allowed his pension funds to build up to $3,000,000, and then died. Assume that the present value of the right to $112,500 a year for his life expectancy at that date was $1,000,000. There would be a 15 percent tax on the $2,000,000 excess.

Note that the $300,000 tax payable in the example would *not*:

a. Qualify for the marital deduction—even if all the money went to a surviving spouse;
b. Qualify for a charitable deduction—even if all of the money went to a qualified charity.

This additional tax on certain retirement plan distributions can be confiscatory because it can be added to the federal estate tax already calculated (which may be taxed at rates as high as 55 percent in 1987 and 50 percent in 1988 and later years). The result in 1987 could be a top tax rate of 70 percent (15 + 55). No part of the unified credit can be used to offset the 15 percent tax.

- **15 percent tax on excess accumulation from retirement
  plan** $_____

- **If I were to die today, my federal estate tax liability would be roughly** $_____
- **My estate's total "liquidity" (cash) needs are at least** $_____ *

Now you know what the federal government will take. It can be a lot —or a little, depending on what you do—or don't do.

Remember, the federal estate tax is a *voluntary* tax. Your heirs won't have to pay much (or anything) when you die—if you take the time to plan—now!

Tax on Generation-Skipping Transfers

The Tax Reform Act of 1986 imposed a tax *in addition* to the regular estate tax and *in addition* to the 15 percent estate tax on excess retirement plan distributions. This third tax, called the generation-skipping transfer tax (GSTT), is the most incideous, complex, and confiscatory of the three.

The generation-skipping transfer tax is imposed at a flat 55 percent rate until 1988 and at a 50 percent rate from that year on. Essentially, the tax will be imposed on transfers to grandchildren or others of that generation or younger.

The following are typical examples of when the GSTT would be imposed:

1. *The Taxable Distribution.* A mother sets up a trust that provided income or principal distributions to her daughter or granddaughter at the discretion of the trustee. A distribution of either income or principal from that trust to the granddaughter would be a generation-skipping transfer. If the trustee distributed $100,000 of trust income in 1987 to the granddaughter, the tax would be 55 percent of $100,000, or $55,500. The granddaughter would net only $45,000. In other words, it could cost as much as $55,000 in tax to distribute $45,000 in assets.

2. *The Taxable Termination.* A parent establishes a trust which provides income to his son for life. At the son's death, property in the trust goes to the parent's granddaughter. If $1,000,000 was placed in the trust, at the son's death, a tax of 55 percent of $1,000,000, or $550,000, would be imposed. The granddaughter receives only

---

*Sums of all lines on pages 132 or 133 with check marks ($\sqrt{}$). (This amount can be substantially higher if your will makes cash bequests or if you've made charitable gifts in cash. The trick is to provide—in your will—that your executor can satisfy gifts you make in your will, to friends, relatives, or charities, in cash or in "kind." That way your executor could give them property and use cash to pay debts and taxes.)

Maximum Credit Table for State Death Taxes

The amount of any state death taxes paid may be subtracted from the federal estate tax as determined under the preceding table, provided, however, that the maximum to be subtracted may not exceed the maximum determined under the following table:*

If the taxable estate is:	The maximum tax credit shall be:
Not over $150,000	8/10ths of 1% of the amount by which the taxable estate exceeds $100,000
Over $150,000 but not over $200,000	$400 plus 1.6% of the excess over $150,000
Over $200,000 but not over $300,000	$1,200 plus 2.4% of the excess over $200,000
Over $300,000 but not over $500,000	$3,600 plus 3.2% of the excess over $300,000
Over $500,000 but not over $700,000	$10,000 plus 4% of the excess over $500,000
Over $700,000 but not over $900,000	$18,000 plus 4.8% of the excess over $700,000
Over $900,000 but not over $1,100,000 . . .	$27,600 plus 5.6% of the excess over $900,000
Over $1,100,000 but not over $1,600,000 . .	$38,800 plus 6.4% of the excess over $1,100,000
Over $1,600,000 but not over $2,100,000 . .	$70,800 plus 7.2% of the excess over $1,600,000
Over $2,100,000 but not over $2,600,000 . .	$106,800 plus 8% of the excess over $2,100,000
Over $2,600,000 but not over $3,100,000 . .	$146,800 plus 8.8% of the excess over $2,600,000
Over $3,100,000 but not over $3,600,000 . .	$190,800 plus 9.6% of the excess over $3,100,000
Over $3,600,000 but not over $4,100,000 . .	$238,800 plus 10.4% of the excess over $3,600,000
Over $4,100,000 but not over $5,100,000 . .	$290,800 plus 11.2% of the excess over $4,100,000
Over $5,100,000 but not over $6,100,000 . .	$402,800 plus 12% of the excess over $5,100,000
Over $6,100,000 but not over $7,100,000 . .	$522,800 plus 12.8% of the excess over $6,100,000
Over $7,100,000 but not over $8,100,000 . .	$650,800 plus 13.6% of the excess over $7,100,000
Over $8,100,000 but not over $9,100,000 . .	$786,800 plus 14.4% of the excess over $8,100,000
Over $9,100,000 but not over $10,100,000 .	$930,800 plus 15.2% of the excess over $9,100,000
Over $10,100,000	$1,082,800 plus 16% of the excess over $10,100,000

*This table resembles the table contained in IRC Section 2011(b), but it is not the same. The table in the Code is based on the *adjusted taxable estate,* defined as the taxable estate reduced by $60,000. This table is based on the *taxable estate.*

$450,000. Here, it cost $550,000 in tax to distribute $450,000 in assets.

3. *The Direct Skip.* A grandparent makes a lifetime gift of cash or other property to her grandson. If the gift was worth $1,000,000 and was made in 1987, the grandparent would be liable for a generation skipping transfer tax of 55 percent of $1,000,000, or $550,000. But because this tax is paid, not out of the gift but out of additional assets of the grandparent, the granddaughter nets the full $1,000,000.

The total cost of making a generation-skipping transfer can cost *more* than the value of the gift! For instance, assume a grandfather in a 55 percent gift tax bracket makes a gift in 1987. Assume the gift is worth $2,000,000 and is made in a manner that does not qualify for the exclusions described below. The GSTT is 55 percent of $2,000,000, $1,100,000. The grandfather is *also* liable for a gift tax—on both the

$2,000,000 gift *and* on the GSTT—of $1,100,000 which he is deemed to be giving! So, he pays a gift tax, at a 55 percent rate, on $3,100,000. The total tax is, therefore, $2,805,000—140 percent of the value of the gift!

There are two important exceptions to the GSTT: (1) A $1,000,000 per donor exemption (which can be doubled if the donor is married), and (2) a *very* limited (only until 1990 and only if the gift to the grandchild is direct and nonforfeitable) $2,000,000 per grandchild exemption.

There are ways to avoid or reduce the impact of the GSTT. Perhaps the most effective is by gifts of up to $10,000 a year per donee ($20,000 if the donor is married) to an unlimited number of donees (regardless of their relationship to the donor) for as many years as the donor lives. For instance, a 40-year-old married individual with 2 children and 3 grandchildren could give each $20,000 for as long as she lives. Life expectancy for a 40-year-old is 42.5 years. Total gifts in that time could amount to $4,250,000, not one nickel of which would be subject to the federal estate tax, federal gift tax, or GSTT. If the beneficiaries invested their $100,000 a year at an average 5 percent after-tax return for those 42.5 years, the total gifts would amount to $13,906,521. At a 50 percent estate tax bracket, this equates to an estate tax savings of $6,953,261! An even better approach would be for the donees to purchase life insurance on the life of the donor with the $100,000 a year. The total wealth transferred would be many times $13,906,521.

Obviously, the GSTT is of concern only to very wealthy individuals. But if you feel it *might* apply to you, run—don't walk—to a highly competent attorney.

Part 2:
State Death Taxation

Many people will not have to worry about the federal estate tax at their deaths. However, the same cannot be said about state death taxes. In fact, the chances of your beneficiaries paying state death tax at your death may be even greater than you think. Twenty-nine states and the District of Columbia impose a tax even if there will be no federal estate tax. Twenty states (Alabama, Alaska, Arizona, Arkansas, California, Colorado, Florida, Georgia, Hawaii, Illinois, Missouri, New Mexico, North Dakota, Texas, Utah, Vermont, Virginia, Washington, West Virginia, and Wyoming) impose a *pickup* tax. This tax is levied only on estates subject to federal taxes. Nevada is a good place to die since it doesn't have a death tax. The laws in the remaining states vary. Each imposes either an inheritance tax or an estate tax (but not both). Fortunately, there are many ways to avoid or reduce state death taxes, but before you can successfully attempt to reduce or eliminate these taxes, you must first know what they are and how they work.

Three Types of State Death Tax

There are three varieties of state death taxes: the state inheritance tax, the state estate tax, and the state credit estate tax.

The inheritance tax

An inheritance tax is a tax on your beneficiaries' right to receive your property. It's the type of tax found in most states.

The amount of inheritance tax payable depends on the value of property each of your beneficiaries receives—and their relationship to you. Typically, beneficiaries are divided into categories.

Those beneficiaries most closely related to you (such as your spouse) and your lineal relatives (essentially your children, grandchildren, parents, and grandparents) will receive the largest exemptions and the lowest rates. Pennsylvania law is a good example. Real property held jointly between spouses with rights of survivorship is totally exempt from state death taxes. But the same property held in the same manner by brothers is subject to a 15 percent tax. Property you own solely in your name that you leave to a child is subject to a 6 percent tax. The same property left to a cousin or aunt or friend generates a 15 percent levy.

Technically, this type of tax is payable by the recipient but actually it is almost always paid by the estate's executor. The executor then distributes the net estate to the beneficiaries.

The estate tax

A state estate tax is imposed not on the right to receive your property but rather on your privilege of transferring it. In other words, a state estate tax is measured by the value of the property transferred. It's similar in that respect to the federal estate tax. Some states impose both an inheritance and an estate tax. The tax is payable by the estate's executor.

The credit estate tax

A credit estate (often called a *gap* or *pickup*) tax is designed to bridge the gap between the state's inheritance (or estate) tax and the maximum state death tax credit allowed under federal estate tax law.

Let's try an example to see how this works. Carl's taxable estate for federal estate tax purposes is $500,000. Using the table on page 140, you'll see that a credit of up to $10,000 is allowed against the federal estate tax for the taxes the executor pays to the state as death taxes.

But what if the state inheritance tax is only $8000? If the federal law allows a $10,000 credit and the state imposes only an $8000 inheritance tax, a second state tax, amounting to the $2000 difference, i.e., the credit estate tax is imposed. That means that the total state death tax is increased by $2000 to $10,000.

How to Reduce or Eliminate State Death Taxes

Many factors will influence the amount of state death taxes your estate will have to pay. These include state exemptions and deductions, multiple state taxation, and tax rates. Planning can lower your taxes considerably.

Avoiding Double Domicile Problems

Dr. Dorance was a scientist-businessman who maintained two large fully staffed homes only a few miles from each other, one in New Jersey and the other in Bryn Mawr, Pennsylvania. The New Jersey residence was maintained for income and property tax reasons, while Dr. Dorance really lived in the socially prominent main line area outside Philadelphia of which Bryn Mawr is the hub.

When he died, both states claimed the right to tax Dr. Dorance. He hadn't helped his case much. He deliberately kept the lights on in his New Jersey home, kept a car out front, maintained his church membership, and even wrote in his will that he considered himself a domiciliary of New Jersey. So, New Jersey levied a state death tax of about $17,000,000. Not to be outdone, Pennsylvania imposed a tax of almost the identical amount.

When the case went to the United States Supreme Court, it held that both sides had the right to tax. So they did. The total state taxes alone were over $34,000,000. That was in 1933. Worse yet, this case is still on the books—it could affect *your* estate!

Dr. Dorance wasn't alone. Many people have both summer and winter homes or have land and other property in states other than where they live.

Typically, our property will only be taxed in one state—but in certain situations, an estate or its beneficiaries could be liable for the taxes of two—or more—states.

The right of a state to impose a death tax depends on the type of property involved. Here's how it typically works.

Your land and buildings are taxed only by the state in which that property is located. Attorneys call this the *situs* of the property.

Tangible (you can touch it) *personal* (non-real estate) property, such as cars, boats, and household goods, is taxed in the state where it is situated. A boat, for example, is taxed where it is permanently docked. Its registry and location for insurance purposes are examined in order to determine its legal location.

The big problem lies with intangible (you don't hold the actual property—only paper representing the underlying asset) personal property. Stocks, bonds, notes, and other securities you own may be taxed, in the absence of interstate reciprocal agreement, by several states.

Generally, intangible personal property is taxed only by the state of your domicile (technically this is the place that you call home and—no matter where you are or for how long—intend to return to). Unfortunately, if you've established residences in more than one state or don't clearly establish which state you want to be treated as your domicile, two or more states can still impose death taxes on the same intangible personal property.

It's easy enough to avoid multiple state taxation: Just remember actions speak louder than words. Look at your driver's license, where you receive your mail, where you spend the bulk of your time, and where most of your home furnishings are. These are just a few of the things tax authorities examine. Don't split your time evenly. Spend more time (and plant more daisies) at your "home sweet home."

Shop for the Best Rates

Rates rate consideration. Many wealthy individuals considering retirement shop around for the state that offers not only a warm sun but also a warm inheritance tax climate. It can make a big difference.

The rates at which transfers or receipts of property are taxed vary considerably from state to state. Some states have graduated or progressive rates similar to the federal estate tax. Others, such as Pennsylvania, have flat rates (the percentage of tax does not grow progressively higher as the size of the estate increases).

Although we don't recommend moving to a state merely because it has a more favorable tax law, it certainly is a factor to consider *before* you move. Talk to your attorney—describe what type of property you own, how it is titled, and who your beneficiaries are. Have your attorney or other tax advisor check to see which states would treat your estate most favorably.

Check Out Exemptions and Deductions

Not all property is subject to state death taxation. Most states exempt property you leave to the federal government, to the state itself, or to certain charitable organizations.

A few states exempt property passing to a surviving spouse. Most totally or partially exempt life insurance. Only eight states tax life insurance owned at death: Massachusetts, Minnesota, New York, North Carolina, Rhode Island, South Carolina, Tennessee, and Wisconsin. One word of caution: If you've named your estate or your creditors as the beneficiary of your life insurance, in most states any exclusion you would have had is lost. For instance, a $100,000 life insurance policy is inheritance tax free in most states—if you've named a beneficiary other than your estate or your creditors. But if the same policy is paid to your estate, the full death tax may be imposed. Pennsylvania doesn't tax life insurance even if it *is* paid to the estate, but we still don't recommend this even to our Pennsylvania clients. Oklahoma taxes all insurance unless it is paid to a surviving spouse.

The difference between a state tax and no state tax often depends on just a few minutes of planning with a knowledgeable advisor.

This chapter deals with the different types of state death taxes. However, every state does not have each type of tax, and the exemptions and rates vary from state to state. For specific information concerning the taxes in your state, we suggest you write to the State Inheritance Tax Department in your state capitol. For free information, the trust department of local banks should also have useful information.

12

Gift Giving Techniques

Advantages of Giving

There are many estate planning reasons why "it is better to give than to receive." Some of these include:

1. If you feel your income and capital exceed your needs, it may be the time to think about *intentional defunding* of your estate. Intentional defunding is another way of saving; it is better to give assets —and income—to keep them from being taxed (and probated) in your estate. So giving (we'll call it gifting) is a way to reduce your probate costs and substantially reduce or even eliminate the death tax on wealth.

   Giving away assets to save estate taxes is especially useful where you have an asset that is likely to appreciate substantially and you'd like to have the growth occur in someone else's hands. For instance, Sam recently formed an insurance agency. He might want to give stock in the business to his children, Sam, Jr., and Lee, before the business becomes successful.

2. Another advantage of lifetime gifting is that you can be sure the person—or charity—that you want to get your gift will receive it. Wills can be broken, and in most states a surviving spouse or child is entitled to a portion of your estate regardless of what your will says. (This is called the right to "elect against" your will.) A lifetime gift is a sure thing.

3. Making a gift while you are alive also gives you the pleasure of seeing the recipient(s) enjoy it. It also makes it possible to see what your donee does with the gift. For example, you can watch how your son handles and invests cash. That can help you make decisions about whether, when, and how to make larger additional gifts, either during your lifetime or at your death.

4. Your lifetime gift is private. No one but the *donee,* the recipient of your gift, has the right to know any of the details. On the other hand, property which passes under your will must be inventoried. That list is filed with the county *Register of Wills.* It, therefore,

becomes public information. This makes your beneficiaries prey to the well-intended (and sometimes not so well-intended) but often harmful advice of those people who always know how to invest someone else's money. This is not a problem with a lifetime gift.

5. A gift provides financial security for loved ones and, at the same time, insulates that property from the claims of your creditors.
6. Many gifts are motivated by potential intra family income tax savings.

To fully understand income tax savings, it is necessary to understand the concept of *combined marginal tax bracket.* Your marginal tax bracket (referred to as your tax bracket) is the tax rate that is multiplied by the taxable income in excess of income taxed at the next lowest bracket. For instance, assume an individual who is married and filing jointly with no dependents has a taxable income of $50,000. Such an individual would pay a rate of 15 percent on the first $29,751 of taxable income and a marginal rate of 28 percent on all taxable income over $29,751. The combined marginal tax bracket is the highest combined federal and state rate on which taxes are collected. An individual who is in a 33 percent federal bracket (as are most taxpayers earning between $72,000 and $180,000), who is also subject to a 5 percent state income tax, will be in a combined marginal tax bracket of about 36 percent (assuming a deduction is allowed against the federal income tax for state income taxes paid).

Sheryl's salary puts her in a 35 percent combined marginal income tax bracket. That means that 35 cents of every additional dollar of salary she earns will be lost in taxes. Worse yet, if she has dividends from stocks or receives rental income or even earns interest from a bank account, at least 35 cents, and maybe more, of every dollar wouldn't go to her but go to the federal and state government. But if she gives the stock to her 14-year-old daughter, Lynn, the income from the stock is no longer taxed to Sheryl. Instead, it is taxed to Lynn at Lynn's much lower bracket. If Lynn was in a 15 percent bracket, the 20 percent difference is kept within the family. (Actually, because *each* child is entitled to a $500 standard deduction, the actual percentage savings—as illustrated in the example below—can be increased significantly beyond the apparent differential.)

If Sheryl gives her daughter $30,000 worth of stock earning 10 percent (in trust or through a custodial account), the *annual* savings would be $675. Together with interest, over just 10 years, this savings alone increases to over $11,834. A slightly lower amount of savings would be realized if each year's income were accumulated by and taxed to a trust for Lynn's benefit.

Giving is an important estate-planning technique because it can save estate taxes and probate costs, guarantee that the party you want to receive your gift will do so, and assure everyone that the details of the gift

Post TRA 1986 Income Shifting: Child 14 or Over

Amount of investment	$30,000
Rate of return on investment	0.100
Years investment lasts	10
Parent's combined (federal and state) tax bracket	0.35
Child's combined (federal and state) tax bracket	0.15
Trust's combined (federal and state) tax bracket	0.15

	Parent	Child	Trust
Interest income	$3,000	$3,000	$3,000
Tax	1,050	375	435
After-tax income	1,950	2,625	2,565
Annual Advantage		675	615
Total savings over 10 Years		11,834	10,782
Total savings over 15 Years		23,591	22,094
Total savings over 20 Years		42,527	39,342

will be completely private. Making a lifetime gift gives you an opportunity to enjoy the pleasure of your recipients and to see how well they handle and manage the gift. Finally, gifts of income-producing property shift the tax on the income and are easy ways to save income taxes.

How to Eliminate the Federal Gift Tax

It will not cost a cent in taxes—even to make substantial gifts—if you qualify for one or more of these:

1. An annual $10,000 per donee gift tax exclusion.
2. The right to split gifts.
3. A marital deduction.
4. A unified credit.

Let's see how to make these four gift tax eliminators work for you.

The Little Giant

Anyone, married or single, can give up to $10,000 in cash or other property each year to any number of parties with no gift tax liability whatsoever. This is called the annual gift tax exclusion. These gifts can be made to individuals (whether or not they are related to you) or to other parties (such as a charity or club). Here's an example:

John, a wealthy 28-year-old bachelor, has three nephews (Jim, Andy, and Nick). John can give each of his nephews $10,000 in cash or other property each year. That means he can remove $30,000 a year ($10,000 × 3) from his estate at no federal tax cost to himself or to them. If John marries his girlfriend, Westie, and, as his wife, she agrees to "split" the gift (split gifts are discussed in more detail later in this chapter), the amount the couple can give—per donee, per year—doubles. So John and Westie together can give up to $60,000 a year—$20,000 to each of John's three nephews.

We call the annual exclusion the *Little Giant* because, over time, it can remove massive amounts of property from your estate. Since John's life expectancy is about 54 more years, he could avoid estate taxes on $3,246,000 ($60,000 × 54). In fact, if his nephews invest the money each year and only earn 5 percent, the $60,000 a year gifts will grow to $15,608,243! If John's top federal estate tax bracket is 50 percent, the federal estate tax savings from these "no cost" gifts will be $7,804,122. This incredible little giant concept can be turbocharged: If John's nephews purchase life insurance on John's life with the gifts, the total wealth shifts would be many times $15,608,243.

How to Split Gifts

Split gifts are just one more of the many pleasures of married life. When a husband or wife makes a gift to a third person (that person does not have to be a relative), the IRS treats the gift as if each spouse made half the gift—even if they didn't. Assume that John and Westie are married at the time John makes gifts to his nephews. Even if all the money that John and Westie give John's nephews comes from John's personal assets, the couple can split the gifts. It's as if John and Westie each gave $30,000 a year, $10,000 to each nephew, even though all the money came from John's personal bank account.

Obviously, doubling the amount you can give away each year is advantageous. But what makes gift splitting even more important is that it causes the gift tax—if there will be one—to be lower. The reason is that the gift tax rates are progressive or disproportionately higher. For example, as you can see in the table on page 150, if John made a taxable gift of $100,000 while he was single, it would result in a $23,800 gift tax. But the same taxable $100,000 gift made from John's money during his marriage would be treated as if each spouse made a $50,000 taxable gift. That drops the gift tax to a total of $21,200 ($10,600 each). Splitting saves $2600.

If you live in a community property state, such as Texas, Louisiana, California, Idaho, Arizona, New Mexico, or Washington, gifts of community property by a husband and wife to a third party are not eligible for gift splitting, since such property has already, in essence, been split. Each spouse is automatically considered to own half the property.

Advantage of the Marital Deduction

Another advantage of marriage—at least from the recipient spouse's viewpoint—is that, before a gift from one spouse to another becomes taxable, a gift tax marital deduction is allowed (over and above any annual exclusion).

Unified Rate Schedule for Estate and Gift Taxes

If the amount with which the tentative tax to be computed is:	*The tentative tax is:*
Not over $10,000	18% of such amount
Over $10,000 but not over $20,000	$1,800 plus 20% of the excess over $10,000
Over $20,000 but not over $40,000	$3,800 plus 22% of the excess over $20,000
Over $40,000 but not over $60,000	$8,200 plus 24% of the excess over $40,000
Over $60,000 but not over $80,000	$13,000 plus 26% of the excess over $60,000
Over $80,000 but not over $100,000	$18,200 plus 28% of the excess over $80,000
Over $100,000 but not over $150,000	$23,800 plus 30% of the excess over $100,000
Over $150,000 but not over $250,000	$38,800 plus 32% of the excess over $150,000
Over $250,000 but not over $500,000	$70,800 plus 34% of the excess over $250,000
Over $500,000 but not over $750,000	$155,800 plus 37% of the excess over $500,000
Over $750,000 but not over $1,000,000 . . .	$248,300 plus 39% of the excess over $750,000
Over $1,000,000 but not over $1,250,000 . .	$345,800 plus 41% of the excess over $1,000,000
Over $1,250,000 but not over $1,500,000 . .	$448,300 plus 43% of the excess over $1,250,000
Over $1,500,000 but not over $2,000,000 . .	$555,800 plus 45% of the excess over $1,500,000
Over $2,000,000 but not over $2,500,000 . .	$780,800 plus 49% of the excess over $2,000,000

For 1984–1987—*In the case of decedents dying and gifts made in 1984, 1985, 1986, and 1987*

Over $2,500,000 but not over $3,000,000 . . .	$1,025,800 plus 53% of the excess over $2,500,000
Over $3,000,000	$1,290,800 plus 55% of the excess over $3,000,000

For 1988 and Later Years

Over $2,500,000 . . . . 50%

Gift tax laws allow one spouse to give another an unlimited amount gift tax free because of the marital deduction. So if John gives Westie $120,000 after they are married (in addition to his $10,000 gift tax annual exclusion), not one dime will be subject to gift tax. If he gives her $1,200,000, it's still 100 percent gift tax free. There's no upper limit on how much you can give during your lifetime—or leave at death—to your spouse and pay no federal estate or gift tax.

The Unified Credit

Even that part of a gift which is taxable may not generate an actual tax liability. A dollar for dollar reduction in the gift tax payable is allowed to every taxpayer. This is called the *unified credit* because it is allowed against gift taxes, or estate taxes, or both. But unlike the $10,000 per donee annual exclusion, which regenerates each year, the unified credit ($47,000 in 1981; $62,800 in 1982; $79,300 in 1983; $96,300 in 1984; $121,800 in 1985; $255,800 in 1986; and $192,800 in 1987 and later years) once used is gone. We suggest you use it as soon as possible to eliminate the tax on lifetime gifts of appreciating property—but to the extent you haven't used it during your lifetime, it will be available later to eliminate all or a portion of the estate tax.

Let's look at the unified credit another way: The 1987 credit is roughly equivalent to an exemption of $600,000. So each spouse could give away—to anyone—or die and leave to anyone (even to someone who is not a relative)—up to $600,000 in assets and not pay one cent in federal gift or estate taxes. This is in addition to annual exclusion gifts. Some attorneys look at the unified credit as a *noninterest bearing bank account at the U.S. Treasury* for each client.

Using All the Tools

If John and Westie make a $1,220,000 gift in 1987 to their son, Russell, each spouse would compute gift tax liability as follows:

	John	*Westie*
Gift (split)	$610,000	$610,000
Less: Annual exclusion	10,000	10,000
Net gift	$600,000	$600,000
Tax on net gift	$192,800	$192,800
Less: Unified credit in 1987	192,800	192,800
Net tax due	0	0

Since the credit used during lifetime reduces the credit available against the estate tax, John and Westie, after having given away a total of $1,220,000, will have exhausted their unified credits. But if the couple had made smaller gifts, the unused credit of each spouse could be used at any time and against any taxable lifetime gift—or it can be used by each spouse's executor to offset any estate tax liability.

A Special Bonus

At one time, any gift you made within three years of your death was brought back into your estate regardless of your motive for making the gift. But this no longer applies. For example, if John should die within three years of a cash gift of $10,000 to a cousin, the gift would not be brought back into his gross estate. It would escape estate tax entirely even though he made it deliberately to avoid the tax.

Because gifts that qualify for the annual exclusion are gift tax free and are not brought back into the gross estate, the trick is to give such outright unrestricted gifts to as many donees as possible each year. You can use this special bonus to avoid estate taxes even if you are on your death bed while you are making the gifts. We suggest that very wealthy individuals in poor health make gifts now even if the size of the gift will require the payment of a gift tax. That's because, once you survive a 3-year period after making the gift, the gift tax is not brought back into the estate for purposes of computing the estate tax. This could result in a sizeable reduction of transfer taxation.

Selecting the Appropriate Property

The best property to give away depends on your circumstances and objectives. Typically, if you are in a high income tax bracket and your donee is in a relatively lower bracket, the best type of property for you to give is high income-producing property.

Another prime property for gifting is an asset that is likely to grow substantially in value. The gift should be made when the gift tax values—and, therefore, the gift tax transfer costs—are lowest. So if John was incorporated and thought his business was about to acquire a substantial customer, a gift of the stock before profits rise (and with it the value of the business) would be an inexpensive way to shift assets to his son, Russell.

You should give property away, even if it's already appreciated, if you are thinking about selling the property and your donee is in a lower income tax bracket than you are. For example, John bought stock ten years ago at $20 a share. Now it's worth $100. John is going to sell it to finance his 14-year-old son's private school tuition. He'd be better off giving it to a custodian for his son (gifts to minors are discussed in Chapter 19) and having the custodian sell it. The $80 of growth would be taxed to his son, Russell, at his low tax bracket rather than to John at his high rates. (This same technique can be used even if your children are not minors.)

Another type of property that makes an excellent gift is life insurance. That's because it has a relatively low gift tax value but a high estate tax value. For instance, if you own a $100,000 term policy on your life, you could remove $100,000 from your estate at practically no gift tax cost (but don't forget you are giving up control) by transferring ownership to your spouse or child or to a trust for them.

Don't give away property which would result in a loss if you sold it. Your donee can't use your loss to offset his/her income. You should sell the property, deduct your loss against other income, and give away the proceeds of the sale.

If you are older or in ill health, *don't* give away appreciated property. Appreciated property you own at death receives a *stepped up* basis. In other words, your heirs will receive a basis (cost for computing gain or loss or for depreciation purposes) that is stepped up to the date of death value of the asset. The bottom line is that all or a substantial portion of any gain will *never* be taxed.

If you own assets in more than one state, give away property in a state other than the one in which you live. That prevents what's known as *ancillary administration* which is a costly and duplicative process involving probate not only in the state of your domicile but also in the state where the property is. If John and Westie owned a sailboat in Maryland and they lived in Pennsylvania, the sailboat would be a better gift to their son (other things being equal, of course) than cash of identical value.

Timing Your Gift

When is the best time to make a gift? One answer is never, if you can't afford to part with the property for psychological or financial security reasons. If you are depending on that property or the income it produces, or think you might need it at some time in the future, don't give it away no matter how much savings you may realize. If you own 51 percent of a corporation, for example, a gift of that business' stock could cost you a loss of control.

But if you are sure you can afford to make a gift, then the time to make the gift is right now. Get it out of your estate as quickly as possible. The reason is to shift the tax on the income to your donee as quickly as you can. That way, income tax savings compound the advantages of making the gift. If the property grows in value, none of that appreciation will be subject to either gift or estate taxation.

Generally, if the assets you own fluctuate widely in value, you should give them away when the market value is low.

How to Make the Gift

There are many ways of making gifts. One of the most simple is outright. John might give Westie $10,000 in cash. If John wanted to give her stocks, he might tell his broker to put the title in her name. Quite often gifts are made by putting real estate or other property in joint names with rights of survivorship. (If John buys land in Wildwood, for instance, and titles it jointly with Westie with rights of survivorship, should one spouse die the other automatically becomes the sole owner.)

Often, the problem with outright or joint gifts with rights of survivorship is that the recipient can't—or doesn't want to—handle or manage the asset. In a nutshell, the form of your gift should match your donee's financial abilities, desires, and circumstances. John may be thrusting an unwelcome burden on Westie that she is ill-equipped to handle if he gives her property outright or if he titles property jointly and then dies.

When the recipient of a proposed gift is a minor or a mentally or emotionally disabled child (or adult), care must be taken to arrange for property management and investment advice. A temporary solution to this problem is the Uniform Gifts to Minors Account. A better long-term solution for minor beneficiaries is a 2503(c) trust (see Chapter 19).

Another consideration is whether you want your donee to have the property immediately and without restriction. Not everyone wants the recipients of their gifts to have absolute and immediate control. John, for example, may want his nephews to reach greater emotional maturity before they receive substantial gifts. Yet, he might want to remove those gifts from his estate and have the income taxed to them immediately. For this reason, many property owners set up trusts. You can set the terms of the trust. The law gives you wide discretion as to how and at what time (or times) or under what conditions the trust property will be paid out to your beneficiaries and still allows substantial estate and income tax savings.

State Gift Tax Laws

Nine states have gift taxes. So be sure to check with your counsel before making a gift if you live in Delaware, Louisiana, New York, North Carolina, Oregon, Rhode Island, South Carolina, Tennessee, or Wisconsin. Keep in mind that the laws of each of these states vary, and an exemption or deduction under federal law may not be available under state law.

In Summary

Gifts—like any other tool or technique you use in planning your family's financial future—must be used wisely. Putting too much in the wrong hands at the wrong time may be more costly in the long run than not making gifts. On the other hand, many estate owners foolishly try to hold on to all their property until the last possible minute. Often, the result is that thousands of dollars of income and estate taxes are needlessly paid (and, therefore, not available to your loved ones).

Both mistakes can be avoided by thinking out the consequences of even the smallest gifts—and talking it over with members of the estate planning cooperative. Discuss the pros and cons of gifts with them and have them chart out a long-term gift giving program that fits into your personal objectives for yourself and your family.

13

Specific Techniques for Eliminating or Reducing Federal Estate Taxes

This chapter details three ways that you can greatly reduce, and in some cases eliminate taxes—mostly death taxes. The federal estate tax *marital* deduction permits a person to leave his/her entire estate to his/her spouse and pay no tax. But is this always the best course to take, and when, if ever, do you pay tax? How the marital deduction trust works is a very important section for anyone whose total estate, including the proceeds of life insurance, fringe benefits, and all other property, will exceed $600,000.

Are you interested in keeping all of the proceeds of insurance on your life, as well as other assets, completely estate tax free to your children when you and your spouse both die? If so, the *inter vivos* (living) irrevocable trust, or supertrust, should be of interest to you. In the section on disclaimers, you can learn how it is sometimes best to refuse to accept property that has been left to you by someone else. It may be hard to believe, but refusing to accept property (if done properly) can in itself constitute estate planning.

The Marital Deduction

Of all the deductions allowed by the estate tax law, the single most important allowed to a married couple is the marital deduction. This is a deduction you are allowed on the net value (gross value less indebtedness) of property you leave to your spouse. This deduction is unlimited. That means you could leave your entire estate to your spouse and pay no federal estate tax.

To take an extreme example, Barry could leave his wife, Alice, his entire $5,000,000 estate. Because of the unlimited marital deduction, no federal estate tax will be due at Barry's death. (Most states do not have a marital deduction so there probably would be a state death tax to pay.) If Barry's estate did not qualify for a federal estate tax marital

155

deduction and had to pay tax on the $5,000,000, the federal tax would be $1,907,200.

Delays But Doesn't Eliminate

There is no free lunch in the tax law, of course. Sooner or later the federal government will come to collect. If Alice doesn't give the money away (she'll pay gift taxes on large gifts) or use it up (perhaps in some cases the best estate planning of all), the $5,000,000 will be taxed in Alice's estate. The point is that the marital deduction does not, per se, eliminate the estate tax. But it does delay it until the surviving spouse dies. The longer your surviving spouse lives, the longer the tax is delayed (and the greater her opportunity to give property away tax free using the annual $10,000 per donee gift tax exclusion).

Not everyone has an estate of $5,000,000. But almost everyone can benefit a surviving spouse by delaying the impact of the federal estate tax through the marital deduction. The use of the tax dollars otherwise payable can provide significant financial security.

There is one very important factor you should know about the unlimited marital deduction. Many wills drawn before September 13, 1981, will not allow your estate to qualify for an unlimited marital deduction. If your will is one of those, your estate's deduction may be limited to the greater of (a) $250,000 or (b) half your adjusted gross estate. Because thousands of estate tax dollars may be at stake, it makes sense to have your attorney make an immediate review of your will and trust.

There are many ways to qualify for the marital deduction. Most of them involve leaving property to your spouse outright or in a manner tantamount to outright.

For instance, if Don names his wife as the sole beneficiary of a $100,000 life insurance policy on his life, his executor can deduct the entire $100,000 and pay no federal estate tax on it. Bob and his wife, Arlene, own their $300,000 home jointly. The estate tax law requires $150,000 of that to be included in Bob's estate if he dies first. But since Arlene becomes the sole owner of the house at Bob's death, and, therefore, owns the house outright, Bob's executors can take a marital deduction for the includable $150,000 and pay no estate tax on the house.

Advantages

Bob's wife, Arlene, may not want or be able to handle large sums of money. So Bob would like to have his probate estate, the assets that will pass under his will, go into a trust that will provide management and investment expertise for Arlene. Yet, Bob would like to qualify those assets for the marital deduction. How does he do it?

There are several ways Bob can obtain the investment and management benefits of a trust and, at the same time, pass assets to Arlene federal estate tax free. The most commonly used is the marital deduction trust, a trust designed specifically to obtain the federal estate tax marital deduction.

Actually, most attorneys will probably draft at least two trusts, a marital deduction trust and a nonmarital trust (some call this a family trust). Assets that go into the marital trust will be in the surviving spouse's estate when she dies. Assets that go into the nonmarital trust will not be taxed when the surviving spouse dies. Here's a diagram of how it looks:

Estate Owner's Assets

Nonmarital Trust "My spouse is to receive all the income from assets in this trust, but at her death, all the assets to go to my children."	*Marital Trust* "My spouse is to receive all the income from this trust. Additionally, she can take all the trust assets whenever she desires or leave all the assets to anyone she names in her will."
Assets in this trust are *not* in the surviving spouse's estate and therefore are *not* taxed when the spouse dies.	Assets in this trust *are* taxed when the surviving spouse dies.

You may be wondering why a nonmarital trust is needed or what goes into it if you can leave your entire estate to your spouse and pay no estate tax. The answer has to do with the credit that an estate is allowed.

This *unified* credit allows each of us to leave substantial assets to anyone we'd like and pay no federal estate tax. In 1987, and later years, the credit will be equivalent to an exemption of $600,000.

Let's say you die in 1987 and your estate, after paying expenses and debts, totals $800,000. Let's say your spouse has assets of $50,000. If you leave everything to your spouse, there will be no tax on your estate because of the unlimited marital deduction. But when your spouse dies, your $800,000 will be added to her $50,000 (a total taxable estate of $850,000). Fortunately, since your spouse is allowed a credit that is equivalent to a $600,000 exemption (assuming she dies in 1987 or in a later year), only $250,000 will be taxed ($850,000 less $600,000). The tax on $250,000 is $70,800. But by not using your credit, you wasted it.

Assume, instead of leaving everything to your spouse, you set aside $600,000 and put that into the nonmarital trust. Estate planners call this a *zero tax* marital deduction because an amount equal to the credit equivalent (see page 137) in the year of your death is held back (actually it goes to the nonmarital trust in order to bypass the estate tax when your spouse dies). So the assets in this trust (often called a CEBT, credit equivalent bypass trust) will bypass the tax at your spouse's death. The rest of your estate, $200,000, goes to your spouse.

The objective of a zero-tax marital deduction trust is to reduce total taxes in both estates to zero—or as close to zero as possible. (Remember, this nonmarital trust is the trust that bypasses taxation in your spouse's estate.) Since the $600,000 is not going to your spouse, it doesn't qualify for the marital deduction. So it is technically taxable. But the entire $600,000 is then exempted from tax because of the credit. You pay no tax on this amount. The remaining $200,000 goes to the marital trust for your spouse. There's no tax to be paid at your death on that $200,000 because of the marital deduction.

When your spouse dies, that $200,000 plus the $50,000 of his or her assets is exposed to tax. But now your surviving spouse's $600,000 exemption shields that entire $250,000 amount. There's no tax at the death of your spouse. Here's a comparison of these alternatives:

The Bottom Line?

	All to Spouse	Zero Tax Formula
Tax at first spouse's death	0	0
Tax at second spouse's death	$70,800	0
Total tax	$70,800	$ 0

Savings with the zero tax formula = $70,800.

This potential saving is another reason you may want to have your attorney review your will. Wills and trusts drawn prior to September 13, 1981, are unlikely to have a zero-tax marital deduction formula.

GPOA versus QTIP—What's It Mean?

A third reason to discuss estate planning with your attorney, if your will was drawn before September 13, 1981, is the QTIP (Qualified Terminable Interest Property) trust.

Before we explain a QTIP trust, let's go back and examine how the typical marital trust generally works.

Tax law allows property you leave in trust to qualify for the marital deduction—if (and only if) the trust meets certain requirements. The key ingredients for success are: (1) Your spouse must be entitled to all of the income produced by trust assets, and (2) your spouse must be given a general power of appointment. That means your spouse must have the right to take everything in the trust (if you've given her a lifetime power of appointment—the right during her lifetime to name anyone she wants as the recipient of trust assets, including herself or her creditors) or to name in her will the ultimate recipient of whatever property you've placed into the trust (if you've given her a testamentary power of appointment).

A trust that meets these requirements is called a General Power of Appointment (GPOA) trust. There's one big problem with the GPOA trust: If your spouse remarries, her second husband (and eventually his children) may end up with the assets you've left to this trust (possibly to the exclusion of your own children).

How? First, your wife could give him or leave him that property. She has the right to do so. But even if she doesn't, her new husband—or his children—may end up with it anyway. The reason is that most state laws give a surviving spouse a *right of election,* a right to take a specified portion of your estate regardless of what your will says. Say your wife left all her property—including the property you left her in the marital trust—to your three children. A second husband could elect against the will and end up (in most states) with at least the amount he'd receive if she died intestate, that is, without a valid will.

That's where the QTIP trust comes in. Prior to 1982, if you left property to your spouse for life and then to your children, you'd get no marital deduction unless you also gave your spouse a general power of appointment. You had a Hobson's choice—you could be sure your children would get the property by saying that your wife was to get the income from the trust property, but at her death the principal was to go to your children. But you'd lose the marital deduction. In other words, a large amount of federal tax would be payable when you died, but if you were willing to pay this tax, you could be sure no one other than the beneficiaries you named would receive your assets.

Alternatively, you could be sure of getting the marital deduction and avoiding the federal estate tax by adding a power for your wife to appoint (direct who gets) trust principal—but then you could not be sure it would go to your children.

Current tax law provides a way to meet both objectives—obtain the marital deduction and be sure your children will receive your assets—through the QTIP trust.

How does the QTIP trust work? It is essentially the same as the nonmarital trust described previously that gives your spouse income for as long as she lives and then passes trust assets to your children (or whoever else you pick). The big difference is, if it's a QTIP trust, your executor can then elect to have this trust qualify for the marital deduction.

Where's the catch? It all seems too simple. Well, there is a cost. Your executor has to agree to have the QTIP trust property taxed in your surviving spouse's estate when she dies—even though she doesn't get the property—or have the right to say who gets it when she dies. But it may be well worth the cost since your spouse may live and enjoy trust income (and principal) for many years. That includes taxes that might otherwise have to be paid when you die. You can be sure that, at your spouse's death, whatever is left after taxes are paid will go to your children or other parties you have specified.

Planning Strategies

The illustrations on page 160 compare marital deduction planning strategy prior to 1982 and current planning techniques.

PRE-1982 PLANNING. (50–50 or ½ + ½)

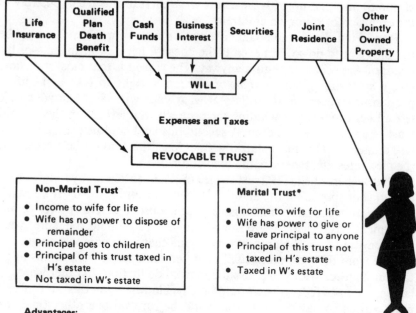

| Life Insurance | Qualified Plan Death Benefit | Cash Funds | Business Interest | Securities | Joint Residence | Other Jointly Owned Property |

WILL

Expenses and Taxes

REVOCABLE TRUST

Non-Marital Trust
- Income to wife for life
- Wife has no power to dispose of remainder
- Principal goes to children
- Principal of this trust taxed in H's estate
- Not taxed in W's estate

Marital Trust*
- Income to wife for life
- Wife has power to give or leave principal to anyone
- Principal of this trust not taxed in H's estate
- Taxed in W's estate

Advantages:

1. Management and investment provided for spouse.
2. Best tax planning prior to January 1, 1982.

Disadvantages:

1. Surviving spouse might leave one-half of estate to a future husband, to children of a different marriage, or to a favorite charity. Problem for remarrieds.

*If wife predeceases husband, the marital deduction is lost.

PLANNING OPTIONS CURRENTLY AVAILABLE

The marital deduction bequest to the spouse can now be:

A	B	C	D
Outright	**Traditional Marital Trust**	**Q.T.I.P. Trust**	**Non-marital (Bypass) Trust**
via	• Income to wife for life	• Income to wife for life	• Income to wife for life
• Simple Will	• Wife has power to dispose of principal during lifetime or at her death to anyone	• Remainder to children (or other party specified by husband)	• Remainder to children (or other party specified by husband)
• Joint Ownership		• Wife has no power to dispose of principal at her death	• Wife has no power to dispose of principal at her death
• Direct Beneficiary			

Pre-1982 planning typically assumed that life insurance, death benefits from qualified retirement plans, cash, any business interest not subject to a buy/sell agreement, and securities would pass by will (after payment of expenses and taxes) to a revocable trust. The revocable trust may have been established during lifetime (an inter vivos trust) or may have been a testamentary trust (one created at death by an individual's will). Assets you owned would be apportioned according to a formula. That formula would pass one-half of the estate owner's property (after taking into account jointly owned and other property automatically passing to the surviving spouse) to the marital trust.

Because of the marital deduction, assets passing to this trust would not be subject to federal estate tax in the estate owner's estate, but would be subject to tax when the surviving spouse died. The reason was that the surviving spouse would be given a general power of appointment over assets in the trust. In other words, she could take the assets herself at her whim or give or leave them to anyone she desired (almost as if she had outright ownership of those assets).

The B Trust

The second trust, the B (established under paragraph B of the trust document) or nonmarital trust, also provided the surviving spouse with income for life, but gave the spouse no power to decide who would receive the principal at her death. The remainderman of the nonmarital trust was selected by the estate owner. Assets going into the nonmarital trust at the surviving spouse's death are taxed when the estate owner dies (because assets passing into this type of trust will not qualify for the marital deduction), but are not taxed when the surviving spouse dies. For this reason, the nonmarital trust was often called the *bypass* trust, since assets in it would bypass taxation in the surviving spouse's estate.

This 50-50 arrangement provided investment and management expertise for the surviving spouse and, at the same time, was the best tax planning available prior to January of 1982.

Problems with prior law planning

Unfortunately, assets in the marital trust were subject to the survivor's absolute power of disposal. That meant that property the estate owner might have wanted to go to his children could (and often would) go to children of the next marriage partner of the surviving spouse, or to a friend or favorite charity of the surviving spouse. There was no way the estate owner could be sure his (or her) dispositive desires would be met.

Now there is much greater flexibility. It is possible to leave tax free any percentage of your estate to your surviving spouse. Depending on your objectives and the size of your estate, you could leave your spouse everything, nothing, half, an amount designed to minimize or eliminate the tax in both your estate and your spouse's (the zero-tax marital deduction formula), or you could leave your estate in any other proportion you desire. All or most of it can pass federal estate tax free if you are married at the time of your death.

Better yet, you can still qualify for that zero-percent to 100-percent marital deduction by leaving property to your spouse outright (by will, joint ownership, or as the beneficiary of life insurance), under the traditional marital deduction trust or through the new QTIP trust (deductible when you die—taxable at your spouse's death even though you pick the eventual recipients of this trust's property).

You could—to any extent you choose—decide to pay an up-front tax. That is, you could decide to take no marital deduction (and therefore pay tax) when you die in return for being certain the property will go to the party you have selected at your spouse's death and the assurance that the assets in this trust will bypass taxation in your survivor's estate.

What action you choose depends on a number of factors that your attorney, accountant, and other financial advisors should discuss with you.

The Inter Vivos (Living) Trust

Bob was looking for a method that would help him provide for his wife, Eileen, and their children, yet reduce his estate and income tax as much as possible. His lawyer told him he could accomplish all he wanted to do if he would set up an irrevocable living trust.

With an irrevocable trust, you can do many of the things a revocable trust can do, but you can also make significant income or estate tax savings possible.

Bob's beneficiary, the person for whose benefit the trust was established and who will receive the benefit of the trust income or principal, is his wife.

In many trusts, there are two types of beneficiary: An income beneficiary and a remainderman. For instance, Bob could have named his wife, Eileen, as income beneficiary. The trust could provide that she was to receive the income from trust property for her life or for a fixed period of years or until a given event occurred. Bob could have provided that his son, Brad, and daughter, Allison, were to ultimately receive the assets in the trust at Bob's wife's death. They would receive what remains at Eileen's death; they would be the *remaindermen*.

Bob could decide to keep a string on his trust so that at his whim he could revoke it, change its terms, or regain ownership of the property in the trust. In that case, Bob has created a revocable trust. Most trusts are revocable, allowing you to change both your mind and the terms—or beneficiaries—of the trust. Alternatively, Bob could set up the trust without retaining the ability to alter, amend, revoke, or terminate it. You make a revocable trust irrevocable by giving up the right to alter, amend, revoke, or terminate the trust.

The Supertrust

A well-known estate planning attorney, Frank Weisz, nicknamed the irrevocable trust the *Supertrust*. The title of his bestselling book by that name is appropriate because it's that good. Here's why: No matter what's in the irrevocable trust, it wouldn't be in Bob's estate—if he's willing to give up the right to:

1. Any income provided by trust assets.
2. Use or enjoy the trust property.
3. Name new trust beneficiaries, or change the ones he's named.
4. Get trust property back.
5. Alter, amend, revoke, or terminate the trust.

That means that, even if the trust holds a $1,000,000 policy on his life, none of the insurance—or any other trust assets—will be taxed in Bob's estate when he dies. This supertrust can even be set up so that there's no tax when Bob's wife, Eileen, dies. That way the insurance proceeds and other assets avoid federal income and estate and generation-skipping transfer taxes and state tax in two estates and pass to Bob's children intact. The supertrust is probably the single most efficient, quick, effective, and safe way to transfer large amounts of capital available under current law.

Perhaps an even greater advantage to this supertrust is that the income produced by any property placed in the trust wouldn't be taxed to Bob as long as he doesn't retain the power to say who will enjoy trust principal or income, and trust income:

1. Isn't paid to Bob or his wife.
2. Wouldn't be accumulated for later distribution to Bob or his wife.
3. Can't be used to pay premiums for a policy on Bob's or his wife's life.
4. Isn't used to support someone Bob is legally obligated to support.
5. Isn't used to discharge Bob's legal obligations.

So who is taxed on trust income if Bob isn't? If a beneficiary receives (or has the right to receive) income, that person is taxed on it. If the supertrust accumulates income, it is taxed on it. Eventually, when that accumulated income is distributed to the beneficiary, that person is taxed on it but receives credit for the taxes the trust paid. Remember that trust income paid to a beneficiary under age 14 will be taxed to that child, *but at the same rate* as if it were the income of the child's parent.

Supertrust gift tax implications

One of the primary laws of tax planning is "there's no free lunch in the tax law." This is true even when using the supertrust.

When Bob puts mutual funds, cash, life insurance, or other property into a supertrust, because he's giving up dominion and control over these assets, he's making a gift for federal tax purposes. (Check to see if your state is among those which impose a state gift tax.)

If the gift is large enough, Bob will have to pay a federal gift tax. Fortunately, the supertrust can be drafted in such a way that all or most of the gift is excluded from the federal gift tax. Estate planners call this a supertrust with *Crummey power,* named after the Clifford Crummey case in which an annual gift tax exclusion was allowed to a taxpayer for gifts to a trust that allowed the beneficiary to make limited yearly withdrawals.

Bob can give his beneficiary the right to take out (gift tax free) the greater of $5000 or 5-percent of the assets in the trust each year. But it's a "use it or lose it" right; it's noncumulative. So if the beneficiary never exercises the right to make withdrawals and lets his or her right go (which is what you are counting on), money Bob puts into the trust can be used by the trustee to pay premiums on a life insurance policy on Bob's or his wife's life. Since the money being used is capital and not income, there are no income tax problems.

One additional tax implication: If Bob transfers appreciated property to an irrevocable trust and that property is sold by the trust within two years, the trust pays the tax on it, but at Bob's bracket. For instance, if Bob bought land in Wildwood for $1000 an acre and transferred it to the trust when it was worth $10,000 an acre, he doesn't pay tax on any gain. But if the trust sells the land within the next two years, any gain it realizes is taxed to it at the same rates it would have been taxed at if Bob personally had sold it. If Bob is in a 33-percent tax bracket and the trust in a much lower bracket, it might pay to wait until more than two years have passed before the trust sells the land.

Additional utility of the supertrust

Does this irrevocable supertrust help in estate planning? Absolutely. Not only does it save income and estate taxes, but it also can be used to provide estate liquidity to help pay estate settlement costs.

The simplest way is for the trust, once it receives the insurance proceeds on Bob's life, to use those dollars to purchase assets (such as stock or land) in Bob's estate from Bob's executor. That gives the estate cash to pay taxes and other expenses and keeps key assets inside the trust for the benefit of Bob's children (but outside of Bob's estate).

An alternative is for the trustee to lend Bob's executor enough cash to pay immediate expenses.

Using Disclaimers

A *disclaimer* is a refusal to accept property that has been left to you by someone else. Now who would give up the right to property—and why?

Let's say you were the first in a succession of heirs under your uncle's will. You might say "no" to money or property you could otherwise have if you were a person with more than adequate income, a modest standard of living, and a large estate of your own. Suppose you knew accepting the property would mean these assets would be added to the property you already have and, therefore, compound your potential estate tax problems. You might disclaim the bequest so that, by default, your daughter, the next recipient under your uncle's will, would receive the property. That way the asset would go directly from your uncle's estate to your daughter, and at your death the property wouldn't be taxed in your estate.

You might say "no" if you were in a high income tax bracket, you wanted your son in college to have both income and financial security, and he was next in line after you in your uncle's will.

Or you might say "no" if your father left property to you instead of to your mother, who was named as the *residual* (take everything that's left) beneficiary under his will. By disclaiming your interest, no only do you shift the property to your mother—gift tax free—but you also enable your father's estate to qualify for the federal tax marital deduction. That might wipe out the federal tax in his estate entirely. Your mother could then make a substantial gift to you—gift tax free—and the amount you'd retain would be enhanced with the significant estate tax savings.

How to Disclaim

There are five major requirements that must be met for a disclaimer to be effective for tax purposes. You have to:

1. Make an irrevocable and unqualified refusal to accept the property.
2. Make that refusal in writing.
3. Have the refusal in the hands of your benefactor's executor or other legal representative within nine months of the date on which you reach age 21, or if later, within nine months of your benefactor's death (or if you are receiving the gift under a trust set up during your benefactor's lifetime, within nine months of the time the property is placed into the trust for your benefit).
4. Make your disclaimer before accepting the property or income produced by it.
5. The property must pass to the next person without any direction on your part. (You can't say who is to receive the property when you disclaim.)

Tax Implications of a Valid Disclaimer

Burke, a successful business owner, has four children. Under the terms of Burke's late Aunt Katherine's will, he is to receive her entire estate if he survives her. If he does not, her will provides that Burke's four children are to receive the estate in equal shares. By making an effective disclaimer, Burke will be treated for tax purposes as if he had predeceased his aunt. That would result in her estate being divided into four equal shares and distributed to Burke's children. Knowing that his children were financially secure, Burke could spend and enjoy his own fortune more freely.

Burke's disclaimer is not treated as a gift to his children for gift tax purposes. So Burke would not be subjected to the gift tax he would have had to pay if he accepted the property and then gave it away. Furthermore, the property he had refused to accept will not be in his estate for federal estate tax purposes. Once Aunt Katherine's property has been disclaimed, any income produced by it is taxed to Burke's low-bracket children rather than to Burke himself at his high income tax bracket.

14

How to Defer and Discount the Tax Payment

Advantages of a Payout

One of the most prevalent ideas about buying and selling property of any kind is that the parties to the transaction, or at least the seller, would be better off if the full price were paid in a lump-sum cash payment. While this method might be the best when buying something relatively inexpensive, there are more sophisticated ways that you should consider when selling property of significant value. A lump-sum payment does have the advantage to the seller of 100 percent security, and the proceeds of the sale can be put to work immediately. But where your objective is to shift wealth to your children or other relatives, and you are willing to take economic risks, there may be better ways of meeting your goals.

The *private annuity* offers potential for amazing income tax and estate tax advantages, especially applicable to family transactions like transferring a home, undeveloped real estate, stocks, or a business interest.

One of the most popular tax planning tools is the installment sale. One of the principal reasons for its success is that it offers tax advantages to both the buyer and seller. The seller may be able to spread gain on the sale of the property over the years in which the installments are paid. Of course, it's much easier on the buyer's pocketbook to be able to spread payments out over a period of years, as opposed to coming up with a lump-sum initial payment.

Under Section 6166 of the Internal Revenue Code, your estate can obtain relief against the problems caused by the fact that federal estate taxes must be paid nine months after death. Code Section 6166 gives estates in which a business interest constitutes a substantial asset an extremely liberal means of stretching out the payments of the federal estate tax.

Each method of payment described in this chapter has its own rules and regulations. If properly utilized, they can greatly reduce taxes or alleviate the harshness of lump-sum cash demands.

The Private Annuity

A private annuity is an arrangement between two parties in which one, the transferor, conveys complete ownership of property to the other, the transferee. In return, the transferee promises to make periodic payments to the transferor for some period of time—usually for the transferor's life or for the life of the transferor and his/her spouse.

Louise used a private annuity. She bought land in West Chester, Pennsylvania, several years ago for $10,000. It's now worth $100,000. Louise wants to sell this property but would like to avoid a large tax in one year. She is in the 33-percent income tax bracket. The private annuity will enable her to defer and spread the tax on her gain over her entire lifetime. (In this respect, the private annuity is similar to the installment sale discussed in this chapter.)

Milt would like to retire and shift control of his business to one of his employees, Michael. He would like to sell the business to Michael and have him take over. But Milt is concerned about adequate income upon his retirement. Unfortunately, Michael can't afford to buy Milt's stock for a lump sum. But Milt could sell Michael his stock in return for Michael's promise to pay him an income he can never outlive no matter how long he lives. In fact, the arrangement could provide that the income will last for Milt's life and then for as long as Milt's wife, Sylvia, lives. This private annuity creates a market for the business where there might not otherwise be one.

Sam owns a large parcel of land. It is appreciating rapidly and will probably be developed in the near future. Sam could sell the parcel to his married daughters in return for their arrangement to pay him an income for life. This arrangement not only will provide Sam with an income but also will remove the value of the land from his estate at no gift tax cost. When Sam dies, the payments stop and nothing but the payments he has already received (and not spent or given away) will be in Sam's estate.

Liz is a widow who owns a large parcel of nonincome-producing property left to her by her husband. She wants to increase her spendable income and reduce her dependence on her son, Frank, who is currently giving her $700 a month. Because of the choice location of the real estate, it is increasing substantially in value. Over the next ten years, it will probably double or triple in value. Frank could stop making gifts. Liz could transfer the real estate to him in return for his promise to pay her a monthly lifetime income. This removes the property from Liz's estate and, therefore, reduces estate taxes at her death. At the same time, it gives Liz financial independence (and frees the dollars she was using to pay real estate taxes on the property). Frank becomes the immediate owner of the real estate, and all the growth in value for tax purposes occurs in his hands.

Louise used the private annuity to reduce overall income taxes. Milt used it to help an employee purchase his business interest. Sam used the private annuity to remove property from his estate. Liz used the private annuity to give her independence and make nonincome-producing property productive (while keeping family land within the family). You might want to use a private annuity—for any or all of these purposes.

Selecting the Right Type of Property

What kind of property should you have to make the private annuity idea work? Although it is possible to use any type of property, the best types of property for this purpose will be income-producing, nondepreciable, and not subject to indebtedness. Many people have transferred a home, undeveloped real estate, stocks, or a business interest in return for a private annuity.

Most important is the ability and the willingness of the transferee to make payments to the transferor. If the transferee has little or no income, then the property in question should be income-producing, or at least be a type that can easily be sold or used as collateral for a loan.

A private annuity example

At age 65, Ed felt that he had worked hard—and long enough. He owned farmland in Chester County worth $100,000, which he had bought 30 years ago for $10,000.

Ed wants his son, Eric, to have the land. Ed does not want to pay any gift taxes on the transfer. He would like to remove the farm from his estate.

Ed asked his attorney to draft a private annuity agreement. The agreement states that the farmland is sold to Ed's son, Eric, in return for his promise to pay Ed an income for life that he can never outlive. (The annuity could have continued for the life of Ed's wife, Joyce.)

At age 65, Ed's life expectancy is 20 years. (See the table on p. 184.)

The promise made by Eric to purchase property worth $100,000 in return for a lifetime annual payment would result in an obligation to pay his father $14,712 a year. (That's the actuarial equivalent of $100,000 today.) Ed will be able to exclude a portion of that $14,712 from income each year. This is because he invested $10,000 in the property, and he is entitled to recover his $10,000 cost, income tax free. The amount he can recover income tax free is found by dividing his $10,000 cost by his 20-year life expectancy, as shown by the table on p. 184. A male age 65 is expected to live 20 years. $10,000 divided by 20 = $500. So out of each $14,712 that Ed receives, he can exclude $500 from income.

The $14,212 balance of each annual payment ($14,712 − $500) will be taxed at ordinary income rates from 1988 on.

Estate tax savings potential

The big advantage of a private annuity is that it removes the property transferred from your estate immediately. This means that Ed has removed $100,000 of property and had no gift tax cost. If he dies the very next day, not one nickel of the $100,000 will be in his estate. Likewise, since his son, Eric, promised to pay to him as long as he lives—and only as long as he lives—Eric's obligation to continue the payments stops at his father's death. Therefore, nothing is in Ed's estate because of Eric's promise, even if he dies after only one payment.

Disadvantages

There is a big disadvantage to a private annuity: The promise made to Ed by Eric can't be secured. There can't be a trust or escrow account to hold title to the transferred property. Once the deal is made, Eric is the outright and absolute owner of the property. Ed becomes a general creditor and has to rely on Eric to make the payment he has said he will make. For this and other reasons, the private annuity will be the right tool in very few estate planning situations (but where it is right, it is very right!).

The Installment Sale

Bob is a real estate investor who is about to retire. Bob just sold some land he's held for many years. His gain on the sale is $100,000, and he's in the 33-percent income tax bracket. Bob could have beaten the tax by dividing the gain and deferring part of it into more than one tax year. In other words, he could have taken the sales proceeds in installments. If he takes $50,000 of the gain this year and $50,000 the first week of next year, he will only pay $16,500 in tax this year on the sale (since, technically, Bob doesn't have to report the remaining $50,000 of gain until April fifteenth of the year after next). Even if his tax liability is $16,500 in that year, he'll have that $16,500 to invest for more than a year before he has to pay it. If his income has dropped, the rate at which the other $50,000 of gain will be taxed also falls. For instance, if in the next year Bob is in the 28 percent tax bracket, the tax will be $14,000, not $16,500—a savings of $2500.

Requirements

Many people should consider the installment sale for estate planning purposes. Essentially, the major ingredient is that the seller agrees to accept the purchase price in installments over a period of years (or agrees to accept no payment in the year of the sale and one or more payments in later years).

Who might find the installment sale concept advantageous? (1) A person (or business) who wants to sell property to someone who may not have enough capital to buy the property outright. Calvin was looking for a way to buy out his employer, Gene. Calvin couldn't pay Gene a lump sum, but in return for a higher price for his business, Gene was willing to accept a long-term payout. In this respect, the installment sale can help create a market for property or a business where none previously existed.

(2) Someone in a high income tax bracket who holds substantially appreciated closely held stock or real estate can spread ordinary income over the period of installments. That pro-rates the tax due, and the seller (for instance, Bob, in a previous example) pays tax only as actual payments from the sale are received. This can make it possible to shift most of the reportable profit from a high income (high tax) year (or years) when the seller is in a lower bracket.

(3) Installment sales between family members provide a way to remove rapidly appreciating assets from the seller's estate. All the growth experienced by the property from the date of the sale is shifted to the family member who buys the asset. So the installment sale may be an effective way to freeze the growth in your estate.

Potential problems

As with every planning tool, the installment sale should be utilized only after consultation with both accounting and legal counsel. This caveat is particularly appropriate (1) where the sale is to a related party, (2) where the property is depreciable, (3) where the buyer is a related party who plans to dispose of the property before completing the installment payouts, (4) where the property in question is mortgaged, (5) where the property is worth more than $150,000, (6) where the seller has substantial business or personal debt, or (7) where the property consists of publicly traded stock or other securities. All of these situations may result in additional, unexpected, and adverse tax consequences.

An alternative to the installment sale as an income and estate tax savings device is the private annuity (previously discussed in this chapter).

Installment Payments of Estate Tax

Suppose you've been financially successful beyond your wildest dreams. The business you started so many years ago with a few thousand dollars of borrowed money is now a multi-million-dollar operation. Your children are rapidly learning the business and are enthusiastic about working with you.

But, there's one major problem. Your accountant or attorney or other financial advisor has shown you that at your death, if the business is left to those children, substantial federal estate taxes would be payable. That's a major problem because you have little liquidity; there's just no cash to pay taxes—it's all been invested in the business.

"Don't worry," says one of your buddies. "I just heard that there's a section in the tax law that enables you to "borrow" money from the federal government to pay taxes. It's called Section 6166, and it can solve your problems."

Is he right? The answer is yes—and no.

Yes, there is a Code Section 6166, and it does provide for installment payments on estate tax. But no, all that glitters is not gelt, and there is no free lunch.

How to qualify for deferred payments

Section 6166 of the Internal Revenue Code provides relief against the general requirement that the federal estate tax must be paid in full (payment must be made in cash—no credit cards, stock certificates, or real estate deeds are acceptable) within nine months of death.

Under 6166, your executor—at his or her discretion—could elect to pay the federal estate tax attributable to your interest in a closely held business (sole proprietorship, partnership or corporation) in installments.

Your executor doesn't pay any tax for the first four years after the tax becomes payable—just interest on the unpaid balance. For up to ten additional years, principal and interest are payable. That does stretch out the payments. But, there are requirements that must be met to qualify for this favorable treatment. The two major requirements are (1) the business must be included in your gross estate; and (2) the value of your business interest must exceed 35 percent of the value of your adjusted gross estate.

If these tests are met, your executor can pay all or a portion of the estate tax in installments. The formula for determining how much can be paid in installments is:

$$\text{Net Federal Estate Tax Payable} \times \frac{\text{Value of Your Business Interest}}{\text{Adjusted Gross Estate}}$$

For instance, Ann's business is worth $600,000. Her estate—after subtracting debts and expenses—is $1,000,000. Since her $600,000 business interest exceeds $350,000, 35 percent of her $1,000,000 adjusted gross estate, her executor is entitled to elect to pay estate taxes in installments.

Ann is single. She is leaving her entire estate to her friend, Barbara. Since the federal estate tax totals $236,000, Ann's executor could elect to pay $141,600 (60 percent of the $236,000) of federal estate taxes in installments:

$$\$236,000 \times \frac{\$600,000}{\$1,000,000} = \$141,600$$

Potential drawbacks

Don't assume that the existence of Section 6166 means you don't need to plan and don't need to assure estate liquidity. It is true that Section 6166 is an excellent post-death tool that an estate's executor should use if it applies and makes sense to use.

But you must not ignore the need your estate will have for cash. First, Section 6166 only applies to active businesses. It doesn't apply to investments, no matter how profitable they may be. The income source you consider a business may be classified as an asset holding company rather than a trade or business. For instance a 100-room apartment house or $10,000,000 office building may not be treated as an active business if you are merely supervising passive investment, rather than performing substantial managerial services.

Second, your business may be worth less than 35 percent of your estate and not qualify for the tax deferral.

Third, your estate may just barely meet the "more than 35 percent" test. Your business might constitute just slightly over 35 percent of your adjusted gross estate. Since 6166 only provides for installment payments of federal estate tax attributable to your business, 64 percent of the federal estate tax may have to be paid immediately. Section 6166 does not allow a deferral of the balance of the federal tax. That must be paid in cash—nine months after your death.

Fourth, only the federal estate tax is deferred; 6166 doesn't allow a deferral of state death taxes. Your executor will also need cash to pay funeral costs, debts, administration expenses, and specific cash bequests to relatives, friends, or charities.

Fifth, unless your heirs will agree to become personally liable for any unpaid tax for the full period of the deferral, your estate has to remain open until the tax is paid. Your executor can't safely pay your beneficiaries their full shares of your estate for many years. Can they do without? Will they want to wait? (Incidentally, the person you have named as executor is fully and personally liable for the tax while it is unpaid. Would *you* want to have that personal liability for over 14 years?) If your business fails and it has to be sold for an amount less than the unpaid tax, your executor may have to pay these taxes out of personal funds.

Sixth, 6166 doesn't provide a source of funds; it merely delays the time payment is due. So you should ask yourself these questions: Where will your executor obtain the cash to pay both the tax and the interest? Will the corporation pay the estate (your estate will be the shareholder of your stock) dividends? Why isn't it paying dividends now? (Will a corporation that's just lost its key profit maker and which may be struggling to survive be able to pay dividends?) Can a portion of the business be sold by your executor? (If more than 50 percent of the business is sold, the unpaid tax becomes due and payable immediately.) Who would buy less than a controlling interest? What price would a minority interest bring? Would that be enough for your family? Would some other asset have to be sold to pay the tax and other immediately payable expenses?

Using 6166 effectively

Section 6166 is quite valuable in spite of the problems it poses. The trick is to have enough estate tax free life insurance (it could be owned by an irrevocable life insurance trust so that it wouldn't be taxed in your estate) so that when you die, the trustee of that trust can use that money to buy assets from your estate. That gives your executor cash and shifts your assets to the trust for your children.

Your executor could pay taxes year by year in installments under Section 6166 and invest the balance of the life insurance received from the sale of estate assets. (There is no requirement that your executor *must* use 6166.)

To some extent, a very favorable 4-percent rate (compounded daily) applies to up to $153,000 of the unpaid tax.

If the federal estate tax owed exceeds $153,000, a significantly higher interest rate is due on the unpaid balance.

But there is a kicker! Interest on the unpaid tax is compounded daily. So if the rate were 16 percent, thanks to daily compounding, taxes and interest you could owe the IRS double in 4.6 years and triple in 7.3 years. The IRS would have a financial time bomb ticking away for it if there's a large sum of money involved.

The idea is to have income on the estate's investments exceed the interest and principal payments on the unpaid tax. This is possible if you purchase adequate amounts of life insurance, arrange it so that it will be estate tax free, and select an executor with investment expertise.

Flower Bonds

There are two ways to pay federal estate taxes at a discount. One way is through life insurance. That's the way to go if you are insurable. But if you are not insurable (most of us are), Flower Bonds are your answer.

Flower Bonds, so-called because they blossom, are traded and can be bought at a deep discount (about seventy cents on the dollar). The federal government will redeem them—buy them back—at one dollar on the dollar in payment of the federal estate tax.

Where to buy Flower Bonds

You can buy Flower Bonds, which are actually U.S. government bonds, through bank trust departments or from stockbrokers.

The only requirements are that they must be bought while you are alive, and they must be owned by you at death. They must be purchased by you or at your direction pursuant to an effective power of attorney. (See Chapter 21.) They can actually be bought at a discount on your deathbed.

Disadvantages

John was told he had a fatal disease and had only a few months to live. His attorney told him that at his death a federal estate tax of about $200,000 would be due.

John quickly purchased a 3.5-percent 1990 series Flower Bond. The price he paid was 73.26; that is, he paid $732.60 for each $1000. So he had to pay $146,520 (73.56 × 2000) for $200,000 worth of bonds (redemption value).

At first glance, it appears that the discount is the difference between the $200,000 of taxes the federal government will accept and the bonds (John paid $146,520). In other words, it seems as if John's estate has made $53,480 on the deal.

The catch (there is no free lunch in the tax law) is that the bonds are included in John's estate at their par value ($200,000 in this case) even though the day before John bought the bonds only $146,520 was in his estate. Since he's in a 37-percent estate tax bracket, 37 percent of $146,520, or $19,787 of the discount, is lost. To add insult to tax injury, whether or not the bonds are actually used to pay the federal estate tax, to the extent they *could* be used to pay taxes, they must be included in John's estate at their par, and not their market value. So even if they are sold after the date of death for their market (discounted) value, they may be included in the estate at their par (higher estate tax payment value).

Another cost is that the bonds generate a very low interest rate (3.5 percent in this example). This makes these bonds a foolish investment for any reason except the payment of federal estate taxes by someone who has a short time to live. In fact, an executor who keeps more Flower Bonds on hand than are needed could be surcharged by the beneficiaries on the grounds that the executor didn't invest estate money as productively as possible.

Given the impending maturity date on many issues of these Flower Bonds and the much lower rates of interest prevalent at the date of this printing, discounts on Flower Bonds have been dropping considerably.

Not everyone has had—or has taken—the opportunity to do all the planning or purchase all the life insurance necessary for liquidity purposes. Flower Bonds are a last-ditch tool, which should not be overlooked by the uninsurable, but they are clearly not a suitable alternative for properly arranged life insurance for anyone else.

PART FOUR

SITUATIONS THAT REQUIRE SPECIAL PLANNING

How to Effectively Plan for Your
Business, Your Children, Retirement,
Old Age, and Disability

15

How to Use Your Business to Enhance Your Personal Net Worth

At your death or disability, no asset tends to deteriorate as quickly and thoroughly as a business. If someone owns an automobile, or a home, or almost any kind of tangible property, the value of that property one month after that individual dies would be relatively the same as at the date of death. But what if the deceased individual owned a restaurant that didn't open for a month, or was a doctor whose office was closed for a month, or owned a small manufacturing plant for which no provision had been made following his death. In all or some of these cases, the precipitous drop in value could be staggering.

If your spouse is in business with another person, how would you like to be associated with that individual if your spouse were to die? (Or, suppose the situation were reversed?) This chapter is about what can happen to a business if something happens to the owner, or one of the owners, and what can be done to eliminate, or greatly reduce, the almost insurmountable financial and personal problems that frequently arise when there has been no advance planning.

A properly drawn and adequately funded buy-sell agreement can be worth even more than the business itself. A fully funded Section 303 Stock Redemption (which we'll define below) can reduce or eliminate the economic hardships caused by federal estate taxes, state death taxes, funeral costs, and administrative expenses. It may even prevent the forced sale of your business.

One way for your business to provide financial security for your family is to set up a survivor's income benefit plan (SIBP).

Your business can make otherwise nondeductible medical expenses completely deductible when you set up a medical expense reimbursement plan.

It sometimes takes almost a lifetime to establish a successful business or professional practice. This chapter contains the information

177

necessary to enable you to stabilize and maximize the value your family will derive from the business in the event of your death or disability. This chapter illustrates specific methods to utilize the business to obtain tax savings benefits for yourself and the members of your family. How can you stabilize and maximize the value of your business holdings? How can you be sure your business will be controlled and run by those people you select? Please read on.

Why You Need a Buy-Sell Agreement

Eddie's shoe store had been a fixture in town for 20 years. Eddie ran the business with the help of his long-time manager, Marty, and two other part-time salespeople. The business provided the sole support for Eddie, his wife, Miriam, and their children, as well as for Marty and his family.

Eddie was an old timer who loved his business, worked night and day, and didn't believe in planning for the future. When Eddie had a heart attack and died within three days, not only was the family hit with the immediate emotional trauma of his death, but they were then hit with problems with the store—economic problems which seemed insurmountable.

Miriam tried to continue to run the business, an operation which she knew nothing about. She told Marty she would continue his salary. However, after just three months in which Miriam took most of the money out of the business to pay Eddie's medical bills, shoe sales declined almost by half. Correctly anticipating that the business would fail and his job would be lost, Marty quickly accepted the offer of one of Eddie's chief competitors. Several months later, Miriam had to sell the remaining inventory. She received less than 50 percent of what Eddie had originally paid for it (and only a fraction of what the business was worth while Eddie was alive). The store closed its doors for the last time.

Jerry's automobile parts shop could have suffered almost the same fate as Eddie's store if Don, Jerry's insurance agent, hadn't made his suggestions to Jerry. At Don's suggestion, Jerry and his manager, Bob, worked out a key man buy-sell agreement. Under the terms of the agreement prepared by Jerry's lawyer, in the event of Jerry's death, or permanent disability, Bob agreed to buy the business from Jerry at a predetermined price they both felt was fair. The agreement provided that they would review the price at least once a year to make sure that it would always reflect a value both individuals considered fair.

In order to have the money on hand to purchase Jerry's interest, Bob bought a policy on Jerry's life in the amount of $75,000 (the value they had originally decided on). When Jerry died, Bob collected the insurance money and paid it to Jerry's widow in return for Jerry's stock. Jerry's widow, therefore, received the full value of the business, and Bob now owned the automobile parts shop, free and clear of any obligations to Jerry's family. Not incidentally, he also protected his job!

Problems Can Occur Even in Family-Run Businesses

As brothers, Joe and Paul could not have been closer. They had been in business together for 25 years and worked very closely together. They were in a service business and had divided their business activities down the middle. Joe was responsible for bringing in the business, as he was a super salesman. Paul ran the day-to-day operation of the business. Joe was conservative and lived with his wife and children in a small apartment. Paul and his wife lived life on a higher scale.

One night, while the brothers were both in their early fifties, Joe died suddenly in his sleep. When the lawyer for Joe's estate sat down with Joe's wife, Lillian, and Paul, he heard the following story.

Lillian told the lawyer that, since Joe had owned half the business, she wanted half. She also wanted to continue to be able to take out of the business the money that Joe had taken, since it was in part due to his efforts that the business had reached the status that it presently enjoyed. In fact, it was absolutely necessary for her to continue to take the same amount of money out, since she had children in college.

Paul felt a very close attachment to his brother's widow and their children. He wanted to do everything he could for them. However, he was not a good salesman, and it was, therefore, necessary to hire a new salesman at a considerable salary to replace Joe, even though no new salesman would be capable of bringing in the volume of business that Joe had. Unfortunately, the business could not now afford to pay three salaries where before it had only paid two. Even Paul's salary had to be cut. Paul's wife was extremely upset at having to reduce her standard of living. She cautioned the lawyer and Lillian that, if the economic strain was too much for Paul and his health suffered, then nobody would realize anything from the business. Therefore, she suggested that perhaps Lillian should go out and find a job to provide for her own needs and her children's education.

It is obvious that regardless of what solution was eventually worked out, it would be unsatisfactory to some family members.

This unfortunate situation could have been prevented if Joe and Paul, their lawyer, accountant, and insurance agent had executed and properly funded a buy-sell agreement. A properly drawn agreement could have provided that, in the event of the death of either partner, the remaining partner would purchase the share of the deceased partner with insurance proceeds from a policy that the surviving partner owned on the deceased partner's life.

Buy-Sell Advantages to Both Parties

Here's what could have happened: On Joe's death, the life insurance policy that Paul owned on Joe's life would have paid Paul the amount they had agreed would represent Joe's interest in the business. Paul would have taken the money, paid it to Lillian, and would then have owned the business outright. From Lillian's standpoint, she would now have the money she needed for herself and her children. She would have had no legal right to question Paul's future business decisions—or the salary or other benefits he provided himself through the business.

Paul's situation would also be greatly enhanced. He would own the business free and clear and, therefore, have the right to all of the income. He would then have funds available to hire a salesman to solicit new business, and should also not have to worry about being pressured by his sister-in-law or his wife—a remarkably appropriate and simple solution to an extremely difficult situation.

Both sides lose if there is no buy-sell

You probably know someone who owns a closely held corporation. You may even own stock in one yourself. If you do, and there are other shareholders, you may want to consider a buy-sell agreement. Why? The best way to answer that question is to look at the basic characteristics of a closely held business.

Gene and Gary each own 50 percent of the stock in the Marcia-D Corporation. Both Gene and Gary are active in the operation of the business. Gene handles the accounting and office work while Gary is in charge of sales. Both Gene and Gary receive most of their income in the form of salaries or fringe benefits. The corporation had never paid dividends and probably never will. Except to the extent that Gene and Gary personally guaranteed loans that the corporation has made, they have limited their liability to corporate creditors.

What happens if either Gene or Gary dies? If either shareholder/ employee dies, the legal structure of the business will probably remain intact. The Marcia-D Corporation will survive as a legal entity. But the personal structure of the corporation will change dramatically.

When a working shareholder dies, the surviving shareholder or shareholders have little choice. In this case, if Gary dies, the surviving shareholder can (1) decide to stay in business with Gary's heirs, (2) buy out Gary's heirs, (3) sell out to Gary's heirs, or (4) accept the individuals who purchased Gary's stock as new shareholders.

What would you do if you were Gene? What would you want if you were Gary—or his heirs? It is inevitable that the interest of the surviving stockholders and the decendent/shareholder's heirs will conflict. Gene, the surviving shareholder, will seek to maintain (or increase) his salary. Why not? He's now doing the work of two men. He will want to re-invest corporate earnings and profits in the business to avoid the need to borrow at high interest rates. Gene will favor expansion, growth, and other steps that build up the financial strength of the Marcia-D Corporation. Typically, dividends are the last thing that Gene will want the corporation to pay out. Paying dividends not only would put a strain on the corporation, but also would be highly taxed before Gary's heir could get to use them.

On the other hand, Robin, Gary's heir, will be very much concerned with dividends. Since she is a minor and not capable of earning a meaningful salary (or for any other reason does not go into the business), dividends will become her major source of income. This is especially true when the heir doesn't have the skill, education, or temperament to carry her part in running the business. (The IRS would disallow the deduction for a high unearned salary even if the business could afford to pay it to her.)

Robin's position is not unusual. Often, heirs can't or don't want to take an active role in the business. Sometimes, a person's heirs will lack a technical understanding of the business. Quite often, they will have little training or experience or are unwilling or unable to handle the severe emotional punishment entailed in modern business management.

Surviving stockholders will seldom want to share corporate control or decision making with individuals who have not worked in the business for some time. (Would you want your co-shareholder's heirs in business with you with an equal voice in major decisions? Would they be happy to accept your heirs?)

If Robin should remain inactive, it places her fate in the hands of Gene, the surviving shareholder. This may be undesirable because the dividends Robin would be likely to receive as an inactive heir would probably not provide adequate income. Gene, in trying to be fair to Robin, may not be fair to himself.

Could Robin sell her stock to an outsider? She could, but it is usually difficult for the heirs to sell their stock, since the price they will want (and often need) is often more than many buyers can afford or would be willing to pay. Frankly, a buyer who is aware of how much Robin needs cash to pay taxes or to provide income will use this knowledge to his advantage (and to Robin's disadvantage).

Robin, like most heirs, will probably be totally unfamiliar with the true value of the Marcia-D stock. Quite often, heirs assume (erroneously) the value of the stock should be a multiple of the deceased/shareholder/employee's salary. This is a misguided, naive, and even dangerous expectation. The result will probably be a forced sale of stock or other property at drastically depressed prices to raise cash for basic living needs.

The problem is aggravated even further since Robin owns only 50 percent of the corporation's stock. Her task would be much easier if she had a controlling (51 percent or more) interest. If she owns less than 50 percent, her minority interest could make it difficult, if not impossible, to find a buyer. The reason is that the minority shareholder has little power or say over any of the major decisions to be made in a corporation. A minority shareholder can't control the hiring or firing of employees or whether the corporation will or will not pay dividends. Someone contemplating the purchase of Robin's stock will be just as powerless as she is (and, therefore, would not purchase it or offer to pay more than a "fire sale" price).

Advantages of a properly drawn agreement

Most attorneys and financial advisors will recommend a legally binding buy-sell agreement. That document would require the surviving shareholders (or the corporation) to buy, and require the estate of a deceased shareholder to sell, the inherited stock interest. Gary and Gene might decide to establish a buy-sell agreement and properly "fund" it for the following reasons. (Funding means providing the appropriate amounts of cash to effectuate the buy-out when it occurs.)

First, looking at the problems from the surviving shareholder's point of view, the corporation is protected against inactive, uninformed, and potentially dissident shareholders who often cause conflict over management policies such as the size of dividends, the amount of salaries or fringe benefits, or company "percs" provided to working shareholders, or risks the corporation should take for growth. Once a buy-sell agreement is executed and properly funded, Gene won't have to worry that Gary's heir, Robin (or her guardian), might try to tell him how to run his business. The buy-sell has kept the closely held corporation "close."

Second, Gene, the active shareholder, can be assured that the profits produced by his efforts will benefit him rather than someone else (such as an inactive shareholder or the person who purchases that shareholder's stock).

Third, by properly funding the agreement, Gene, the surviving shareholder, is assured of all or the bulk of the cash he will need to purchase Robin's interest.

Fourth, Gene knows that he will not have to pay more than a fair price for the stock.

Fifth, only a buy-sell agreement can guarantee the surviving or remaining shareholders that the transition of management and control will be fluid and complete.

Sixth, the buy-sell agreement can be used by Gene as a convenient means of fulfilling the natural sense of obligation that he may have toward Gary and his family.

A legally binding and properly funded buy-sell agreement makes sense from the viewpoint of the deceased shareholder's family too.

From Gary's point of view, once the agreement is in effect, he knows that Robin will receive a reasonable price for the stock. This would be especially important if Gary held less than a 50 percent interest.

Second, after Gary and Gene sign the agreement, the economic future of Gary's heirs (as well as Gene's heirs) would no longer be tied to the fate of the business. Robin will be free from worry about the financial success or failure of the business.

A third reason that a buy-sell agreement is advantageous from Gary's viewpoint is that he knows once Robin receives the cash from the buy-out the pressure on her to liquidate other estate assets to pay estate taxes and other settlement costs would be decreased. Valuable family heirlooms would not have to be sold to pay taxes. Money from the sale of the stock at a shareholder's death is assured. Death, the event that creates the need for cash, creates the cash to satisfy the need.

Fourth, if a buy-sell agreement is arranged properly and the price or the formula which establishes the price is fair when the agreement is drawn, it will practically eliminate an after-death dispute with the Internal Revenue Service as to the value of the stock. A properly drawn buy-sell helps establish the federal estate tax value.

Fifth, at Gary's death, funds paid by the corporation or by Gene to Robin in payment of her stock interest can be entirely income tax free.

Objectives to be met

Specifically, what is it that a buy-sell agreement should do? What are the objectives that the parties want to meet in funding such an agreement?

A corporate buy-sell agreement should be funded by a method that will facilitate a trouble-free transfer of the business interest in one of four situations: (1) at some time before retirement, (2) at normal retirement age, (3) in the event of a disability of a shareholder, and (4) at the death of a shareholder.

Ideally, Gene and Gary's advisors will be able to figure out a way to provide funds to meet those contingencies. Optimally, the method used to provide such funds will:

1. Have relatively low cost.
2. Be simple for Gary, Gene, Robin, and any other party to the agreement to understand.
3. Be easy to administer.
4. Not adversely affect the working capital or credit position of the business.

Funding your buy-sell

Steve, the insurance agent who handles all the Marcia-D Corporation's insurance, told Gene and Gary that they should consider the possibility of a buy-out at a stockholder/employee's termination, retirement, death, or disability. Both Gene and Gary were shocked when Steve showed them actuarial tables illustrating the possibility of either death or disability before age 65. He told them that, expressed as the number of chances out of 100, at least one out of two business owners in relatively good health will die or become disabled before age 65. The figures are:

Chances of Death before 65	Ages of Business Owners
48.5	30/30
47.4	35/35
45.8	40/40
43.5	45/45
39.8	50/50
38.0	30/35
46.6	35/40
44.7	40/45
41.7	40/45

Adapted from *Tools and Techniques of Estate Planning*, 6th Edition, The National Underwriter Company, Cincinnati, Ohio.

Steve mentioned that the probability of disability would be even greater. (See the table on the facing page.)

Both Gene and Gary immediately asked Steve how they would create the cash for the buy-sell. Steve explained that there were four alternatives available for funding the buy-sell: (1) cash, (2) borrowing, (3) installment payments, and (4) life insurance. They asked him to compare the four methods.

Cash has the apparent advantage that no immediate outlay of cash is required. The problem is neither partner knows who will be the survivor. You don't know precisely when you will need the cash or how much cash you will need. This means you will always have to keep a large amount of cash available to meet the anticipated need.

Worse yet, you will have to use after-tax dollars. In other words, either you or the corporation will have to earn the money, pay taxes on it, and then use what is left to go through with the buy-out. Obviously, more than one dollar must be earned to net a dollar of purchase money. For instance, if the corporation is in a 34 percent bracket, it must earn $151,520 to net $100,000 since the buy-out is nondeductible. If the shareholders are in a 33 percent bracket, they must earn $149,250 to net $100,000.

Also, money that you or the corporation hold in reserve to meet that potential need can't possibly earn a return as high as it might earn if it were invested in the business. (But, of course, if you invest it in machinery, equipment or other business assets, it wouldn't be available.)

Gene and Gary then asked about borrowing. Why couldn't the survivor go to a bank and borrow the necessary money? Steve's answer to that was that a bank may not be willing to lend money to a corporation that has lost one of its key employees and is probably struggling to survive.

But even if a bank did lend your corporation or the surviving shareholder money to buy out the decedent shareholder, it could be terribly expensive. Steve pointed out that the annual cash flow needed to pay off

Long-Term Disability of Business Owners: The Odds

This table presents the odds of at least one long-term* disability occurring before age 65, expressed as number of chances out of 1000:**

One life		Two lives		Three lives			
Age	Chances	Ages	Chances	Ages	Chances	Ages	Chances
30	289	30–30	494	30–30–30	640	35–45–60	558
35	284	30–35	491	30–30–35	638	35–50–50	597
40	278	30–40	487	30–30–40	635	35–50–55	582
45	267	30–45	479	30–30–45	630	35–50–60	548
50	250	30–50	467	30–30–50	621	35–55–55	567
55	222	30–55	447	30–30–55	607	35–55–60	531
60	158	30–60	401	30–30–60	574	35–60–60	492
		35–35	487	30–35–35	636	40–40–40	624
		35–40	483	30–35–40	633	40–40–45	618
		35–45	475	30–35–45	627	40–40–50	609
		35–50	463	30–35–50	618	40–40–55	595
		35–55	443	30–35–55	604	40–40–60	561
		35–60	397	30–35–60	571	40–45–45	612
		40–40	479	30–40–40	630	40–45–50	603
		40–45	471	30–40–45	624	40–45–55	588
		40–50	459	30–40–50	615	40–45–60	555
		40–55	438	30–40–55	601	40–50–50	594
		40–60	392	30–40–60	568	40–50–55	579
		45–45	463	30–45–45	618	40–50–60	544
		45–50	450	30–45–50	609	40–55–55	563
		45–55	430	30–45–55	595	40–55–60	527
		45–60	383	30–45–60	561	40–60–60	488
		50–50	438	30–50–50	600	45–45–45	606
		50–55	417	30–50–55	585	45–45–50	597
		50–60	369	30–50–55	551	45–45–55	582
		55–55	395	30–50–60	570	45–45–60	548
		55–60	345	30–55–55	534	45–50–50	588
		60–60	291	30–55–60	496	45–50–55	572
				35–35–35	633	45–50–60	537
				35–35–40	630	45–55–55	557
				35–35–45	624	45–55–60	520
				35–35–50	615	45–60–60	480
				35–35–55	601	50–50–50	579
				35–35–60	568	50–50–55	563
				35–40–40	627	50–50–60	527
				35–40–45	621	50–55–55	546
				35–40–50	612	50–55–60	509
				35–40–55	598	50–60–60	469
				35–40–60	565	55–55–55	529
				35–45–45	615	55–55–60	491
				35–45–50	606	55–60–60	448
				35–45–55	592	60–60–60	403

*Lasting 90 Days or more
**Based on the 1971 Experience Modification of the 1964 Commissioners' Disability Table

a loan of $100,000 at 10 percent would be $25,500 in the case of a five-year loan and as much as $15,864 a year in the case of a ten-year loan. The total cost of such a loan would be $127,482 in the case of a five-year loan and almost $158,581 if the loan was outstanding for ten years. Since it takes one dollar in sales to net ten cents in corporate surplus, it would take over $1,585,000 in sales just to pay off a $100,000 loan!

Although a loan assumed by the buyer may relieve the deceased shareholder's family, it puts an extremely heavy weight on the buyer who must pay off that loan—mainly with after-tax dollars. Worse yet, interest would likely be considered *investment* interest. That means it's deductible only to the extent the buyer has investment income (which many buyers wouldn't).

Will installment payouts be the answer? Could the corporation or the surviving shareholder buy out the deceased shareholder's interest through installment payments?

Steve's answer to this was that it could be used, but the installment payout method would not provide the large sums of cash that might be needed by the deceased shareholder's family for settlement costs. The big problem is that it leaves substantial sums at the risk of the business. And from the surviving shareholder's viewpoint, the installment payment creates almost as much nuisance value as if the deceased shareholder's heirs still owned the stock.

Steve then showed Gene and Gary the cost of a ten-year installment payout of $100,000, assuming 10 percent interest was paid on the balance. To repay $100,000 over ten years, $58,581 would be interest (which may to a great extent be nondeductible as investment interest not offset by investment income). This would significantly increase the cost and, therefore, the cash flow problems of the buyer, making a total payment of $158,581. But if the surviving shareholder were in a 40 percent combined federal and state income tax bracket, to pay $158,581 would require that the stock purchaser earn as much as $264,302. It would be paying for stock with very expensive dollars.

Steve explained that life insurance is the only means of guaranteeing that death, which creates the need for cash, will also create the cash to satisfy that need.

Determining the right amount of life insurance

Gene wanted to know how much insurance should be purchased. Steve recommended that the buy-sell agreement should, if possible, be fully funded. That means that each partner should purchase enough life insurance to allow the survivor to purchase all the stock of the other.

In fact, you may even want to purchase more than the business is currently worth. That's because the value of your business interest and, therefore, the liability of the surviving shareholder will increase—not only with the real value in the price of your stock, but also with inflationary growth. If the business grows at 10 percent, the price that will have to be paid will (approximately) double every 7.2 years. (The rule of 72, that is used by bankers and other financial planners, can be used to find out quickly how long it takes an asset to double in value by dividing whatever growth rate you assume into the number 72.) He illustrated that a business currently worth $500,000 would be worth $1,296,871 in ten years at a compound rate of 10 percent. In 20 years, a $500,000 business would be worth over $3,300,000.

Gene and Gary then asked Steve how to proceed. Steve mentioned that a joint meeting should be held as soon as possible with all the members of the estate planning "cooperative"—the insurance agent, the attorney, the CPA, Gary, and Gene.

The cross purchase buy-sell

At that meeting, their attorney explained that there are two types of buy-sell agreements, a so-called *cross purchase* agreement and a *stock redemption* agreement. A cross purchase (criss cross) agreement is used where the shareholders have decided to assume the obligation of purchasing a deceased co-shareholder's interest personally. Each stockholder owns, pays the premiums for, and is the beneficiary of an appropriate amount of life insurance on the lives of the other shareholders. Since Gene and Gary are each 50 percent shareholders, the agreement would obligate the survivor to purchase the shares of the decedent. If each has a business interest worth $100,000, Gary would purchase at least $100,000 of insurance on Gene's life, and Gene would purchase at least $100,000 worth of insurance on Gary's life. If Gary dies first, Gene receives $100,000 of insurance. He then uses that insurance to buy Gary's stock from his estate or beneficiary. Gary would do the same if Gene died first.

The stock redemption buy-sell

Their attorney explained that in some cases he drafts the buy-sell agreement so that the corporation, rather than the individual shareholders, is obligated to purchase (retire or redeem) the stock of the deceased shareholder. In that case, the corporation purchases, pays premiums on and names itself the beneficiary of an appropriate amount of life insurance on each shareholder's life. When a shareholder dies, the corporation receives the insurance proceeds and then uses that money to purchase the stock from the estate or heir of the deceased shareholder.

The wait and see buy-sell

A third type of buy-sell was popularized in the book *The Wait and See Buy-Sell*. The authors, Attorneys Morey S. Rosenbloom and Steve Leimberg, explained that the Wait and See Buy-Sell is more flexible than either the cross purchase or the stock redemption plan since the buyer of the stock at death or disability could be (a) the remaining shareholders or (b) the corporation or (c) both the shareholders *and* the corporation. Since change (in tax law as well as your needs and circumstances) is the only certainty, flexibility in buy-sell plan designs is the most logical answer.

The beauty (and source of the name) of the wait and see buy-sell is that no decision is made as to who the buyer of the stock will be *until* the triggering event (death, disability, or retirement) occurs. That's the very time when the most is known about how the tax law will impact upon the circumstances—and the buyout can then be structured in the most advantageous manner for all concerned. Life insurance to fund the buyout can be owned by the corporation, by the shareholders, by both the corporation and the shareholders, or by a third party such as a trust or pension plan and loaned to the corporation or shareholders to effect the buyout.

Taxation

Gene asked if the premiums were deductible. Steve's response was that no deductions were allowed where a stockholder, to fund obligations under a cross purchase agreement, purchases insurance on the life of another stockholder. Gary then asked if a stock redemption agreement made it possible for premiums to be deductible. Steve's answer was that the tax law denies deductions for premiums paid on a life insurance policy used to finance the purchaser's obligation under a buy-sell agreement, no matter who owned or was the beneficiary of the policy.

Steve also explained the taxation of premiums to stockholders. In a nutshell, he said, premiums paid by a co-stockholder do not constitute income to the insured under either a cross purchase or a stock redemption type of agreement.

The proceeds the policy owner receives when one partner dies will be income tax free. The proceeds are income tax free regardless of whether you use a cross purchase type of agreement or a stock redemption agreement. No matter how much money you receive, it will be entirely income tax free.

A portion of the insurance proceeds received by a corporation may be subject to the alternative minimum tax (AMT) payable by the corporation on *preference* items.

Because of the AMT (greatly oversimplified, a 10 percent tax on the proceeds), many attorneys are suggesting that corporations use the additional cash flow generated by the drop in corporate brackets (from 46 percent down to 34 percent to purchase 10 to 15 percent more coverage or that buy-sell insurance be owned by the shareholders personally).

Estate tax treatment of insurance proceeds

In the case of either a cross purchase or a stock redemption agreement, in a properly drawn plan, only the value of the deceased shareholder's corporation stock is includable in his estate.

Under a cross purchase agreement, each shareholder owns a policy on the other's life. So the value of the policy the decedent owns on the life of the surviving shareholder will be included in the decedent's estate.

In the case of a stock redemption agreement, when a corporation receives the insurance proceeds, it may have the effect of increasing the value of the business interest for estate tax purposes. How much, if any, it increases the value of the stock for estate tax purposes depends on how the buy-sell agreement is drawn by the firm's attorney. This is another reason you may want to consider having the life insurance owned outside of the corporation.

Taxation of the seller

Regardless of whether the buyer is the corporation (stock redemption) or the surviving shareholder (cross purchase), the estate of the deceased shareholder is selling and not giving away the stock. Unless it is arranged properly, that sale could result in a tax disaster.

Fortunately, current tax law makes it possible for a sale by a decedent shareholder's estate to a surviving shareholder to be entirely income tax free in most cases. Extreme caution should be used in the case of a stock redemption, however, since highly complex tax laws can make the *entire* amount received by the estate or heir subject to ordinary income tax. The problem is especially acute where the shareholders are related to each other. (We recommend that family-owned corporations use a stock redemption type buy-sell only after very careful examination and full consideration of the alternatives by competent tax counsel—and even then with great caution). The wait and see buy-sell provides a convenient and safe means of assuring the most favorable tax treatment when a decedent's stock is purchased at death.

Section 303 stock redemptions

Gary asked if it was necessary for his estate to sell his entire interest in Marcia-D Corporation. Steve's response was that favorable tax treatment in the case of a partial redemption (purchase of less than all the shares of Gary's stock) by the corporation was possible without the corporation's distribution being considered a dividend, but only if Gary's estate qualified. Steve called this partial purchase a Section 303 redemption.

From a business owner's viewpoint, Section 303 can be a key section of the Internal Revenue Code. It allows a corporation to purchase enough stock so that the deceased shareholder's estate can pay federal and state death taxes, funeral costs, and allowable administrative expenses. In most cases, the estate will realize no gain on the sale of stock after the death of the shareholder. Therefore, the transaction will be income tax free to the deceased shareholder's estate.

Section 303 requirements

Section 303 applies only at death, and not every estate can qualify for the protection of a Section 303 stock redemption.

First of all, only stock includable in your estate at the time of your death will qualify. So if you give stock away more than three years before your death, since it is not includable in your estate, it does not qualify for a Section 303 redemption.

Second, the protection of Section 303 only applies if the estate tax value of that stock in your estate is *more* than 35 percent of your "adjusted" gross estate (technically, your gross estate less allowable funeral, administrative expenses and debts). If your adjusted gross estate were $1,000,000 and the value of your stock were exactly $350,000 or some lesser figure, it would not qualify. An easy-to-use form designed by The American College in Bryn Mawr, Pennsylvania, an organization that provides tax education for thousands of estate and financial planning professionals each year, can be found on the next page. Why not check to see if your estate will qualify for a Section 303 redemption and see how much stock can be sold to your business?

What happens if the corporation buys less than all of the decedent's stock, but the tests of Section 303 are not met? The result might be that the *entire* payment made by the corporation to the deceased shareholder's estate would be a dividend taxable as ordinary income. But if the Section 303 more than 35 percent test is met, the seller would realize no taxable gain, and the corporation could buy enough stock so that the seller could pay off estate administrative expenses and federal and state death taxes.

Funding a 303 redemption

As is the case with a typical buy-sell agreement, a partial buy-sell (Section 303 stock redemption) should be properly and adequately funded with life insurance. One way is for the corporation to own insurance on the life of each shareholder. At the least, the amount of insurance would be the total of the estimated combined death and generation-skipping transfer taxes and funeral expenses.

Perhaps a better approach is to have some third party, such as an irrevocable trust or an adult child, own insurance on the life of the shareholder and then have that third party, at the shareholder's death, lend money (fully secured and at a reasonable rate of interest) to the corporation. The corporation could use the loan to purchase the deceased shareholder's stock.

One advantage of the third-party insurance ownership is that the insurance would not increase the estate tax value of the stock. Another advantage is that interest paid by the corporation to the lender would provide income that could be used for food, clothing, shelter, and other current living expenses. The corporation could deduct the interest payments it makes. Eventually, it would pay off the loan out of earnings.

Determination of Whether Estate Qualifies for
Section 303 Stock Redemption

Husband's/Wife's Estate When He/She Dies First/Second

(1) Federal estate tax value corporate stock included in gross
    estate $_____

(The value of stock of two or more corporations can be
aggregated if 20% or more of the value of the outstanding
stock of each such corporation is included in the
decedent's gross estate)

(2) 35% of adjusted gross estate $_____
_____ Does Qualify   _____ Does Not Qualify

If line 1 exceeds line 2, a redemption under ection 303 is
considered a sale or exchange rather than a dividend to the
extent the selling stockholder's interest is reduced directly
or the stockholder is bound to contribute to the payment of:

(a) Deductible funeral and administrative expenses $_____
(b) Federal estate and generation skipping taxes $_____
(c) State death taxes $_____
(d) Interest collected as part of above taxes $_____

Maximum allowable Section 303 Redemption $_____

How to make sure your estate can use Section 303

Assume your adjusted gross estate is $1,000,000. Your business interest
is worth exactly $350,000 (which does *not* meet the requirement that the
business interest must be worth *more* than 35 percent of your adjusted
gross estate to qualify for Section 303 protection). What can you do to
make sure your estate will qualify?

The easiest way is to make your corporation worth more—relative to
the rest of your estate. One way to do that is to have the corporation
purchase and own life insurance on your life to help swell the value of
the business relative to other estate assets. Certainly, a $100,000 policy
will help put the value over the more than 35 percent minimum.

Another way is to give away assets (other than stock) such as cash,
land, or other property. But to keep it from being too easy to qualify
under this favorable tax law provision, the Internal Revenue Code says
property you give away within three years of your death doesn't count in
meeting the more than 35 percent test. So the trick is to give it away—
now. Since you can give up to $10,000 per year per donee gift tax free
($20,000 if your spouse consents to split the gift), there are no federal
gift tax costs to reduce your estate to the required level.

Remember, it's not easy for your estate to qualify, and without
enough money to make a Section 303 redemption work, it doesn't matter if your corporation is qualified to purchase stock. There must be cash or

life insurance to enable the corporation to make a purchase of stock under Section 303, or it's worthless.

Survivor's Income Benefit Plan (SIBP)

The idea is to provide for your family's security with corporate funded tax deductible dollars to the extent the law allows. The Survivor's Income Benefit Plan (SIBP) is one way to accomplish that objective. (Your attorney may call the SIBP a salary continuation plan, and your insurance agent may call it a death benefit only [DBO] plan.)

A SIBP is an agreement between your business and you as an employee. Your corporation agrees that, if you die before retirement, it will pay a specified amount—or an amount determined by a specified formula—to your spouse (or other survivor). Your corporation could make that death benefit a multiple of your salary or a specified amount. It could pay your survivors a lump sum or specify that payments will be made in installments (the more typical case).

One thing that a SIBP does not do is provide you with retirement income.

When is a SIBP indicated?

Ed is a widower. Ed is in a very high estate tax bracket. He is looking for a way to provide substantial security for his two daughters if he should die before they are financially self-sufficient.

Bob is the president of a fast-growing corporation that is looking for a special employee benefit plan to lock in three key employees and attract two new sales managers from a competitor. He's already covered most of his 100 employees with a pension plan. Bob now wants to cover just these few special people.

Ron of the RonDell Corporation recently hired Sam, a young, hardworking supervisor. Ron would like a plan that would provide immediate financial security for Sam's family, but could easily be turned into a retirement plan if Sam remains with his firm.

A SIBP plan could meet all these objectives.

How the SIBP works

Let's say you are 40 years old; you are an executive of a corporation that would like to provide your family with financial security (and provide you with the knowledge that you are more financially secure).

The corporation makes a legally binding promise that, in return for your agreement to continue working for the firm, if (and only if) you should die while employed by the company, it will pay your surviving spouse a special amount or percentage of your salary (for instance, $50,000 a year for ten years). This equates to a total of $500,000 of security for your family.

What does it cost the firm?

We suggest that all or a substantial portion of the firm's potential liability under this plan be met with corporate-owned life insurance. It could work like this: Assume the firm insures you for $500,000. At your death, the insurer would pay that money—tax free—to your employer. The money is the corporation's. It could invest that money in any way it wants. Assume the money is put into tax-free municipal bonds earning 8 percent. The income is $40,000 a year—tax free.

Now assume that at the time the payout begins the corporation is in a combined federal and state tax bracket of 40 percent. Since payments to your widow are treated as a continuation of salary, they are deductible by the corporation. That means it costs—after taking a deduction—only $30,000 a year (40 percent of $50,000—$20,000—is deductible) to pay your widow $50,000 a year. So, $30,000 a year is going out of the corporation.

$40,000 comes in—$30,000 goes out—so $10,000 a year more stays in than goes out. In ten years, $100,000 more comes in than goes out. And don't forget, at the end of the ten years—after your widow has received $500,000—the company's obligation is over, but it still has a $500,000 tax-free municipal bond (or other investment).

Additional tax implications

Before you decide whether the SIBP is right for you, consider that no deduction is allowed to your corporation for premiums it pays. On the other hand, life insurance proceeds the corporation will receive (no matter how large the amount) are income tax free (aside from the no more than 10 percent portion which may be subject to the corporate alternative minimum tax). Then, when the corporation actually makes payments to your widow (or other employer-designated beneficiary), every dime it pays is deductible, if and to the extent that (a) the payments represent reasonable compensation for services you had rendered, and (b) the plan serves a valid business (as opposed to purely stockholder) purpose. For example, if the plan is designed to lock a key employee into the firm, it meets a business goal.

If the plan has been drafted carefully (don't even think about trying it without both your attorney and your accountant), and if you own 50 percent or less of the business, none of the death benefit will be in your estate. Even if the death benefit is includable in your estate for some reason, if your spouse is your beneficiary, the unlimited estate tax marital deduction shelters your estate from federal estate tax. Even failing that, the first $600,000 of assets includable in your estate is protected by the unified credit described in Chapter 11.

Second, since the insurance isn't technically tied into the plan (it's treated merely as a corporate asset that the employer may or may not use to satisfy its liability under the plan), you don't have any rights to it. That's good because it means that you're not subject to income tax each time your employer pays a premium. You pay no tax at all while you are alive and working.

How are beneficiaries taxed each time they receive a payment? Dollars your spouse receives are treated just like salary; only it's as if the salary were paid to your spouse. It's taxed as ordinary income, at her (or his) tax bracket.

Can you think of a better way to provide estate tax free financial security for your family through your business?

Medical Expense Reimbursement Plan (MERP)

A medical expense reimbursement plan is an agreement provided by an employer (including a professional corporation) to reimburse one or more employees for dental expenses, cosmetic surgery, and other medical expenses which are not covered under Blue Cross/Blue Shield or any other medical plan available to all employees.

A MERP will reimburse you for the medical expense you incur as an employee. It will also pay for medical expenses incurred by your spouse and dependents.

The nicest thing about a MERP is that it can be tax free to you as an employee, and tax deductible by the corporation. In other words, as long as the plan does not discriminate in favor of highly compensated employees, you pay no current income taxes regardless of how much your medical expenses are reimbursed. No matter how much the corporation pays, that amount (assuming it is reasonable) will be deductible against its ordinary income.

Could you use a MERP? Certainly, if you own or are a shareholder in a closely held corporation and all or most of the corporation's employees are members of your family, a MERP makes sense.

If your business does *not* have a MERP, the bulk of your family's medical expenses are paid either by insurance or out of your own pocket with expensive (after tax) dollars. After your corporation installs its MERP, those out-of-pocket expenses aren't paid out of your pocket any more—the money comes from the corporation. And the money it uses has never been taxed to you, and never will be. Best of all, the expenses will be deductible by your corporation. So a MERP makes otherwise nondeductible medical expenses completely deductible. This is particularly valuable since, under the 1986 Tax Reform Act, medical expenses are not deductible except to the extent they *exceed* 7.5 percent of your adjusted gross income. For instance, if your adjusted gross income is $40,000, you can only deduct those medical expenses which exceed $3000 (7.5 times $40,000).

Let's see how a MERP works and who should set up a MERP: Morty is the president and chief executive of the Fly High Kite Manufacturing

Company. Morty and his wife, Mary, are the only full-time employees of the corporation. Before establishing the MERP, expenses Morty or his wife incurred over and above their group health insurance limits had to be paid for with expensive after-tax dollars. To pay $10,000 in dental and cosmetic surgery costs, Morty (who is a 40 percent combined federal and state income tax bracket) had to earn nearly twice that amount.

Dr. Edward is an ophthalmologist who recently formed a professional corporation. He has two nurses who are receiving salaries of $15,000 each. Edward's salary is $150,000 a year. He covers both of his nurses as well as himself and his family. The MERP makes what might otherwise be nondeductible medical expenses incurred by his family deductible to Edward.

Charlie employs 16 people in his closely held corporation. All but three are not related to Charlie. Charlie believes that it is his responsibility to provide significant and tax-favored benefits to his employees. He also believes that providing such benefits will help attract and retain the type of employees he needs to run his highly specialized electronics corporation. He already has provided coverage for these employees under basic Blue Cross/Blue Shield and an insurance company sponsored major medical plan but would like to provide additional protection for them.

MERP requirements

What does a MERP cost? There are requirements that must be met to qualify for the favorable tax treatment afforded to a MERP. A MERP can be insured by an insurance company or can be self-insured by the employer. Self-insured means your corporation makes the promises and takes the risk. So if a covered event occurs, you pay (you can provide a ceiling on the amount of money the corporation will pay). In either case, the plan must be nondiscriminatory. It can't discriminate either in coverage or operation in favor of shareholders or highly compensated employees.

A MERP that discriminates will cause all or a portion of the reimbursements to be included in the income of key employees.

What expenses can a MERP cover?

The answer is—any medical expense that is deductible on your income tax return (including prescription eyeglasses and dental work) can be covered by a MERP plan. Why not sit down with your attorney and your accountant and see if a MERP makes sense for you and your corporation?

Deduction for Health Insurance Costs of Self-Employed Individuals

The Tax Reform Act of 1986 provided that—until 1990—self-employed individuals would be allowed a deduction equal to 25 percent of the annual cost of medical care insurance on the proprietor, spouse, or dependents.

But there are a few catches: First, the deduction can't exceed the proprietor's earned income. Second, if you provide health insurance for yourself, you must also provide it to your employees on a nondiscriminatory basis. Third, you can't take the deduction if you are also covered by a plan maintained by another business. In fact, if your spouse is employed by another employer and her employer's plan covers you, you are ineligible for this deduction.

Key Employee Insurance

Key personnel are the most important assets a business has. No business owner would conceive of not insuring their buildings, machinery, and equipment. Why then not insure the most essential asset of all: The one or two individuals whose presence makes or breaks profits.

How much key employee insurance should a business have?

The IRS, the courts, and business management consultants have long recognized that the loss of a manager, scientist, salesperson, or other key individual will almost always have a serious effect on the earning power and sometimes on the very stability of a business. Although the principle applies in publicly held businesses, it is particularly true in a closely held corporation where profits are dependent on the ability, initiative, judgment, or business connections of a single person or small group of owner-employees.

There is no universally recognized and accepted formula for computing the economic effect of the loss of a key person. One used in several court cases utilizes a discount approach: A percentage discount is taken from the going concern value of the business.

Some authorities feel that if the business will survive the death of the key employee, and in time a competent successor can be found, a discount factor of from 15 to 20 percent should be used. Where the business is likely to fail, or be placed in serious jeopardy upon the death (or disability) of the key employee, a discount of from 20 to 45 percent is more appropriate. The exact discount factor should be arrived at through consultation with the officers of the company and the firm's accounting and legal advisers.

Some questions that should be answered in the process of determining the factor (or range of factors) to be used include:

1. How long will it take for a new person to reach the efficiency of the key individual?
2. How much will it cost to locate and situate a replacement? Will the new employee demand more salary? How much will it cost to train the new person?

3. What mistakes is a replacement likely to make during the "break in" period, and how much are those mistakes likely to cost the company?
4. What proportion of the firm's current net profits are attributable to the key employee?
5. Is the employee engaged in any projects which, if left unfinished at death or disability, would prove costly to the business? How costly? Would a potentially profitable project have to be abandoned or would a productive department have to be closed?
6. Would the employee's death result in the loss of clientele or personnel attracted to the business because of his or her personality, social contacts, or unique skills, talents, or managerial ability?
7. What effect would the key employee's death have on the firm's credit standing?
8. What portion of the firm's actual loss is it willing to self-insure, if any?

Key Employee Valuation

Fair market value of business with key employee	$75,000
Discount percent without employee	0.20

Discount Percent	Value without Key Employee	Value of Key Employee
0.16	$630,000	$120,000
0.17	622,500	127,500
0.18	615,000	135,000
0.19	607,500	142,500
0.20	600,000	150,000
0.21	592,500	157,500
0.22	585,000	165,000
0.23	577,500	172,500
0.24	570,000	180,000

There are a number of ways—other than the discount approach—to value a key person's contribution to a corporation's profits. One way is to measure the number of working years remaining to the executive (say 10). Estimate the annual loss of earnings attributable to that person (say $30,000 per year). Then discount (using a present value calculator) the value of that annual loss (for example at 10 percent). This will result in the present value of the key person's services, about $113,000.

Alternatively, computation of goodwill could be adjusted to measure the goodwill produced through the efforts of the management team, and this total would then further be apportioned (perhaps by relative salaries) among the key employees.

For instance, assume a firm had an average annual asset value of $450,000 and an average annual earnings after taxes of $75,000. If 10 percent were thought to be a fair rate of return on tangibles, then $45,000 ($450,000 × .10) of the $75,000 would be attributable to tangibles. The remaining $30,000 would be attributable to goodwill. Assume 60 percent of this ($18,000) could reasonably be allocated to management. If it takes five years to replace the entire management team, then $18,000 should be multiplied by five, or a total of $90,000. If the executive in question drew 80 percent of the total salaries of the management team, then that person's worth would approximate $72,000 ($90,000 × .80).

The discount approach used in the chart shortcuts a number of the difficulties posed in these alternatives.

Business Overhead Insurance

If you are in business or in a professional practice, we strongly suggest that you talk to your insurance agent about business overhead insurance. Why? Because if you are disabled, this type of coverage will keep your office afloat.

A business overhead policy will cover expenses such as staff salaries, rent, telephone, utilities, professional dues, malpractice insurance, or any other expenses necessary to keep your office open. (It will *not* cover new purchases, principal payments on practice loans, or salaries to other professionals who fill in for you while you are disabled.)

Business overhead insurance costs only about one-third as much as personal disability coverage. But it's less expensive because the coverage is restrictive, and the payout is limited to, in most cases, no more than two years.

The latest versions of business overhead policies should have these features:

1. The policy should be noncancellable and guaranteed renewable. This means the company cannot cancel your policy, and premiums will remain the same as long as you keep the policy.
2. The policy should cover most of your fixed expenses (none will cover your own compensation).
3. The premium should be discounted if you carry both your office overhead policy and your disability coverage with the same company. Discounts of up to 15 percent are common.
4. Most policies have an initial waiting period of 31 days. After you've been disabled beyond that initial waiting period, benefits should be retroactive to the first day.
5. Many policies provide a *total liability* clause. This extends benefits beyond the stated period if they are not used up. For instance, if your policy provides for $4000 a month for 12 months, and you only used $3000 a month, the remaining $12,000 of benefits would be available for the next 12 months.
6. Some policies will pay partial benefits on partial disability.

16

Incorporating: Reducing Taxes by Increasing Taxpayers

Tax rates (income, gift, and estate) are *progressive*. That means the more you earn, the more you give away, or the more you own when you die, the more tax you pay. But progressive doesn't mean only more tax; it means the *rate* of tax increases faster and faster. The more successful you become, the more the IRS takes.

Let's turn this concept around: Spreading income or wealth among family members will save taxes.

If you have any doubt about that statement, make this simple test. Check income tax rates and you will see that married taxpayers with two exemptions filing joint returns will pay a tax of $3000 on taxable income of $20,000. If the same couple earns $60,000 of taxable income, the tax is $12,932, a difference of much more than 3 × $3000. A single taxpayer earning a taxable income of $20,000 will pay a tax of $3279. A single taxpayer with a taxable income of $60,000 will pay a tax of $15,322. Therefore, a single taxpayer earning $60,000 pays more in taxes than three single taxpayers each earning $20,000.

Divide and Conquer

How to use the *divide-and-conquer* concept to increase spendable income for you and your family is what this chapter is all about.

When you form a corporation, you have created a separate taxable entity. As an employee of the corporation that you have created, you are now entitled to the same type of fringe benefits as an employee of General Motors—with the same tax advantages. At the same time that you can avail yourself of the tax savings consequence of incorporating, you are also in a position to realize the other advantages of incorporating, such as the ease of transferring your ownership interest by giving away or selling shares of stock.

If you want some of the advantages of incorporating, but you want to avoid the tax at the corporate levels and have corporate income taxed directly to you, at your low personal bracket, then an *S corporation* might be excellent tax planning. And last, if you are extremely successful financially, consider setting up a *personal holding company.*

Not all of these ideas apply to everyone, but, if any one is suited to your situation, the tax savings that result can be tens or even hundreds of thousands of dollars annually.

Tax Advantages of Incorporation

A corporation is a super tax shelter. If you are looking for an effective way to accumulate, conserve, and distribute assets, here's what you attain by incorporation:

1. As an employee of your own corporation, you will be entitled to a number of fringe benefits, most of which are tax deductible by the corporation and not taxable to you. These include: (a) pension/profit sharing plans, (b) group life insurance, (c) group health insurance, (d) disability income coverage, and (e) medical reimbursement plans.

2. Your liability is, to some extent, limited. A creditor of the corporation can't proceed against the corporation's shareholders (unless you personally sign as guarantor, or agree to be personally responsible).

3. Before you incorporate you have had no ability to "time" or divide income; it is all taxed to you just as soon as you earn it. It will be taxed to you personally at your top income tax bracket.

But after incorporation, you personally will pay tax only if and as you receive salary, which can be timed within limits to avoid bunching too much income into any single tax year. Furthermore, the salary paid to you is deductible by your corporation. A great deal of the remaining corporate income can be siphoned off into tax deductible (by the corporation) and tax free (to you) fringe benefits.

The lowest corporate rates are very low (only 15 percent on the first $50,000 of corporate taxable income). It's likely that taxable income of most closely held corporations will be subject to 15 or 25 percent levels.

4. Incorporating gives you a relatively simple and inexpensive way to transfer the ownership of your business. All you have to do to make gifts

1988
Simplified Schematic of Corporate Taxation

Gross Income

minus

Ordinary deductions from gross income

minus

Special deductions allowed only to corporations such as the 80 percent dividends received deduction

equals

Taxable Income

Corporate
1987 Tax Table

Taxable Income ($)	Base Amount ($)	Base Tax Owed ($)	Percent on Excess
0	25,000	0	15.0
25,000	50,000	3,750	16.5
50,000	75,000	7,875	27.5
75,000	100,000	14,750	37.0
100,000	335,000	24,000	42.5
335,000	1,000,000	123,875	40.0
1,000,000	1,405,000	389,875	42.5
1,405,000 and above		562,000	40.0

Corporate Tax Calculation Worksheet

	Example:
Step 1: List taxable income _____	$200,000
Step 2: List base tax _____	24,000
Step 3: Compute "excess" over base amount _____	100,000
Step 4: List % on "excess" _____	.425
Step 5: Multiply step 3 × step 4 _____	42,500
Step 6: Total step 2 + step 5 _____	66,500

Corporate
1988 Tax Table

Taxable Income ($)	Base Amount ($)	Base Tax Owed ($)	Percent on Excess
0	25,000	0	15.0
50,000	75,000	7,500	25.0
75,000	100,000	13,750	34.0
100,000	335,000	22,250	39.0
335,000		113,900	34.0

Corporate Tax Calculation Worksheet

	Example:
Step 1: List taxable income _____	$200,000
Step 2: List base tax _____	22,250
Step 3: Compute "excess" over base amount _____	100,000
Step 4: List % on "excess" _____	.39
Step 5: Multiply step 3 × step 4 _____	39,000
Step 6: Total step 2 + step 5 _____	61,250

is to endorse shares of stock over to your donees and record the transactions in your company's books. You can make gifts to friends, nieces, nephews, and charities quickly and easily.

5. Through gifts of stock, you can give family members an interest in the family business without giving up control. (You "call the shots" as

long as you keep at least 51 percent of the company's stock.) You also shift the growth of the business to your children and, by dividing shares among several family members, you can shift a portion of your estate to your children's lower estate tax brackets.

6. You maintain privacy. The transfer of stock in a closely held corporation is not public information. You can, therefore, keep your business and your family's financial affairs from public scrutiny.

7. Legally, your business can continue without you. This *continuity of operation* is one of the major advantages of incorporation. Within limits, the corporation may continue its business when you die with little or no hindrance from the probate court. The corporation's other officers could continue to make business decisions without the necessity or delay of the judicial process. (As a practical matter, absent careful and thorough planning, most small corporations—and even some large ones—die with the death of their principal shareholder.)

The 80 percent dividends received exclusion

To some extent, a corporation is like a magician's magic money box. Dollars that would be taxable to anyone else are tax free or almost tax free to the corporation.

For instance, say you receive a $1000 dividend on stock you owned, and you are in a 33 percent income tax bracket. You'd pay $330 in tax and have $670 left to invest or use for your personal needs.

Now assume you formed a corporation and transferred the stock to it. Suppose your corporation owned the same stock and received the same $1000 dividend. A corporation is entitled to a special deduction known as a *dividends received* deduction. This deduction reduces the corporation's gross income by 80 percent of the dividends it receives from certain other corporations. In other words, your corporation pays tax on only 20 percent (100 percent – 80 percent) of the dividend it receives. In our example, that's $200 ($1000 × .20). Since the maximum corporate tax rate is 39 percent, the most tax the corporation could possibly pay (it doesn't reach the 39 percent level until it has over $100,000 of taxable income) on the $200 exposed to tax is $78—39 percent of the $200. That means the corporation would have $922 ($1000 – $78), (instead of $670) to invest or use for its needs (including payment of tax-deductible fringe benefits).

The bottom line is that the maximum rate on dividends received by a corporation which has invested capital in other corporations is 7.8 percent ($78 out of $1000 received) as compared with a top tax of 39 percent top rate on other types of income.

This seems too good to be true, but it is—true, that is. There is a limit to how much money, securities, or other investments a corporation can shelter at its lower tax brackets. But current law allows accumulations of up to $250,000 for most business corporations ($150,000 for most professional corporations) even if you form or use the corporation to avoid personal income tax by allowing earnings and profits to accumulate at favorable corporate rates.

Sophisticated shuffles

Once you incorporate, you can shuffle the corporate structure at various times to help you accomplish your people and tax planning objectives. In other words, your attorney, accountant, and other financial advisors might suggest that you *recapitalize* the corporation (exchange one type of stock for another type of stock, exchange one type of security for another type, or change voting or dividend provisions).

Why would you want to do this? Because, through a recapitalization of an existing corporation you could:

1. Give younger, more active employees/shareholders a larger share of the business, encouraging them to work harder and stay with the business.
2. Shift control from you to a family member.
3. Provide more active shareholders with greater voting rights.
4. Transfer control to a family member working in the business and, at the same time, provide income for your retirement.
5. Provide a key employee with a voice in management.
6. Help freeze the value of your stock for federal and state death tax purposes, and shift the growth in the value of the stock to the family member of your choice.
7. Make it easier for a co-shareholder to buy you out.
8. Prevent nonworking, minority shareholders from voting on important business matters.
9. Provide retirement income for you and, at the same time, shift the growth in your business to your children who are working in it.

Recapitalization

One way a recapitalization can work is like this: Larry and Dorothy own all the shares of common voting stock of the LD Corporation. Larry wants his son eventually to become the owner and key employee of the business. Larry wants to encourage his son to stay with the firm and have the benefit of what he expects to be rapid appreciation in the business's value.

Larry and Dorothy could exchange all their voting common stock (say its worth was $1,000,000) for a combination of voting stock (worth say $100,000) and preferred stock (assume this worth $900,000). The preferred stock will be worth about 90 percent of what the stock they exchanged was worth. That means that the common stock (which carries both the growth and voting rights) would be worth 10 percent of the value of the stock surrendered.

Larry and Dorothy could give (or sell) that common stock to their son, as they see fit, over a period of time. This means control could be shifted as slowly or as quickly as they felt appropriate. Because of its currently low value, Larry and Dorothy would pay little, if any, gift tax on the transfers of the common stock.

Larry and Dorothy would keep the preferred stock. They could receive dividends on the preferred stock to help provide retirement security.

The "recap" has provided retirement income for Larry and Dorothy and, at the same time, provided them with a way to shift the future control and growth of the corporation from themselves to their son.

A preferred stock dividend, in which each shareholder who owns common stock receives tax-free preferred stock, can be used to accomplish the same objective.

S Corporations

Within days of the passage of the Tax Reform Act of 1986, many accountants and attorneys established S corporations for hundreds of their clients.

Why? You might ask Rodger, president of Rugged Steel Foundries. When he founded the steel company, Rodger knew he and his associates would be putting hundreds of thousands of dollars into a high-risk business that was subject to wide market swings and profit volatility. His accountants told Rodger that the company might show losses in the first few years of business. Rodger wanted the legal protection against creditors offered by corporate status but also wanted to be able to deduct what he expected would be several years' losses against his outside income. (He knew the business itself wouldn't have enough income to take advantage of the losses.)

By electing S corporation status, it became possible to pass through corporate losses to Rodger's personal tax return (to the extent of the capital investment and loans he had made). That way Rodger could use corporate losses to reduce his personal income tax liability.

When the business turns the corner and begins to make a profit, Rodger and the other shareholders may terminate the S election. That would make the corporation's profits taxable to the corporation—at its initially relatively low tax brackets. Future profits will all be taxed to the business.

As long as the S corporation election is in effect, Rodger and his fellow shareholders can enjoy many of the typical benefits and advantages of a corporation. At the same time—if each shareholder is in a low tax bracket—he might want corporate income taxed directly to him. This is very different from regular corporate taxation, where income earned by the business is taxed once to the corporation and then is taxed a second time when paid out as a dividend. An S corporation election, therefore, provides a way to beat the double tax. Let's look at a simplified example of the tax savings potential.

There are five equal shareholders of the ABC Corporation which is currently earning profits of $50,000. The federal corporate tax, in 1988, is $7500, 15 percent of the first $50,000 of earnings. This means the amount which could be distributed to the S corporation's shareholders is $42,500 ($50,000 – $7500). Each stockholder's share is $8500 ($42,500 ÷ 5). Of course, this amount is further reduced by personal taxes. Assuming each owner has outside income and is in approximately a 33 percent tax bracket, individual taxes will be about $2805. The aggregate income tax on all five individuals' income will be $14,025. In total, the taxes paid are $21,525 ($7500 of corporate tax plus $14,025 of personal taxes).

Assume the corporation has elected S status. The election, of course, does not change corporate profits, which are $50,000. However, the $50,000 is now passed directly through to the shareholders (the character of the income also is passed through), and there is no corporate tax to pay. The net profits subject to distribution are $50,000. Dividing that figure by five, each shareholder's share is $10,000. Personal taxes are, therefore, increased to $3300 each. The aggregate tax payable is $16,500.

Taxes before S Election	*Taxes after S Election*
$21,525	$16,500

The S election saves $5025 annually.

The following chart compares the 1988 income tax payable by a corporation operating under regular corporate rates (a C corporation) to one operating as an S corporation. This chart assumes business earnings pass through the corporation and are taxed directly to a sole shareholder who is filing a joint return with two personal exemptions:

Taxable Income	*Tax as a* C Corporation	*Tax as an* S Corporation
$25,000	$3,750	$3,750
50,000	7,500	10,132
100,000	22,250	25,538
1,000,000	340,000	281,092
2,000,000	680,000	561,092

Why else might Rodger's advisors recommend S corporation treatment? Perhaps the biggest reason many S corporations are formed is that they have the potential for shifting income (and therefore spreading taxes) within a family unit. That's because the income earned by an S corporation is taxed by percentage ownership to the parties who own stock (even if they don't actually work in the business). So (assuming Rodger was taking a reasonable salary) if each of his three children (each over age 14) owned 30 percent of the stock (a total of 90 percent) and Rodger owned 10 percent, he'd be taxed on only 10 percent of the corporation's net income, while the children would each report 30 percent. If the corporation earned $100,000, $10,000 would be taxed—in addition to Rodger's salary—to him. But the remaining $90,000 would be taxed to his three children in their lower tax brackets.

By gifting (or selling) S corporation stock to family members, it is possible to shift the corporation's income to a larger number of relatively low-tax bracket individuals. The result is income tax savings that go on year after year.

An S Corporation as a wealth shifting device

Looking at the S corporation from a nontax standpoint, it's a regular garden-variety corporation. It looks (and is) different only because it has elected to be taxed differently from other corporations. That difference makes all the difference.

An S corporation computes its taxable income in much the same way as a C corporation. It receives a deduction for salaries it pays to employees (including shareholder-employees).

One big difference between an S and a C corporation is that, once taxable income is computed, it is not subject to the regular tax imposed on the taxable income of a corporation. (See pages 201 and 205.) Instead, taxable income is charged directly to the corporation's shareholders as it is earned (even taxable income that is not actually paid out is taxed on a pro-rata basis to parties who own stock).

That leads to one of the biggest planning techniques of all—the S corporation gift. If you own 100 percent of the S corporation stock but give it away—say 10 percent of it—to your child or another relative, that person must report 10 percent of the corporation's income. This makes substantial intra-family income tax shifts possible. You can shift income to any family member you choose. (See Chapter 19 for the rules on shifting income to children.) Of course, your gift of stock is an irrevocable gift, and if it is large enough, there may be gift taxes to pay. But probably, any tax you pay will be far outweighed by the year-after-year income tax savings.

Furthermore, since both the value of the stock you've given away and the after-tax income is in your child's estate rather than yours, significant estate tax savings can be realized.

Drawbacks and limitations

If owners of an S corporation do not materially participate in the business, any losses experienced by the business can only be used by them to offset income from other *passive* investments. Active owners of S corporations will receive *active* income or losses which can't be used to offset passive income or losses.

Another drawback of S corporation status pertains to employee benefits. If you own more than a very small percentage of the corporation's stock, no deduction is allowed to the corporation for the payment of typical employee benefit costs such as group insurance or medical expense reimbursements. But these problems can be alleviated by increasing your salary, thereby allowing you to cover these costs personally.

Personal Holding Company (PHC)

Gary has an estate worth $7 million. Five million dollars worth of Gary's estate consists of highly appreciated and readily marketable securities. He wants to reduce the federal estate taxes attributable to those assets. Gary currently reports income from dividends from the securities in the tax year he receives that income. He would like to achieve a more advantageous method of timing income. He would like to achieve all these things and, at the same time, retain substantial economic control and flexibility in making investment decisions. The solution to his planning goals may be the *personal holding company.*

Estate "freezing" advantages

Most accountants think of a personal holding company as something to avoid. That's because there is a tax, separate from and in addition to the existing corporate tax, on the undistributed income of the personal holding company. The tax is 70 percent. That means the total of the special personal holding company tax and the corporate tax can be as much as 100 percent (or more) of the corporation's income. So a personal holding company is a bad—not a good—thing? No. If it is used properly, a PHC can be a very good thing.

Let's go back to the case of Gary, the wealthy investor just described. Gary purchased shares of Computer-a-go Company many years ago. These Computer-a-go Company shares are now publicly traded and worth one hundred times what he paid for them. They are also continuing to grow rapidly. If Gary retains the stock, the shares will be includable in his estate. If he gives them away, he will incur a sizable gift tax. Furthermore, the gifts will be considered *adjusted taxable gifts.* That means they will increase the rate at which his taxable estate will be taxed. Another reason Gary doesn't want to make gifts of his stock is that some of his beneficiaries are minor children and he doesn't want to make outright gifts. But he does not want to use a trust because of certain administrative problems associated with a trust.

Gary could form a corporation. He could retain 100 percent of its stock. He could then transfer a million dollars' worth of the publicly listed Computer-a-go Company stock to the newly formed personal holding corporation.

The new PHC would have a two-part capital structure. Part one would consist of $900,000 worth of voting dividend-paying preferred stock. Part two would consist of the new capital structure, $100,000 worth of voting common stock. (This breakdown is arbitrary and can be varied as to the appropriate mix.)

Since one of Gary's main planning objectives is to limit future appreciation in the value of his estate, he would retain the voting dividend-paying preferred stock. But simultaneously he would begin a gifting program with the voting common (which carries with it the appreciation in corporate value). He and his wife, Anne, could give $20,000 worth of voting common to each of his five children and grandchildren. Since Gary has retained $900,000 worth of voting preferred stock, he can direct and control the investment program.

The beauty of this arrangement is that, because the common stock has a relatively low current value, its gift tax cost is minimal. If the gifts are made outright or in trust in a manner that enables them to be presently enjoyed by the recipients, the annual gift tax exclusion would eliminate the gift tax entirely. And because the common stock carries with it most or all of the financial growth of the business, all future appreciation occurs in the hands of the donees rather than in the hands of its original owner.

There are other alternatives. Gary could sell rather than give the common stock to his children. They could pay him for the stock by issuing serially maturing notes. These notes would have a total face value equalling the fair market value of the stock Gary's children receive, $100,000. Gary could forgive all or a portion of each note as it matures. This would enable Gary to make gifts with minimal (or no) gift tax cost and delay the impact of the gift tax at his whim.

The two techniques described above are called estate *freezing* devices. This is because they enable Gary to give away the future appreciation in his marketable securities through the personal holding company mechanism. This siphoning device freezes assets at their present value for estate tax purposes with minimal gift tax implications.

How to use the PHC to obtain a gift or estate tax valuation discount

The courts have consistently allowed federal estate and gift tax discounts of 15 percent or more (in one case, as much as 55 percent) on the theory that stock of a personal holding company is less attractive to an investor than a similar stock invested on an exchange with ready access to the investing public.

For example, if Gary makes a gift of 100 shares of Xerox stock, that gift is worth more than a gift of a 10-percent interest in a personal holding company which has as its only asset 1000 shares of Xerox. Why? It would seem that the two are equal. But the truth is that an investment in a personal holding company is less desirable than an investment in the underlying Xerox shares. That's because the underlying assets (the Xerox shares in this example) can easily be traded in the stock market. Shares in the personal holding company cannot. This is why there is a discount from the net asset value of the underlying shares for federal estate and gift tax purposes. In the example, Gary's million-dollar portfolio may be valued at less than the one million dollars that the underlying assets are worth.

The result of a lower value is lower gift or estate taxation. Furthermore, if the stock Gary gave away is a minority interest, a further discount could be allowed because of the lack of voting control. A 10-percent interest would not be enough to allow the owner of the personal holding company's stock to control or even have a major influence on what the company did or did not do.

Additional advantages of a PHC

There are many advantages to a properly arranged personal holding company. One is what is known as the *80-percent dividends-received* deduction. Ordinary income can be substantially or totally avoided by this deduction which is allowed to a corporation that owns stock in another domestic corporation. In essence it allows 80 percent of any dividends it receives to be excluded from income taxation. Only the remaining 20 percent is subject to tax. For example, a corporation could receive a $10,000 dividend, exclude $8000 of it, and pay tax on only $2000. In the worst possible situation, the corporation would pay tax in the 39 percent bracket, which would result in a $780 tax. That would leave $9220 to invest. If the owner of the personal holding company had received that $10,000 dividend personally and he was in a 33-percent income tax bracket, there would only be $6700 left for him to invest. This is an annual advantage of $2520. Over a period of ten years at a net after-tax return of 6-percent, the savings amount to $35,209. In 20 years the future value of the annual savings would be $98,262!

To the extent the individual forming a personal holding company actually performs bona fide services for it, he/she is entitled to receive a salary. Assuming the salary paid is high but reasonable, an individual would be taxed at a 28-percent bracket, and the corporation will be able to deduct the entire payment. (Compensation above a reasonable level is subject to taxes at the corporate level and again subject to tax at the individual level. In other words, no deduction is allowed for that portion of salary paid which is deemed to be unreasonable.)

The taxable income of a personal holding company can be lowered even further by providing a working stockholder and working members of his/her family with various fringe benefits (the cost of which would be tax deductible by the corporation). In other words, Gary could work for the corporation and by performing reasonable services become entitled to be covered under the corporation's tax deductible qualified pension and/or profit-sharing plan.

In fact, all the advantages of incorporation are possible if the estate owner performs meaningful and active services for a corporation after placing his investment portfolio in it.

Potential problems with the PHC

Most accountants are fearful of personal holding company status because, if it is not properly handled, there is a potential for an onerous 50-percent personal holding company tax (in addition to the normal corporate tax). But this is only on the income that is not expensed or paid out by the corporation. In many cases, all or most of the corporation's income can legitimately be siphoned off through salaries and various fringe benefits.

There is also potential for double taxation, once when the corporation sells the securities it holds and again when the shareholder receives the proceeds or other property as a dividend or on the liquidation of the corporation. But this potential for double taxation can be minimized or eliminated altogether by carefully controlling the type of investments made and the type of expenses incurred.

One other problem is the imposition of state capital stock or franchise taxes on the value of the personal holding company stock or on the net income remaining in the corporation each year.

The problems inherent in a personal holding company can be solved—and should be solved—in advance. It is necessary to understand that the personal holding company concept is difficult for many accountants and attorneys to understand. Therefore, it should be attempted only with the advice of seasoned and knowledgeable estate-planning, tax-oriented practitioners, and used only after a careful study is made of the pros and cons.

17

Tax-Sheltered
Retirement Plans

A pension or profit-sharing plan can be the ultimate tax shelter if the situation is right.

HR-10 plans permit an unincorporated business to set aside money for its employees' retirement on a tax-favored basis. The new tax law permits everyone to have an individual retirement account. But the deductibility (and, therefore, the utility) of IRAs has been severely limited for middle class and more affluent individuals.

If you are self-employed, the SEPP, a *Simplified Employee Pension Plan,* might be the way you want to go. You are entitled to receive tax deductions when you pay money into most of these plans. The interest on your investment can accumulate income tax free and be paid to you at retirement on a favorable tax basis.

Some deductions (like medical expenses or automobile repairs when our cars are used for business) help at tax time, but the money spent is gone forever. Deductions for money to be used to provide a more secure future for your family and yourself are, therefore, so much more valuable.

Qualified Pension and Profit-Sharing Plans

Imagine that your corporation makes a large tax deductible contribution to a special fund that will provide security for your retirement.

Assume, no matter how much interest these funds earn or how much growth they experience, not one penny will be taxed until you begin receiving benefits. Even if the fund sells an asset and realizes a large gain, you pay no current tax.

Picture taking the money at retirement under special tax rules that allow you favorable five-year income averaging if you take a lump-sum or special annuity reporting that enables you to spread your tax over your entire retirement lifetime.

If you are an employee of a corporation—even if you are a stockholder/employee—you are eligible for all of these tax benefits through a "qualified" pension or profit-sharing plan.

Requirements to make a plan "qualify"

For you to obtain the benefits of a pension or profit-sharing plan, the plan must be *qualified*. That is, it must meet a number of requirements to qualify the favorable tax treatment just discussed. These requirements include:

1. The exclusive benefit rule: The plan must be for the exclusive benefit of employees. Shareholders who are not employees cannot participate.
2. The primary purpose of a pension plan must be to offer employees a retirement benefit. A profit-sharing plan must provide employees with a share in the company's profits.
3. The plan cannot overly favor officers, stockholders, or highly compensated employees. That doesn't mean these people can't participate. It means that certain guidelines must be followed in order to obtain the substantial benefits described above.
4. The plan has to be in writing, and employees must be given information about how the plan works, the benefits it provides, and how and when they'll enjoy those benefits.
5. The plan must be permanent. This means the plan must contain no set ending date.

What's available

You shouldn't attempt to set up a pension or profit-sharing plan yourself; it should be a joint project attempted only after you've had your accountant, attorney, and employee benefit planner study its feasibility, and report on the direct tax implications and the indirect effects it has on other employee benefit plans. An employee benefits consultant can provide you with a number of plan designs with varying cost-benefit ratios from which to choose.

To make the right decision, you should know something about the various types of plans available.

Essentially, there are two types of pension plans: The *defined benefit* and the *money purchase* plan.

Defined benefit plans

A defined benefit plan is one in which you start with a promise that a specified benefit (for example, $3000 a month for life) will be paid when you reach normal retirement age. A predetermined formula is used to define the benefit each participant will receive. Your corporation then makes an annual contribution large enough so that at retirement the plan can provide that benefit. In other words, the corporation's contribution is based on the actuarial determination of the cost of benefits promised. This type of plan generally favors an older employee with relatively few years until retirement.

Defined contribution plans

A defined contribution plan (some people call this a money purchase plan) is the second type of pension plan. This arrangement bases the retirement benefit upon an employer's commitment to make an annual contribution. Benefits are dependent on how long you participate in the plan and how much money has been contributed on your behalf each year. Your benefit also grows in relation to the earnings and appreciation of the money contributed. This type of plan generally favors a younger employee with a number of years until retirement.

Target benefit plans

There are specifically designed hybrids of these two called *target benefit* plans. A target plan starts with a defined benefit plan. You figure out what you'd like to end up with. Then you figure out how much is needed to get there. But instead of giving you just the promised amount, the target plan then turns into a money purchase plan. That way you contribute what the corporation should have contributed in each year under a defined benefit plan, but you end up with what you would end up with if the plan was a money purchase plan. In other words, if the plan's interest assumptions are exactly met, it's like a defined benefit plan. But if earnings and other assumptions were conservative and the plan does better than expected, all plan participants share in the gains. (Of course, if the plan does less favorably than anticipated, plan participants receive less at retirement.)

Profit-sharing plans

In a profit-sharing plan, your corporation shares a portion of its profits. It's a type of defined contribution plan. A profit-sharing plan doesn't have to have a set formula for determining how much profit will be shared— your directors can decide that on a year-to-year basis. But once that decision is made, there must be a definite formula for dividing these profits among the participants. Furthermore, if there is no definite formula for deciding what contribution will be made each year, the corporation must make recurring and substantial contributions. That means that you can't make contributions in one year and then arbitrarily, without regard for profits, skip contributions until your corporation feels like making more.

Your firm doesn't necessarily have to choose between these types of plans; it can set up more than one. Many firms superimpose a profit-sharing plan on top of a modest pension plan so participants will have both growth possibilities and guaranteed income at retirement.

Tax implications

Dr. Jonathan Frank owns 100 percent of the stock in the J. F. Professional Corporation. His corporation has established a pension plan for its employees, Jon, and his two nurses.

Contributions made by the pension toward each of the three employees' retirements will be fully deductible from the corporation's income.

As the money is invested within the plan for the covered employees, it grows income tax free. This, of course, boosts the preretirement yield considerably.

Neither Jonathan nor either of the two nurses have to include the corporation's contribution on his or her behalf in their income, even if their rights to benefits in the plan can't be forfeited. (Tax practitioners refer to complete nonforfeitability as a "fully vested benefit.") Jonathan pays no tax until he actually receives a benefit payment.

If the plan includes life insurance protection, Jonathan will be treated as if he had received a taxable distribution each year (tax people call this a *current economic benefit*). That "distribution" is essentially the employer's contributions or trust earnings that have been applied during the year to provide "pure insurance" (term insurance) on the employee's life. Jonathan would enter this cost together with other income on his tax return just as if he had received a bonus of that amount. Tax practitioners refer to this reportable income as the "P.S. 58" cost (because the rates from which this reportable income is calculated are found in Pension Service Table Number 58).

Jon may choose to take his pension money at retirement in a lump sum or as an annuity. If he takes the money in a "lump sum" (essentially, this means taking whatever he's entitled to at retirement—and taking that money within one taxable year), the distribution will be entitled to favorable five-year income averaging. (Essentially the same as if you had earned a portion of the income in each year of a five year period rather than all at once. For instance, if you received taxable income of $300,000 all in 1988, you would pay $84,000 (.28 × $300,000), but if you qualify for five year averaging, the tax is only $72,398, an average effective rate of about 24 percent).

Five-Year Averaging

Net Lump-Sum Taxable Amount ($)	Tax 1987 ($)	Effective Tax Rate 1987	Tax 1988 ($)	Effective Tax Rate 1988
20,000	1,140	.06	1,500	.08
50,000	6,540	.13	6,900	.14
75,000	10,890	.15	11,250	.15
100,000	16,720	.17	16,398	.16
150,000	31,770	.21	30,398	.20
200,000	49,270	.25	44,398	.22
250,000	66,770	.27	58,398	.23

Note: If you were age 50 before January 1, 1986, and you receive a distribution in 1987 or a later year, you may elect to use 10-year averaging using the tax rates in effect in 1986 instead of 5-year averaging with current rates. Income averaging for lump-sum distributions is discussed in more detail later in this chapter.

What if Jon chooses to receive payments as an annuity, that is, in the form of an income for life that he can never outlive? In that case, Jon would be taxed under the "annuity" rules. These rules tax payments as ordinary income when received. A portion of each payment will be income tax free, and a portion will be taxable. For instance, if Jon contributed $20,000 in the example above, and would receive retirement payments at the rate of $4000 a year, a portion of every $4000 payment he receives is tax free while the remainder is taxable.

The formula for computing the tax free portion of each payment is:

$$\frac{\textit{Your investment in the plan (if any)}}{\substack{\text{Total return you can expect (actuarially)} \\ \text{over your lifetime}}} \times \text{Annual payment you receive}$$

For example, assume a 65-year-old receiving $125 a month from a life annuity. Assume he had paid $16,000 for the annuity. His life expectancy is 20 years. Fifty-three percent of each payment he receives is excludable:

$$\frac{\$16,000}{30,000} \times \$125 = \$67 \text{ (excludable)}$$

This leaves $58 a month ($700 a year) taxable.

Impact of death taxes

At Jon's death, there are (at least) three taxes to consider: (1) the federal estate tax, (2) the federal income tax, and (3) the 15 percent tax on *excess accumulations*.

Even though the death benefit from a qualified pension profit-sharing plan or an IRA is in your estate, it wouldn't generate any federal estate tax—no matter how large it is—if it is payable to a surviving spouse either outright or in a manner tantamount to outright. This is because of the federal estate tax unlimited marital deduction.

Even if the marital deduction is unavailable, if your estate—including the estate tax includable portion of the pension distribution—is under the "exemption equivalent" ($600,000 in 1987 and later years), your beneficiary should elect special five year income tax averaging. That's because the federal law allows each of us to pass an amount of property equal to the "exemption equivalent" to any beneficiary we choose and pay no federal estate taxes. That way there's probably no federal estate.

There are income taxes to be paid by a beneficiary receiving death benefits from a qualified pension or profit-sharing plan.

The entire amount attributable to employer contributions is subject to income tax (that's because you never paid tax on that amount). That tax will be paid by the beneficiary who receives the payments.

If the plan's death benefit was financed through life insurance, the "net amount at risk" (this is the "pure insurance" amount, the amount in excess of the life insurance policy cash values just before the insured's death) is entirely income tax free. Only the balance is (with certain exceptions) subject to income tax.

Second, the corporation pays the premium with what in essence are tax deductible dollars.

Third, if you are in poor health, any *rating* (extra premium due to your below normal health) would be paid with corporate dollars. But you report P.S. 58 costs as if you were in normal health. In other words, you do not have to report extra P.S. 58 income even if your corporation pays a substantially higher than normal premium on your behalf because of the health (or other) rating.

Lump Sum Distributions

Before you take a distribution from a qualified pension or profit-sharing plan, be sure to check with your CPA, CLU, ChFC, or CFP. You may be able to defer the income tax or reduce it considerably.

If you were age 50 or older on January 1, 1986 (that is, if you were born prior to 1936), you have two options not available to others:

1. Ten-year forward income averaging.
2. Capital gains treatment on pre-1974 contribution earnings.

Persons born before 1936 have a choice; they can elect ten-year averaging at 1986 tax rates or elect five-year averaging at the new tax rates.

Only five-year income averaging is allowed for persons born in 1936 or later. Here's how the tax works at various amounts:

1986 Ten-Year Averaging Rates

Amount of Lump-Sum Distribution ($)	Tax ($)	Effective Rate
50,000	5,874	.12
100,000	14,471	.14
150,000	24,570	.16
200,000	36,922	.18
500,000	143,682	.29
1,000,000	382,210	.38
5,000,000	2,382,210	.48

1987 Five-Year Averaging Rates

Amount of Lump-Sum Distribution ($)	Tax ($)	Effective Rate
50,000	6,540	.13
100,000	16,720	.17
150,000	31,770	.21
200,000	49,270	.25
500,000	162,320	.32
1,000,000	354,820	.35
5,000,000	1,894,820	.38

1988 Five-Year Averaging Rates

Amount of Lump-Sum Distribution ($)	Tax ($)	Effective Rate
50,000	6,900	.14
100,000	16,398	.16
150,000	30,398	.20
200,000	44,398	.22
500,000	128,398	.26
1,000,000	268,398	.27
5,000,000	1,388,398	.28

The Right Way to Borrow

Your company's pension plan can provide for loans of limited amounts to participants. The loan must be made in accordance to specific plan provisions allowing loans. A reasonable charge must be made for the use of plan assets, and the borrower must give adequate security for the money borrowed. Loans must be available to all participants on a reasonably equivalent basis. With the exception of loans to purchase a principal residence, all loans must be repaid within five years. The loan must be repaid in level amounts over the repayment period.

Interest payments on loans to key employees are not deductible.

HR-10 (Keogh) Plans

If you are self-employed, you may be able to set aside up to $30,000 a year, take a tax deduction from your highest marginal tax bracket, have the money accumulate income tax free, and take it at retirement under favorable conditions.

Just remember the letters and numbers HR-10. HR-10, Keogh Plan, Self-Employed Retirement Plan are all the same.

You cannot rely on social security alone to provide retirement income. If you are a self-employed individual, a sole proprietor, or partner who owns 10 percent or more of a partnership, you are allowed to take a tax deduction for money you put aside for your own retirement (as well as a tax deduction for dollars you put aside for the retirement of your employees—including a spouse or child who works for your business).

Contributions to an HR-10 plan make sense because it defers paying money that would currently go in taxes to the federal government—and you can put these dollars to work—tax free for your own retirement. That means you can couple the power of compounding interest with the advantage of tax-free growth. The chart on the next page shows you just how impressive this can be.

Coverage requirements

If you are an owner/employee (a sole proprietor who owns 100 percent of the business or profession, or a partner who owns more than 10 percent

THE AMOUNT AN ANNUAL CONTRIBUTION WILL BE WORTH ASSUMING A 10-PERCENT RATE OF INTEREST

	$ 1,000	$ 2,000	$ 10,000	$ 15,000	$ 30,000
10 years	$ 15,937	$ 31,874	$ 159,374	$ 239,061	$ 478,122
15 years	31,772	63,545	317,724	476,587	953,174
20 years	57,275	114,550	572,749	859,124	1,718,249
25 years	98,347	196,694	983,470	1,475,205	2,950,411
30 years	164,494	328,988	1,644,940	2,467,410	4,934,820
35 years	271,024	542,048	2,710,243	4,065,365	8,130,731
40 years	442,592	885,185	4,425,925	6,638,888	13,277,776

of either the capital interest or profit interest of the partnership) and your business employs other people full-time, they must be included in the plan, too.

Selecting the right type of plan

The maximum annual deductible contribution to a *defined contribution* HR-10 plan (one in which the amount you get at retirement depends on how much you've put in and how fast and long it grows) is the same as a corporate pension plan, up to the lower of (a) 25 percent of your net earnings from self employment, or (b) $30,000 a year. (Technically, this first part is 20 percent of your net before deducting any contribution or 25 percent of your net after deducting the 25 percent contribution.) So Sam, a self-employed salesman with a net income of $60,000 a year, could contribute and deduct $12,000 a year (option a). His retirement fund at age 65 would depend on the amount to which his contribution grew, together with the interest.

A second type of HR-10 plan is the *defined benefit* plan. This type of HR-10 plan starts with a given level of retirement benefits and works backwards. In other words, Sam's contributions would be based on actuarial calculations designed to accumulate enough of a reserve to pay the benefits promised by the plan.

The maximum annual retirement benefit that can be funded for a qualified pension or HR-10 plan designed with a defined benefit formula is $90,000. But note, $90,000 is based on an age 67 retirement for persons born after 1938. This $90,000 limit may be significantly reduced if you retire before age 67 or if you have not participated in the plan at least 10 years. Although official figures have not been released as of this printing, an estimate is:

Retirement Age	Maximum
55	$38,700
60	60,200
62	72,000
65	90,000

It may pay to have your tax advisor investigate a defined benefit plan since your deductible contribution can, in some cases, be significantly higher than the allowable limits under a defined contribution plan.

Generally, a defined contribution plan will favor younger individuals while older "late starters" will obtain greater financial security through a defined benefit plan. (It makes sense to consider both types and have a comparison made.)

Once contributions have been made, funds can be invested in life insurance contracts, mutual funds, savings accounts, variable annuities, government bonds, or a combination of these funding vehicles.

If you die prior to retirement, the amount in the plan can be paid (in most cases probate free) to the person(s) you have specified. Since you never paid tax on either the contributions or the income that money earned, your beneficiary must report the amounts he/she receives as ordinary income. If the plan was partially financed through a life insurance policy, at least a portion of the death benefit will be income tax free (amounts in excess of the cash value of the policy at the date of your death).

Regardless of how much is payable when you die or how it is taken, none of the money in your HR-10 will cause a federal estate tax problem if it is paid to your spouse. That's because of the unlimited federal estate tax marital deduction.

In most smaller estates, a beneficiary who is someone other than the spouse should elect special (favorable) five-year income averaging, since there wouldn't be much estate tax to pay in the self-employed person's estate. For example, Steve died in 1988. His estate was worth about $450,000. He also had $100,000 benefits under an HR-10 plan payable to his 28-year-old son, David. Because of the estate tax credit allowed to every taxpayer, equivalent to a $600,000 exemption in 1987 and later years, there would be no federal estate tax in Steve's estate, regardless of who Steve had named as his beneficiary.

If Steve lives until retirement, he reports the amounts he receives as ordinary income.

Tax penalties

Congress wanted to discourage individuals from "raiding" their HR-10 plans prior to retirement years. It also wanted to encourage owner/employees to continue making payments to the plan. So the tax laws provide that an HR-10 plan that includes an owner/employee must require that no payments can be made to the owner/employee before he or she reaches age $59^1/2$ (except where death or permanent disability occurs).

A 10 percent tax penalty is imposed if a withdrawal is made by an owner/employee before age $59^1/2$. If no withdrawals are started before age $70^1/2$, a 50 percent tax is imposed on the amount which by law should have been withdrawn but hasn't.

Once, the prestigious legal counselors' tax advisor, U.S. Tax Week, wrote that an IRA is "the most basic tax shelter existing today." It wrote on to say, "it may also be the safest and the wisest." Sadly, this is no longer true.

Why? An IRA still allows you to defer your otherwise reportable earned income, invest it (income tax free), and enjoy the rewards later.

It's still true that, at a 10 percent compound interest rate, money put in this year will double itself in about seven years. At 12 percent, it will double over six years. If you were 25 years old and put $2000 a year into an IRA each year until you were 65, you'd retire with $1,700,000.

But since TRA-1986, few individuals can take full advantage of "the people's pension." You can still use an IRA even if you already participate in your employer's pension or profit-sharing plan, or if you are a sole proprietor or partner and have your own pension plan. But if you are an active participant in almost any type of employer-provided retirement plan (whether or not your benefits are vested), your deduction will likely be cutdown severely or eliminated entirely. If you are single, you begin to lose your IRA deduction when your adjusted gross income (AGI) reaches $25,001 and lose it completely when your AGI reaches $35,000. If you are married and filing jointly, the loss of the deduction starts at $40,001, and no deduction is allowed when your AGI reaches $50,001.

Active plan participants can make deductible IRA contributions only if their income falls within certain income limits, as shown below:

IRA Deduction/Compensation Limits
(Taxpayer or Spouse Active Plan Participant)

	Full IRA Deduction	Reduced IRA Deduction	No IRA Deduction
Individual	up to $25,000	$25,001–$35,000	$35,001 or over
Married couple, joint return	up to $40,000	$40,001–$50,000	$50,001 or over
Married, filing separately	not available	0–$10,000	$10,001 or over

The reduction in the IRA deduction for those affected is computed by multiplying the IRA limit ($2000) or 100 percent of compensation by a fraction equal to

$$\frac{\text{Taxpayer's adjusted gross income over full deduction limit}}{\$10,000}$$

There is a $200 floor under this equation; if the result comes out to less than $200, the taxpayer can contribute and deduct $200. Let's look at some examples:

A married couple, one of whom is an active participant in a regular qualified plan, files a joint return and has an adjusted gross income of $43,000.

$$\frac{\$3000}{\$10,000} \times \$2000 = \$600$$

$2000 - $600 = $1400 IRA deduction limit

A single person, an active participant in a qualified plan, has an adjusted gross income of $34,500

$$\frac{\$9500}{\$10,000} \times \$2000 = \$1900$$

$2000 - $1900 = $100

However, the individual may contribute $200, the floor amount.

The spousal IRA deduction limit of $2250 is proportionately reduced in the same manner.

You are considered an active participant if either you or your spouse (assuming you file a joint return) participate in a regular qualified plan, a tax deferred annuity plan, a simplified employee pension (SEP), or other federal, state, or local government plan.

Should you make a nondeductible contribution? We think not. Aside from a tax deferred buildup, there are no advantages and many disadvantages. These include stiff tax penalties for excess contributions, early withdrawals, and insufficient withdrawals at 70$^{1}/_{2}$. We suggest you consider IRA alternatives such as annuities, tax-free municipal bonds, single premium whole life policies, universal or variable life plans.

If you do not actively participate in an employer-sponsored retirement plan, current law allows you to deduct the lower of (a) $2000 a year, or (b) 100 percent of your compensation. That means that, if you earned only $2000, you could contribute and deduct the entire amount. This rule makes it possible to shelter all or a large part of your family's second income if neither you nor your spouse are active participants in an employer-sponsored retirement plan.

Naturally, if you have a working spouse, another $2000 can be contributed and deducted if that spouse's income is high enough. That boosts your family's limit to $4000 a year. It wouldn't take long at that rate to build a sizable nest egg as the chart on the next page illustrates.

If you both work and you earned, say $20,000, and your spouse earned only $1000, you could deduct a total of $3000.

If you are working, but your spouse is not, you are entitled to a spousal IRA or SPIRA. That means you can set aside and deduct up to $2250 (instead of just $2000) even if your spouse has no employment income.

Unless you die or become disabled, you can't take your money out before you are 59$^{1}/_{2}$ without (a) paying the normal income tax rates on the money you've taken, and (b) paying a 10-percent penalty tax. For example, if you take $5000 out of your IRA at age 50 (a so-called "premature distribution"), you have to pay a $500 penalty tax in addition to the normal tax

The Amount an Annual IRA Contribution Will
Be Worth Assuming a 10-Percent Rate of Interest

| Years | Annual IRA Contribution | | |
	$1,000	$2,000	$4,000
10	$15,937	$31,874	$63,750
15	31,772	63,545	127,090
20	57,275	114,550	229,100
25	98,347	196,694	393,388
30	164,494	328,988	657,976
35	271,024	542,048	1,084,097
40	442,592	885,185	1,770,370

on the $5000 itself. That's a technical way of saying that you are in essence tying your money up until at least 59 1/2. (That forced savings may be a big advantage if you have trouble saving money.)

You must begin to take the money by age 70 1/2 or face a tax equal to 50 percent of the difference between (a) what you are required by tax law to take out and (b) what you in fact did take out each year.

An IRA is obviously not for everyone. Even if you are allowed to deduct all or a large portion of your contribution, you should take a careful look at the pros and cons of an IRA and the alternatives.

Where to invest your IRA money

If you've decided an IRA is the way to go and you are eligible to make a deductible contribution, your next decision is what type of IRA to set up. Talk to your CLU, ChFC, or CFP. Compare each type of IRA according to its ability to meet your specific needs, the quality of the service offered, and the knowledge level provided. This last point pertains to whether you are dealing with an under-informed clerk or with a highly trained and well-schooled financial planning professional. The advice you receive can save you considerable aggravation as well as tax dollars.

Assume you've made an investment, and you later find it wasn't the wisest of all decisions. IRA law allows you to *rollover* your IRA investment as often as once a year into a new IRA investment medium. That can help minimize the cost of an investment error.

If you can use the same bank, insurer, broker, or mutual fund manager to change your investment (say from one type of mutual fund account to another), it can be done tax free and the exchange wouldn't count as a rollover.

Timing your contribution

You have until the time you have to file your income tax return to set up and contribute to your IRA. That gives most taxpayers until April fifteenth of next year to take a deduction for this year's income. We recommend you make your contribution as early as possible each year so that interest will compound tax free as long as possible. Over 20 or more years, the difference between a beginning of the year contribution and contributions made in December can amount to thousands of dollars. For instance, if you save $2000 a year at 10 percent for 30 years, you'll have $361,887 if you start your investment at the beginning of each year but only $328,988 if you don't invest until the end of the year, a difference of $32,899.

Simplified Employee Pension Plan (SEPP)

A SEPP is a "super IRA," a retirement savings program with most of the same rules but higher limits than a regular IRA. The SEPP is available only to employees (including yourself if you are self-employed).

Just as in the case of an IRA, contributions to a SEPP are currently deductible, earnings grow income tax free, and you pay no tax until you begin to receive benefits.

How much can you contribute to a SEPP? The answer is 15 percent of your compensation or $7000, whichever is less.

If your income is:	You can contribute and deduct up to:
$ 20,000	$3,000
30,000	4,500
40,000	6,000
50,000	7,000
60,000	7,000
70,000	7,000
80,000	7,000
90,000	7,000
100,000	7,000
150,000	7,000

Limitations

Just as is the case with much of the tax law, there is no free lunch when it comes to SEPPs. The cost of the boost in deductible limits is that to have a SEPP there must be:

1. An employer (can be a corporation, partnership or sole proprietorship).
2. That employer must make a contribution to the SEPP on behalf of each employee who is 21 or older.
3. That employer's contribution can't discriminate in favor of employees who are highly compensated. That means contributions, as a percentage of pay, can't be more (can't be a higher percentage) for officers, shareholders (who own more than 10 percent of the value of the corporation's stock), self-employed individuals, or

highly compensated employees than for others. For example, if Sue, the owner of Skyfly Travel Agency, a sole proprietorship, wanted to set up an SEPP for herself, she would also have to include any of her employees who have one or more years of service. If she had no other employees, she could set up the SEPP just for herself.

4. The SEPP must be in writing, and it must spell out any requirements for participants and how each employee's share is determined.

In spite of these rules, SEPP should be considered as an alternative to a full blown corporate retirement plan in the typical family or "Ma and Pa" business.

In Summary

If your estate documents were drafted before 1987, you should ask your attorney to review the dispositive arrangement for the death payment from your pension or profit-sharing plan. Most people should now name their spouse or a trust for their spouse as beneficiary of all (or all but an amount equal to the equivalent of the credit discussed on page 114) their pension proceeds.

Money left to your surviving spouse, regardless of amount, can qualify for the estate tax marital deduction and, therefore, wouldn't generate any federal estate tax.

Check with your attorney or CPA to be sure you wouldn't be exposed to the 15 percent excise tax on excess distributions. Have your attorney also check out the potential that your estate will have to pay the 15 percent tax on excess accumulations. This tax was imposed by TRA-86. It is *in addition* to the federal estate tax (so in 1988 a payment could be taxed as high as 65 percent) (15 percent excise tax plus 50 percent estate tax). It's totally nondeductible and can't be offset by any credits (see discussion in Chapter 11).

Most of the plans described in this chapter have one thing in common: They involve the systematic process of setting monies aside that can be tax deductible, if you pay them, or not reportable as income, if an employer provides the annual consideration. The plans have to be "qualified," which means approved by the federal government in accordance with the criteria established for each plan. But deductions, however attractive they may be, are not an end in themselves. The real beauty of the retirement planning tools described in this chapter is that, when you are ready to stop working and realize the benefits you have in your plan, there is indeed greater financial security. You will then be able to receive and enjoy the benefits derived from the deductions you so eagerly took during your working years.

18

Making Fringe Benefits
Work Harder

If you work for someone else, then you may not have the opportunity to form your own corporation, set up your own pension plan, HR-10 plan, or group life insurance and health plan. However, chances are that you have a compensation package where you work that may include a pension or profit-sharing plan, group life insurance, health insurance, and other benefits. In fact, your company benefits can help to provide a substantial part of your future financial security.

Why are some of these plans so beneficial? In part, because they force you to do what you might not otherwise do. They put you *first!* And, they put you at the *top* of your own payroll. How? By (1) allocating part of the pay you might otherwise spend (so the money instead of being currently taxed will accumulate tax-free for you), (2) by buying life insurance for you, or (3) by asking you to save money in a plan in which they agree to match your contribution dollar for dollar up to a certain level. In many of these plans, the dollars financing your personal security are deductible by your employer and tax free to you.

Fringe Benefits as a Recruiting Tool

Shirley got started on her career a little late in life. After raising two children and obtaining a divorce from her husband of 15 years, she went back to college in order to eventually obtain a better job. Now, in her late thirties, she has several job offers to consider. Because of her personal situation, Shirley is extremely interested in obtaining the best overall compensation package available. Although money for day-to-day expenses must be her top priority, she is also concerned about her future security.

Shirley has two offers that she is seriously considering. The first is with Barney, a very successful manufacturer's representative, who feels that Shirley's credentials will make her valuable to him as an administrative assistant. Barney represents several quality manufacturers and has offered Shirley an excellent starting salary. Shirley likes Barney, and especially likes the money she can make working for him. But she is concerned because Barney has no benefits to offer her, and also because Barney has only been in business for two years.

Her other employment offer is from a medium-sized corporation, which would like Shirley to be the administrative assistant in one of its departments. The company has a long and stable history and good prospects to continue to do well in the future. That corporation has offered Shirley a starting salary that is several thousand dollars less than the one offered by Barney, but the complete compensation package that Shirley will receive in addition to the salary includes a pension plan and group life, health and disability benefits.

Confused as to which offer to accept, Shirley talks to her friend and accountant, Mary. Mary reviews with Shirley the information on the pension plan that the company supplied to her. Mary explains that this is a *noncontributory* plan which means that Shirley does not have to contribute any of her salary to the plan. She also does not have to report as taxable income the monies that the company puts into the pension plan for her. Mary estimates the amount Shirley could receive at age 65, if she chose to retire, based on her present salary and also assuming that she receives periodic raises. Of course, these figures aren't exact, but they give an indication of the value of the plan to Shirley.

Mary explains the plan's *vesting* provisions to Shirley. Companies have different vesting schedules, subject to the limitations of federal law. These schedules indicate how much of the assets in Shirley's plan she has the absolute right to take if she leaves the company. Shirley's plan schedule indicates that Shirley has to work five years to have the right to keep all of the money in the plan, regardless of whether she is still working for the company at retirement age. If Shirley leaves the company before five years, then only a certain percentage of the monies deposited each year by the company will be available to Shirley, either to take at the time she leaves the company (subject to taxation) or to hold until retirement.

The plan also contains a life insurance feature, and if Shirley dies, these insurance benefits will be available to her children. Mary explains that the interest earned on the pension monies set aside for her are not taxed until she begins receiving benefits. Mary also explains the special lump-sum tax rules (explained in Chapter 17—Pensions, Profit-Sharing Plans) that Shirley can use at retirement to spread the tax out. Mary estimates that the plan is worth at least $1250 a year to Shirley.

Mary also reviews with Shirley the insurance package. Shirley must have medical insurance on herself and her children, which would cost an estimated $800 a year. This is provided for Shirley by the company in a group plan that is more comprehensive than the one Shirley could buy as an individual. The group life insurance plan offered by the company permits Shirley to buy extra insurance if she wants to, and the total cost to Shirley is less than if she were to purchase it on her own. In addition, the plan provides disability coverage for Shirley that would continue her income if she became disabled. Shirley would like this coverage, but, if it were not offered by her employer, she feels she could not otherwise afford it.

Shirley's decision, after her discussion with Mary, was that the company's benefits plus the salary were equal to the salary offered by Barney, but in addition provided her with the security that she wanted for her own future, and also for her children in the event of her death.

Thrift (401[k]) Plans

A 401(k) plan is a retirement plan that allows employees to defer taxes on a portion of their annual income. Income earned on your 401(k) account is tax-deferred until it is withdrawn. Better yet, many employers will match all or a portion of what you put into the plan up to a specified percentage. If you are covered by such a plan at work, you can elect to put up to 25 percent of your pay into the plan before taxes (up to a $7000 limit).

The amount put into the plan can be placed in various investments such as common stock, mutual funds, or annuities, or in a fixed plan with a guaranteed interest rate. As an employee, you may often be able to choose the type of investment you prefer, depending on whether you wish a guaranteed return or the flexibility of an equity type (hedge against inflation) investment.

The same rules apply for vesting with regard to the contributions made by the company only. You are always permitted to get back any contribution you make to any qualified plan when you leave your employer, regardless of the reasons for terminating your employment.

Steve works for the Acme Computer Company, which has a qualified savings plan. Steve elects to have the maximum amount available deducted from his salary, which under his plan is 10 percent of salary. Steve reduced his $30,000 salary by $3000 a year which is contributed by payroll deduction into the plan. The plan provides that the company will match Steve's contribution to the plan dollar for dollar, up to 3 percent of salary. Therefore, on Steve's salary of $30,000, the company contributed $900 to the plan. Not only is Steve investing $3000 in the plan, with interest on his savings accumulating tax free, but in addition he immediately receives a non-currently taxable "bonus" of $900 from the company—an added feature that makes this a very worthwhile investment. Income on employer dollars also grows income tax free.

The Tax Reform Act of 1986 provided that the maximum amount an employee can elect to defer annually under all 401(k) arrangements in which the employee participates is $7000 (even if the regular limits—the lesser of 25 percent of compensation, or $30,000—would have resulted in a higher contribution). This law severely restricts the attractiveness of 401(k) plans if you are highly compensated. So, 401(k) plans will continue to be attractive for rank-and-file employees, but owners and high level executives would be better off with regular profit-sharing or defined contribution pension plans, or a SERP (Selective Executive Retirement Plan).

Money you withdraw from a 401(k) plan prior to retirement or age 59^1/$_2$ will be subjected to a 10 percent penalty (over and above any regular tax). You cannot take out money to purchase a home since penalty free withdrawals are now limited to "hardships" such as medical bills.

SERPs

A SERP is an employer-sponsored plan which provides both death and retirement benefits for selected executives. The plan can cover as few as one executive. Amounts provided, terms of the agreement, and who will be covered are entirely within the discretion of the employer. Most such plans are in addition to pension or other fringe benefits and do not require a contribution or reduction of salary by the employee. A SERP works like this:

The selected employee enters into an employment contract with his or her employer. The contract stipulates that specific payments (for instance, $50,000 a year for 10 years or 30 percent of salary for 10 years) will be made to the employee or the employee's beneficiaries in the event of death, disability or retirement. This creates a direct enforceable obligation. The employer must provide the agreed upon benefits. In return for this promise, the selected employee agrees to continue in the service of the company.

Often the employer will purchase universal, variable, or interest sensitive life insurance (alone or in combination with other savings vehicles, such as a fixed or variable annuity or a mutual fund) to provide the required amounts. The business would apply for and own the policy (or other security) on the life of the employee. The business would pay the premiums and be named the policy beneficiary. The business would completely control and own the policy (as well as any other asset used to finance the employer's obligation under the agreement).

The purpose of the life insurance policy or other asset is to provide funds necessary to pay death and retirement or disability benefits called for under the contract. Policy cash values can be used for this purpose. Alternatively, the policy can be held by the corporation until the employee's death, and the employee can be paid the agreed upon deferred compensation out of other corporate assets. Should the employee die prior to retirement, the life insurance will be received by the corporation and then can be used to provide death benefit payments to the employee's family.

The employee will pay no tax during employment years assuming the SERP is properly arranged. At retirement, all payments under the SERP are ordinary income. At death, payments made to the executive's widow could qualify for the estate tax marital deduction. She would, however, have to pay income tax year by year as she received each annual payment. Up to $600,000 of payments not qualifying for the marital deduction might be shielded from federal estate tax by the unified credit.

Group Insurance

Many large companies offer group insurance to their employees in the form of life, health, and disability. The group life insurance usually takes the form of term insurance and is purchased by the employer on a group basis from an insurance company. Premiums for the insurance are determined on an overall basis by the age composition of the employee group in the plan. Additional charges may be added if the work performed is considered by the insurance company to be more or less risky than usual.

Is this group life insurance a good deal? In most cases, yes, but there are exceptions. For the younger employees, it might be cheaper and safer in the long run to obtain their own coverage because group rates are averaged out. Often, younger, healthier employees pay more than they would have to pay if the insurance were purchased individually. Older, less healthy employees often pay less than they otherwise might pay.

If your plan requires you to contribute toward the cost of the insurance, you should check with your own agent to see if it would be better for you to purchase the insurance on your own. That way you would own the policy, whether or not you terminated your employment.

Group life policies are usually convertible within 30 days if you terminate your employment, but they are convertible (you can change it to whole life) at the age you are when you leave the company and usually only to a whole life policy. The cost may, therefore, be quite high, or even prohibitive, at that time because of your age.

Of course, if you do not have to contribute toward the cost of the coverage, you should take all you can get. The best solution is often to purchase your own insurance and also keep the group insurance.

Stock Options

One fringe benefit not always available to all employees, but a popular one, is the stock option. A stock option is a right to buy stock in the company you work for within a certain period of time, and at a fixed price, regardless of what the stock is selling for at the time the option can be exercised. The details of each plan must be carefully reviewed with your tax advisor before you make a decision to exercise the option.

A relatively new type of benefit is the *incentive stock option* (ISO). It works like this: Amy is an executive of a large chemical company. She is granted an incentive stock option to purchase ten shares of the company stock at $10 per share on March 15, 1987. If she exercises her option and buys the stock on March 15 when its value is $12 a share, she pays tax only when she actually sells the stock. This ability to control the timing of a taxable event enables her to report the gain in a year when her tax bracket is low.

The "spread" by which the fair market value of the ISO at the time of option exercise exceeds the stocks option price is a tax preference under the alternative minimum tax (AMT) rules. The Tax Reform Act of 1986

simultaneously made ISO law more flexible but ISOs less desirable because of the repeal of the long term capital gains deduction.

Social Security

One fringe benefit that almost everybody who works has is social security. We suggest that you don't count on social security to provide you and
your family with a secure financial future. At best, social security can
provide a floor of protection upon which you should build economic
independence. Since you are paying for it, you should know what benefits
you and your family can expect to receive, or at least hope to receive *if* the
system remains financially sound.

You pay social security taxes during your working years, which are
pooled into special trust funds, but not earmarked specifically for you
and your family. Benefits are then paid on your retirement, at your death,
or in the event of disability. Part of the contributions you make go into a
separate hospital insurance trust fund to provide coverage for hospital
bills, which we know more familiarly by the name *Medicare.*

Social security, even more emphatically than your other insurance
benefits, forces you to accept its benefits by its nonvoluntary nature. If
you work in a covered employment, you must participate and pay your
social security (FICA) taxes.

You cannot borrow against your future benefits. These benefits will
begin with the date you elect to retire (which depends, of course, on the
date on which the plan will permit you to retire).

Social security retirement benefits provide a monthly income starting at
age 65 (or whatever age is elected and then in effect) for the rest of your life.
The amount of monthly benefits will be determined by a formula based on
your average monthly wage over your working years. The amount of benefits you will receive from social security and the contributions you make to
the plan are constantly changing. Updated schedules can be obtained from
the social security office or your insurance representative.

Wives are also entitled to benefits equal to a percentage of their husband's income depending on their age—or a mother's benefit if the wife
has dependent and unmarried children under age 18. Unmarried children
under age 18, or under 22 if a full-time student, are entitled to benefits
equal to 50 percent of retirement benefits. In certain cases, husbands of
working women drawing primary retirement benefits are also eligible on
the same basis as the wife would be. There are specific rules as to the
amount of time you must have worked and contributed to social security
before you and your family are eligible for the various types of benefits.

Social Security Death Benefits

At your death, social security can provide your family with survivorship
benefits equal to a life insurance policy worth several hundred thousand
dollars. How much will be paid, and who will receive the survivorship
benefits, depends on the status of your family at the time of your death.

Social Security Guesstimator

The Guesstimator will give you a *rough* idea of monthly benefits you'll receive when you retire. These figures are deliverately conservative and assume that you have (1) worked regularly, and (2) received average pay raises throughout your working career, and (3) your present earnings will stay the same until you retire, and (4) the general level of salaries and wages in the country will not rise (the value of your retirement benefit in today's dollars is guesstimated):

Monthly Benefits at Retirement (Age 65)

		Your Present Annual Earnings		
Your Age	*Who Receives Benefits*	*$20,000*	*$30,000*	*$44,000 & up*
65	You	$ 670	$ 730	$ 760
	Spouse or child	330	360	380
64	You	680	750	780
	Spouse or child	340	370	390
63	You	690	760	790
	Spouse or child	340	380	390
62	You	710	780	810
	Spouse or child	350	390	400
61	You	710	780	820
	Spouse or child	350	390	410
55	You	720	800	860
	Spouse or child	360	400	430
50	You	730	820	900
	Spouse or child	360	410	450
45	You	700	800	890
	Spouse or child	340	390	440
40	You	690	790	900
	Spouse or child	340	390	440
35	You	690	800	920
	Spouse or child	342	390	450
30	You	680	780	910
	Spouse or child	330	380	440

Survivors' benefits will be paid to your family if, at the time of your death, you have survivors who would fit into the following categories:

- Monthly benefits are payable to a surviving spouse as mother's or father's benefits. This payment is made to the widow or widower regardless of age assuming that person is caring for at least one child who is under age 16 or who was disabled prior to age 22. Note that benefits for children age 18–22 who attend college or a post-secondary school were completely phased out in April, 1985.
- A child's benefit is payable monthly for each child who is under age 18 and for children over age 18 who were disabled prior to age 22.
- A widow(er)'s benefit is payable monthly to the surviving spouse (or

surviving divorced spouse) of an insured worker when the survivor is age 60 or older.

- A disabled widow(er)'s benefit is payable monthly for disabled surviving spouses age 50 to 60.

Up to one-half of the social security benefits received by taxpayers whose incomes exceed certain base amounts is subject to income taxation.

You should be aware that social security benefits for survivors were recently, and quietly, reduced. These reductions could be substantial and may mean your children's college education years' security has been seriously undermined. Check with your CLU, ChFC, or CFP to see if you have suffered a shortfall of security.

The 1987 Social Security tax earnings base is $43,800. Self-employed individuals must pay 12.3 percent ($5,387.40 maximum). Employers and employees must each pay 7.15 percent ($3,131.70 maximum), a total of 14.3 percent ($6,263.40 maximum).

Social security also provides disability benefits. You are eligible to receive those benefits if you have a physical or mental impairment that is so severe that you are unable to engage in any substantially gainful work or employment. The disability must last six months before benefits are paid, and at that time, benefits are payable if the disability can be expected to last for at least twelve months from when it began, or will result in death, or if it has already actually lasted twelve months. In the event that you qualify for disability benefits, your wage position is frozen for the purpose of determining your future retirement or survivor benefits, so that you will not be penalized for the period of time when you are out of work because of disability.

Medicare

Part of your social security taxes goes to fund the health insurance plan of social security known as Medicare. Nearly everyone over 65 is eligible for Medicare, which provides benefits for in-patient hospital care and other medical expenses. There are many private hospital insurance plans that are designed to supplement Medicare payments, and because the Medicare benefits will be used to pay the bills first, and the additional insurance will be supplementary, the premiums for this supplemental insurance are usually quite reasonable and, therefore, recommended.

The security of social security

We have purposely avoided using anything but very rough "guesstimates" in discussing social security. Because of the size of the group (almost all Americans), the changes in the tax contributions and the continual adjustments in the amount of benefits paid, any specific figures would be quickly outdated. Regardless of the specific amounts to which you or your family would be entitled under one of the categories of payments, the amount

Social Security Guesstimator

The following guesstimator will give you a *rough* idea of the monthly benefit payable to your family members if you should die. The figures are deliberately conservative and assume that you have worked steadily and received average pay raises throughout your working career:

Monthly Benefits If You Should Die

Your Age	Who Receives Benefits	Your Present Annual Earnings		
		$20,000	$30,000	$44,000 & up
64	Spouse, age 65	$ 680	$ 740	$ 760
	Spouse, age 60	480	530	540
	Child, spouse caring for child	510	550	570
	Maximum family benefit	1200	1300	1340
57–62	Spouse, age 65	$ 700	$ 760	$ 780
	Spouse, age 60	500	540	560
	Child, spouse caring for child	520	570	590
	Maximum family benefit	1230	1340	1380
55	Spouse, age 65	$ 700	$ 760	$ 790
	Spouse, age 60	500	540	560
	Child, spouse caring for child	520	570	590
	Maximum family benefit	1230	1340	1380
50	Spouse, age 65	$ 700	$ 780	$ 800
	Spouse, age 60	500	550	570
	Child, spouse caring for child	520	580	600
	Maximum family benefit	1230	1360	1410
45	Spouse, age 65	$ 700	$ 790	$ 830
	Spouse, age 60	500	560	590
	Child, spouse caring for child	530	590	620
	Maximum family benefit	1240	1390	1460
40	Spouse, age 65	$ 700	$ 810	$ 860
	Spouse, age 60	500	580	620
	Child, spouse caring for child	530	610	650
	Maximum family benefit	1240	1430	1520
35	Spouse, age 65	$ 700	$ 820	$ 910
	Spouse, age 60	500	590	650
	Child, spouse caring for child	530	620	680
	Maximum family benefit	1240	1450	1590
30	Spouse, age 65	$ 710	$ 830	$ 950
	Spouse, age 60	510	590	680
	Child, spouse caring for child	530	620	710
	Maximum family benefit	1250	1460	1670

Social Security Disability Guesstimator

The guesstimator will give you a *rough* idea of the benefits available if you become disabled. The figures are deliberately conservative and assume: (1) you have worked steadily and received average pay raises throughout your working career; and (2) that there are no child-care years for persons age 24-37, which would increase the benefit slightly:

Monthly Benefits at Disability

Your Age	Who Receives Benefits	Your Present Annual Earnings		
		$20,000	$30,000	$44,000 & up
64	You	$ 680	$ 750	$ 750
	Child (or children & spouse)	340	370	370
57–62	You	$ 700	$ 760	$ 775
	Child (or children & spouse)	350	380	380
55	You	$ 700	$ 770	$ 790
	Child (or children & spouse)	350	380	390
50	You	$ 706	$ 780	$ 800
	Child (or children & spouse)	350	390	400
45	You	$ 708	$ 790	$ 820
	Child (or children & spouse)	350	390	410
40	You	$ 708	$ 810	$ 850
	Child (or children & spouse)	350	400	420
35	You	$ 710	$ 820	$ 880
	Child (or children & spouse)	350	410	400
30	You	$ 710	$ 830	$ 920
	Child (or children & spouse)	355	415	460

paid would be subject to a *maximum family benefit*. That amount is now in excess of $1000, but is again dependent on age and the period of time of full coverage.

We think the system is definitely going to survive regardless of any change in funding or benefit payments (although some call the system "social insecurity"). But our assurance is tempered with this repeated word of warning: *Don't rely on social security to solve your future financial problems.* Regardless of what happens to you and your family, it is hard, if not impossible, to imagine that social security can provide you with the material things and the intangible peace of mind that you are looking for. At the very best, it will provide minimum protection for you and your family—and you wouldn't be reading this book if you would settle for that.

Don't rely on social security to keep accurate records

Social security—like any other government administration—is human and will make errors. We suggest (so that they don't make errors with *your* security) that you request a statement of earnings from your social security record at least every three years. This information is free. Be sure to request that the statement verify how many quarters of coverage you have. Send the statement received to *your* nearest Social Security Administration Data Operations Center. Write to the Wilkes-Barre Center (P.O. Box 20, Wilkes-Barre, PA 18703) to obtain the address of the center nearest to you.

	FOR SSA USE ONLY		
REQUEST FOR STATEMENT OF EARNINGS (PLEASE PRINT IN INK OR USE TYPEWRITER)	**AX**		•
	SP		•

I REQUEST A SUMMARY STATEMENT OF EARNINGS FROM MY SOCIAL SECURITY RECORD

NH Full name you use in work or business

First | Middle Initial | Last

SN Social Security number shown on your card | **DB** Your date of birth — Month | Day | Year | **A**

MA Other Social Security number(s) you have used | **SX** Your Sex ☐ Male ☐ Female

AK Other name(s) you have used (Include your maiden name)

FOLD HERE

PRIVACY STATEMENT

The Social Security Administration (SSA) is authorized to collect information asked on this form under section 205 of the Social Security Act. It is needed so SSA can quickly identify your record and prepare the earnings statement you requested. While you are not required to furnish the information, failure to do so may prevent your request from being processed. The information will be used primarily for issuing your earnings statement.

I am the individual to whom the record pertains. I understand that if I knowingly and willingly request or receive a record about an individual under false pretenses I would be guilty of a Federal crime and could be fined up to $5000.

Sign your name here: (Do not print) | TELEPHONE NO. (Area Code) | DATE

SEND THE STATEMENT TO: (to be completed in ALL cases.)

PN Name

AD Address (Number and Street, Apt. No., P.O. Box, or Rural Route)

City and state | **ZP** Zip Code

Form **SSA-7004-PC-OP1** (9/85)
Destroy prior editions

Veterans' benefits

If you were on active duty in the U.S. armed forces and received an honorable discharge, then you and your family may be entitled to VA benefits. Benefits include burial in a National Cemetery or a cash burial expense allowance and eligibility for a headstone.

Widows or widowers, and dependent children under 18 of deceased veterans who died as the result of service-connected disabilities, are eligible for medical care under the Veterans Administration. There is a pension benefit available to widows or widowers of nearly all deceased veterans, with benefits restricted according to income.

There are legal benefits provided for widows, widowers, and children of veterans who died while serving in the armed forces. These benefits include a death gratuity and monthly pension benefits. You might also have life insurance coverage under either Servicemen's Group Life Insurance (SGLI) or Veterans' Group Life Insurance (VGLI). To find out the current status of the VA benefits available to you and your family, contact your local VA office.

Civil service

If you work for the federal government, then you and your family may be entitled to civil service benefits. Retirement and survivorship benefits are available to covered persons and their families, and if you are not familiar with the benefits to which you and your family are now entitled, you can write to the Civil Service Bureau of Retirement Insurance and Occupational Health at 1900 E Street, N.W., Washington, DC 20415.

Disability

What happens to all your great plans for the future if something happens to you? You have life insurance to take care of your family if you die, but what happens if some unforeseen tragedy, a serious illness or crippling illness strikes. Just suppose you were the victim of a permanent or long-term disability. Have you protected yourself and your family adequately?

Jerry and Sally were both earning substantial salaries. Jerry was a successful lawyer and Sally was a teacher. The couple had three children, ages 4, 7, and 10. Jerry was a firm believer in life insurance. He had analyzed his tax situation and felt that he had taken all the necessary steps to safeguard his family's future. When Jerry went out to interview a potential new client who was injured in an accident and couldn't leave her home, Jerry's financial house was completely in order. He had money in the bank and plans were made to send the children to camp and to take a long-awaited vacation. Jerry's practice was improving, and the mortgage payments on their new home were not proving to be the burden he had anticipated.

But fate had other plans for Jerry. Coming home from the client's apartment, he became the victim of a holdup. He was struck on the head, his wallet was taken, and he lay on the sidewalk for some time before he was finally taken to the hospital. He was in the hospital for more than two months.

When Jerry was finally discharged from the hospital and permitted to go home, there was really nothing he could do. The blow on his head had injured his brain, and he spent much of the rest of his life at home while Sally attempted to find the highest-paying teaching job available to cover the family's expenses. Jerry's social security disability payments provided for basic food and clothing, but even when added to Sally's income, they could not cover the large mortgage payments, and eventually the family had to move to a much smaller home.

Frequently, a long-term disability can be even more costly and traumatic than a death. Not only must the remaining healthy family members be able to survive financially, but there is the additional cost of taking care of the disabled member. Together with the economic hardship, the mental effect on the disabled person of being unable to contribute anything to the family is another serious result of the problems caused by prolonged disability.

Fortunately, there are plans designed to alleviate the burden caused by the type of disability that Jerry suffered. As discussed previously in this chapter, if Jerry had been employed by a large corporation, chances are he might have had a disability policy that would have covered him, at least for a minimum period of time. A company might also have offered a long-term disability policy that would have been extremely beneficial in these circumstances.

The chart below, based on actuarial tables used by insurers, shows the odds of disability (which lasts 90 days or more) expressed as the number of chances out of 1000:

Age	Probability
30	289
35	284
40	278
45	267
50	250
55	222
60	158

How to protect your income

What could Jerry have done to guard against long-term or permanent disability? He could have obtained his own individual disability income insurance in addition to any group disability plan from his office or through his bar association. Disability plans provide a specific amount of income to be payable over a set period of time (or for life). The plans often differentiate as to whether the disability was caused by accident or sickness. You should be familiar with the major provisions of disability income policies.

Noncancellable guaranteed renewable contracts

The company's right to cancel the policy is extremely important. We recommend the type of policies that are noncancellable (by the insurer) *and* guaranteed renewable to age 65 or for life. Under these policies, the premium is guaranteed *and* the coverage is guaranteed for the length of the renewable period. You are, therefore, assured that coverage will be there if you need it.

Cost is a factor. Less expensive policies can be purchased that are *guaranteed renewable*. Under these policies, the insurer retains the right to change the amount of the premiums on a class basis rather than an individual basis. Policies that are *renewable only at the option of the insurer* are those under which the insurance company has the right to refuse to renew the policy on its anniversary date. We recommend against this type of coverage.

Upon hearing of Jerry's injury, his accountant, Len, immediately purchased his own disability policy. The policy provided a monthly income benefit of $1000 and had an elimination period for total disability due to sickness of 90 days and for total disability due to injury of 90 days. The maximum duration of the monthly income benefits if the disability was due to sickness was ten years, and if the disability was due to injury, the benefits could last for life. The policy was noncancellable and guaranteed renewable to age 65, and its definition of total disability was as follows:

> *Total disability* means the complete inability of the insured due to sickness or injury to perform any and every duty pertaining to his occupation until monthly income payments have been payable under the policy during any period of disability for 60 months or for a period for which monthly income benefits are payable, if less; and (b) after monthly income benefits have been payable under the policy during any period of disability due to sickness or injury for 60 months, then during the remainder, if any, of the period for which monthly income benefits are payable, "total disability" means the complete inability of the insured due to sickness or injury, as the case may be, to engage in any and every gainful occupation for which he is reasonably fitted by education, training or experience.

Let's review the different features to find out what options are available when purchasing an individual disability income policy. The following checklist will enable you to calculate your disability needs and disability income.

The amount of monthly benefits that you purchase should be based on these factors: (1) your needs, (2) your ability to pay premiums, and (3) the insurer's maximum limits.

The total income needs of your family should be calculated and then reduced by (a) other benefits that will be available, as well as (b) expected income from your spouse, if any, and (c) the return you anticipate

Disability Needs Checklist

	Current	Could Be Reduced to
a. Rent or mortgage (include taxes and insurance)	$_____	$_____
b. Food	_____	_____
c. Utilities (water, heat)	_____	_____
d. Transportation (car payments, maintenance, repairs, insurance, gasoline)	_____	_____
e. Education	_____	_____
f. Insurance premiums	_____	_____
g. Clothing	_____	_____
h. Household items (appliances, furnishings, tools)	_____	_____
i. Recreation (dues, hobbies, entertainment)	_____	_____
j. Medical and dental expense	_____	_____
k. Installment payments	_____	_____
l. Pocket money	_____	_____
m. Savings	_____	_____
n. Other	_____	_____
TOTAL MONTHLY NEEDS	$_____	$_____

Disability Income Calculation Form

	Amount	After a Waiting Period of: (in months)	For a Period Lasting until . . .
1. We (I) *need* each month:			
a. Group disability income insurance	$_____	$_____	$_____
b. Individual disability income insurance	_____	_____	_____
c. After-tax government benefits (social security, workers' compensation, veteran's benefits)	_____	_____	_____
d. After-tax income from other sources (stocks, bonds, spouse's income)	_____	_____	_____
2. We (I) *have* each month	$_____	_____	_____
3. We (I) *still* need (or can drop)	$_____		

receiving on income-producing investments (be conservative and use after-tax rates of return).

Insurance companies place a maximum on the amount of benefits that will be paid, based on a percentage of a person's total income. In other words, the company might be willing to give you 70 percent of your total income if you become disabled, but would not agree to paying benefits that would be equal to or greater than your income had you still been working. Most insurers will not allow coverage to exceed 60 percent of your monthly earnings.

Suppose you have elected a *waiting* or *elimination period* of 90 days both for sickness and accident. This is the waiting period *after* you become disabled but *before* benefits begin. In arriving at this elimination period, you may have made a determination that a disability lasting three months or less would not critically affect your family's financial position. The longer your waiting period, the lower your premium. The premium for the policy with the 90-day elimination period is considerably lower than one with benefits commencing after one or two weeks. Going to a 180-day waiting period cuts your premium by about 15 percent.

In selecting coverage that would last for ten years in the event of sickness and for life in the event of accident, you may base your decision mainly on the cost of the insurance. All things being equal, you certainly should have coverage for the longest possible time.

We feel coverage to age 65 is adequate for most individuals since after that your investment income should be sufficient if you are disabled. However, after reviewing disability plans offered by several prominent companies, and considering the cost of the extended benefits for sickness, you may feel that you would rather increase the amount of monthly benefits as opposed to having a policy that covers you up to 65 for sickness and lifetime for accident. Unless you can afford both the maximum amount *and* the maximum payment period, you must select more of one than the other.

You should demand an absolute guarantee that, in the event of disability, the coverage you purchase will be available with no possibility that the company can either cancel the policy or increase the premium. Although you can save money by foregoing either or both of the above guarantees, we feel this is a dangerous choice.

Your insurance agent should point out the difference in the definitions of disability found in this type of policy. Your agent should also tell you that a company which defines total disability as *inability to engage in any and every gainful occupation* is providing more limited coverage than one that defines disability as *the inability to perform any and every duty pertaining to the insured's own occupation.*

For example, a surgeon might give up surgery after a heart attack. If he's still able to teach at a local medical school, the "any occupation" definition will cut off his benefits entirely once he starts earning income

as a teacher. The "your own occupation" provision would not stop benefits. To save premium dollars, a compromise may be necessary. Consider
a policy that contains the latter definition of disability for the first two to
five years, and then limits it to cover "any occupation" thereafter.

Group disability coverage

We recommend you do *not* rely on group disability as your sole coverage.
Group policies don't give you the right to pay the same premium for the
life of the policy. In fact, the more stable and older the group, the higher
the rates will become. If the group's coverage is cancelled or changed, you
may have no recourse—or protection.

Riders to consider

Some policies increase your monthly benefits if you cannot collect from
social security. We suggest you avoid riders that require you to litigate
for social security benefits since it will be at least a year before you can
collect (during which time you'll receive no benefits from this extra cost
rider). Worse yet, benefits are *not* retroactive.

Another rider provides an increase in benefits to keep pace with
inflation. If the increase in premiums is 15 or 20 percent, is it worth the
extra cost? Certainly not when inflation is low, but consider that at even
5 percent, inflation gouges the buying power of your benefits in half in
less than 15 years. If you do take this rider, be sure benefit increases are
linked to the CPI (Consumer Price Index) rather than arbitrarily decided by the insurer.

"Partial disability" is a provision that can be extremely valuable. If you
have this provision, benefits can continue even after you've returned to
work part-time. In fact, such a provision may make it economically feasi-
ble to do just that. Typically, this rider requires that you must be totally
disabled for a specified period of time (generally as long as the elimination period) before any partial disability benefits could be paid.

"Waiver of premium" in a disability policy means the insurer will
waive the condition that you have to pay premiums once a disability
occurs. Read the provision carefully. The sooner the waiver takes effect,
the better off you are. Check also to see if the insurer will refund any
premiums you pay during the initial period of disability.

Be sure you have your agent shop for you and make a comparison of cost
and provisions offered by at least three companies. Some insurers specialize in coverage for professionals. Demand that your agent do some *extra*
homework if you are a doctor, lawyer, accountant, teacher, or other professional. There are disability income policies specially designed for you.

In Summary

In this chapter, we have discussed many job-related benefits, social
security benefits, and how to guard against being removed from the

workforce. Obviously, before doing anything, you should first take an inventory of what you already have. Many people have never taken the time to understand all of their job-related benefits. Once you know what you have, you can then fill in the gaps to reduce, to the greatest extent possible, the effect of any future event that could hamper or destroy your lifetime goals.

It should be pointed out that there are other benefits that can be available to you depending on the circumstances. If you have a job-related disability, then you could be eligible to receive workers' compensation benefits in accordance with the laws of your state. If you are injured in an automobile accident, and your state has a no-fault insurance law, then you might automatically be entitled to wage loss benefits from your automobile insurance company.

There are "accident-only" policies that provide lump sums for losing specific parts of your body, which are extremely limited in scope and have a relatively small premium. Many more people are removed from the workforce because of sickness than because of accident, and many more people die from illness than as a result of an accident. That's why accident-only disability policies, and accidental death insurance, require relatively lower premiums (and are less likely to pay off) when compared with policies that provide protection against both sickness and accident and with regular life insurance policies.

Make sure that your protection will not be limited to your becoming sick by narrowly defined diseases or being injured only in certain specified ways or times. Policies that cover you only if cancer strikes, or only if you are injured riding in a public conveyance on weekdays, and on which you suffer a loss of at least two limbs, are out of date (and can be dangerously expensive if you contract a disease or develop a sickness or are injured in a manner that is not covered).

There are excellent products that can be tailored specifically to fit your needs. Don't settle for second best. You work hard for your money, and the one asset that requires your concerted attention is yourself. Nothing else in your inventory gives you a better return than your own personal efforts, and, therefore, that "money making machine" (you as a working individual) must be protected to the greatest possible extent.

A Last Comment . . .

With today's high cost of hospitals, you are criminally underinsured if you do not have major medical coverage and grossly underinsured if your protection is less than $500,000 (we suggest you try to obtain at least $1,000,000 of coverage or find a plan with unlimited benefits).

19

The Smart Ways to Send Children to College and Provide for Their Financial Security

There are tax advantages to having money in your children's name as opposed to your owning it, and, in some cases, there are important nontax considerations for placing money or property in your children's names. The Uniform Gifts to Minors Act (UGMA) illustrates how you can make gifts to a minor while avoiding many of the problems and expenses of other methods of giving property to them. The 2503(c) Trust is another excellent vehicle in which to transfer money to children.

Kiddie Tax Rules—Children Under 14

Before we tell you about income shifting techniques (yes, it is *still* possible to shift income and save income taxes by both outright gifts and gifts in custodial accounts and trust), we will consider the "kiddie tax" rules provided in the Tax Reform Act of 1986.

The key rule is this: All unearned income of a child who has not reached age 14 before the close of the tax year will be taxed to the child—but at the parents' tax bracket. In other words, the tax payable by the child on unearned income is essentially the additional amount of tax the parent would have had to pay if the child's unearned income had been added on top of the parents'. Note that this rule applies to all unearned income received by the child; it doesn't matter *who* transfers the income-producing assets to the child or *when* the transfer is made.

The easiest way to see the effect of the kiddie tax rules is to picture three levels of tax on children under 14. At the bottom level, there will be no tax on the first $500 of unearned income. At the second level, there will be a tax to the child on the next $500 of unearned income, but the tax will be at the *child's* rates. The third level consists of unearned income in excess of

243

$1000. Unearned income in excess of $1000 is taxed to the child—but at the parents' rate.

If there are two or more children with unearned income to be taxed at the parents' marginal tax rate, all of the childrens' unearned income is added together, and the tax (at the parents' rate) is calculated. The tax is then allocated to each child based on the child's pro rata share of unearned income. In the case of unmarried parents, the custodial parent's taxable income is used.

Kiddie Tax Rules—Children 14 or Over

Unearned income received by children 14 or older is taxed to them at their rates. This may mean that income is taxed as low as 15 percent. Since single taxpayers can receive up to $17,850 before they are pushed into the next highest bracket, the 28 percent level, if the child's parents are in the 33 percent bracket (most couples with a combined taxable income of over $71,901 will be in the 33 percent bracket), the income shifting savings will be 18 percent (33 less 15). Even if parents are in the 28 percent bracket, the leverage is still 13 percent (28 less 15). This is the same as if the couple could earn an additional 13 percent on its money. So, if you are in a 33 percent bracket, it makes sense from a tax viewpoint to continue to shift income to your children until they have reached a 33 percent bracket. But that point is not reached until each child has received $43,150 of taxable income in a given year.

Uniform Gifts to Minors Act

You'd like to give money or property to your children, but you don't think your child is capable of managing it wisely yet. And you don't want to go to the trouble and expense of setting up a trust.

Perhaps you'd like to shift the burden of paying taxes from your tax bracket to your child's to the greatest extent possible. Your accountant has told you that, since you're in a federal tax bracket of 33 percent, you'll pay a tax of 33 percent of the income and net less than your 14-year-old child who isn't working would net—far less. In fact, he/she tells you that, if you make a $10,000 gift to your child through the Uniform Gifts to Minors Act and your child's custodian invests that $10,000 at 10 percent, only income in excess of $500 will be taxed, and the entire $500 balance is taxed at the child's 15 percent rate (a tax of $75 on the $1000 income). But if you personally invested the same $10,000 at the 10 percent return, you would pay an annual tax of $330, a $255 a year difference. If the difference is invested at a 5 percent after-tax return, in 4 years the tax savings is $1302. If you are looking for a way to drop the tax on family income to your child's lower bracket, keep reading.

You'd like to make irrevocable gifts to your child to move assets—and the appreciation of the assets—from your estate, but you don't want to incur any gift tax if you can help it.

If these are your goals and you don't object to your child receiving money or other property at majority (age 18 or 21 in some states), the Uniform Gifts to Minors Act (UGMA) or its more flexible statutory counterpart, the UTMA (Uniform Transfers to Minors Act), may be your solution.

Selecting the appropriate property to transfer

Most states have passed laws allowing you to put money, securities (stocks; bonds; evidences of indebtedness; certificates of interest or participation in an oil, gas mining title, or lease), life insurance and annuity contracts into an account for a minor.

The UGMA and UTMA provide that as an adult you can give these types of property to a minor (even if you are not related to the minor). This is accomplished by delivering it to—or having it registered in the name of—an adult or a trust company as custodian for that minor. You can even give it to yourself as custodian. But we recommend that you name someone else (such as a spouse, relative, or friend). The reason is that, if you die at a time when you are custodian and the child has not reached the age of majority, the property you have given away will be includable in your estate for federal estate tax purposes.

Custodial gift laws were designed to accomplish a very simple objective: To make it possible for you to make gifts to a minor but, at the same time, avoid many of the problems and expenses of other transfer methods, such as outright gifts, trusts, or formal guardianship arrangements.

Although (as in the case with *all* of these tools and techniques) you should consult your attorney and your accountant before doing anything, a UGMA or UTMA gift is simple. You transfer the cash or other property to the person you have selected as custodian, or you call your stockbroker and tell him to purchase stock, mutual funds, or money markets, and make the person you have selected the custodian for your child. That person holds the property "as custodian for (name of minor) under (your state's) Gifts to Minors Act" (or Uniform Transfers to Minors Act).

If you have more than one child, and you'd like to make a gift to each, you should appoint a custodian and have that custodian keep a separate UGMA or UTMA account for each child.

Keep two things in mind. First, once you make a gift it is irrevocable. You can't get it back. So don't give more than you are sure you can afford to give. Second, don't give property you may need personally or may regret giving (such as controlling interest in your family corporation).

How to save gift tax

Mel transfers his hundred shares of Purple Lady, Inc. stock to his wife, Sonia, as custodian for their daughter, Melanie, age 11. Mel does it by having the ownership of the stock registered on the company's books as follows: "Sonia Young, as custodian for Melanie Young under the Tennessee Uniform Gifts to Minors Act."

Assuming the value of the stock is $10,000 or less ($20,000 if Sonia agrees to "split" the gift and sign her consent on a gift tax return), Mel wouldn't have to pay any gift tax or use any of his gift tax credit. In fact, Mel could make a gift of similar value every year and never pay any tax.

Assuming Mel keeps each year's gifts under the $10,000 limit ($20,000 if split with Sonia), none of the gifts will be in either his or Sonia's estate even if Mel dies within three years of making the gift. In just five years, giving $20,000 a year, Mel could remove as much as $100,000 from his estate (plus the income and appreciation on the annual gifts) with absolutely no adverse gift or estate tax implication (check to see if your state has a state gift tax).

Melanie doesn't pay any income or gift tax on receiving the gift. But since the stock belongs to Melanie once Sonia accepts it as custodian, if Melanie dies it will be in her estate and not in either Mel's or Sonia's estate.

Typically, whether or not she actually receives it, any income produced by the stock will be taxed at Melanie's tax bracket. There is one important exception. If income is used to discharge Mel and Sonia's support obligations (for instance, to pay for Melanie's food, clothing, or shelter), it will be taxed to Mel and Sonia. That problem is solved by using such income to pay for non-necessities such as summer camp, a trip to Europe, toys, or pleasure reading books for Melanie.

Who can be custodian?

Most states' laws provide that you can name any adult or trust company or bank with trust powers as custodian.

If the custodian you have named wants to resign, many states allow that custodian to name a new custodian in writing (the document must be signed by the resigning custodian and should be witnessed by someone other than the new custodian).

What if the custodian dies or becomes incapacitated? In that case, the successor custodian named by the original custodian takes over. If no successor custodian was ever named, typically the minor's guardian will be appointed the successor. If the child is age 14 or over, and no successor custodian has been named, and no guardian has been appointed, the child can name a successor custodian.

Disadvantage of the UGMA

The major disadvantage to making gifts through the UGMA (or UTMA) is that, by law, the property must be distributed to the child when he or she reaches a set statutory age, 21 in most states. In some states, the age at which the minor must receive the property is as low as 18 but can be extended to age 21 by the donor.

The 2503(c) Trust

Internal Revenue Code Section 2503(c) is a blueprint for income, gift, and estate tax savings if you want to accomplish those objectives by making significant gifts of income-producing property to minors.

Ask your attorney about the 2503(c) trust if your income tax bracket is high and your donee's bracket is relatively low. It's also highly useful if you own an asset that is likely to appreciate substantially over a period of time and you don't want it includable in your estate.

The illustration below assumes an annual contribution of $10,000 to a 2503(c) trust by a person in a 33 percent tax bracket. The rate of return is 5 percent. It also assumes the trust ends when the beneficiary reaches age 21. At that time, trust assets would be worth $331,714, a $53,236 advantage—solely from tax savings—over the $278,478 amount that would have been realized had the same donor accumulated the money on his own. The 2503(c) trust technique results in almost a 20 percent increase over the alternative of doing it without a trust:

2503(c) Trust Income-Shifting Worksheet

Annual contribution	$10,000
Rate of return	0.050
Donor's tax rate	0.330
Beneficiary's age (first year)	1
Beneficiary's age (at termination)	21
Future value of trust amount	**$331,714**
Future value outside of trust	**$278,478**
Future value of tax savings from trust	**$53,236**
Savings as a percentage of FV outside trust	**0.191**

Why trust 2503(c)?

Why use a trust to shift cash or other property to your children? Why not give it to them outright? The answer is that there are a number of very realistic objections to outright gifts to minors. Your stockbroker wouldn't deal with securities owned directly by a minor. That's because the law allows a minor to disaffirm either a purchase of stock that subsequently falls in value or a sale of stock that later increases in value.

Another objection to putting property in your child's name directly is that by doing so you freeze the title; your minor child's signature on a real estate deed doesn't give a buyer any assurance that he has acquired a permanent title.

Sure, you could petition a court to have a guardian appointed for your child. Once a legal guardian is appointed, many of the objections to an outright transfer could be overcome, but think of the aggravation and cost: Your child's guardian has to post bond and periodically must account for every transaction to a local court.

Requirements of a 2503(c) trust

Setting up a 2503(c) trust requires an attorney; the trust should be tailor-made to your situation. It should meet three requirements:

- The trust must provide that income and principal may be expended by or on behalf of your beneficiary at any time prior to the time the beneficiary reaches age 21 (21 is the age to be used no matter at what age a minor becomes an adult in your state).
- The trust must require that any income and principal will be payable to the beneficiary upon reaching 21. (Actually, you can have the trust last longer than your child's 21st birthday. It can last as long as you want it to provided that your child is given the right, when he/she reaches age 21, to take the money and other property in the trust. You could provide, for example, that your child has an absolute right to the property at that age, but if the principal is not withdrawn by a written request within three months of the child's 21st birthday, it remains in the trust until he/she is whatever age you select.)
- If your child dies before age 21, the principal must go to your child's estate or the person selected in his/her will.

Taxation of income

If the trust pays out income to the trust beneficiary, that income will be taxed to the beneficiary at his/her bracket (assuming the beneficiary is age 14 or older). If the beneficiary is under age 14, income paid out to such a child will be taxed under the kiddie tax rules discussed at the beginning of the chapter.

Sometimes income is accumulated by the trust rather than paid out. In that case, it is taxed to the trust. Eventually, when the accumulated income is paid out, your child is taxed on the money as if—in each of the years it was actually received by the trust—it had been received by your child. But your child, of course, receives credit for taxes paid by the trust. There's also a rule that exempts from tax all distributions of income accumulated in years he/she was under 21.

Watch out for tax traps! The key one is that the income earned by the trust will be taxed back to you if trust income is—or may be—used to pay premiums on a life insurance policy on your life or your spouse's life. (It is OK to use trust principal.) Trust income can be used to purchase insurance on the life of your child or anyone else, including your business associates. This may make it possible to set up a buy-sell agreement and enable a child working in the business to purchase a deceased business associate's interest.

Trust income will also be taxed to you if it is used to support your child, that is, to pay for his/her food, clothing and shelter. (In a few states, there are cases which hold that parents who can, with ease, meet the support needs of even an adult college-age child, may be considered obligated to provide such support, including college education funds, instead of drawing on a 2503(c) trust. If 2503(c), UGMA, or UTMA income is used to send a child to college, in some states the parent may be taxed on that income. Worse yet, in a few states, the trustee or custodian may be violating fiduciary duty by using such funds to pay for a college education when it is the parents' duty (thus making funds unavailable for the very purposes for which they were intended). We suggest you consult with an attorney who specializes in tax and trust law in your state before using trust income for college payments.

Gifts to a 2503(c) trust qualify for the gift tax annual exclusion. As long as the three requirements described previously are met, your gifts (up to $10,000 a year per donee if you are single or $20,000 if you are married) can be gift tax free.

Once a gift is made, all the future growth occurs in your child's estate—not in yours. Neither the gift nor the appreciation will be in your estate even if you die within three years of the gift.

Dr. Bruce, a foot surgeon in the 33 percent income tax bracket, and his wife, Eileen, set up a trust for each of their three children, Rickey, Steven, and Kim. Bruce put $5000 in cash into each of these trusts for his children. This year, since the trusts meet all the requirements of Section 2503(c), Bruce's gifts are tax free. Bruce pays no federal gift tax on the transfer, and the children pay no gift or income tax either.

If each $5000 investment earns 10 percent, the trust will receive and can pay out $500 per child. No tax will be paid on any of the $1500 total ($500 times three children). But if Bruce had not set up the trusts, he would have lost 33 percent of $1500, or $495, in taxes each year. Stated another way, over a ten-year period, $4950 in tax savings will help put Bruce and Eileen's children through college. Furthermore, none of the $15,000 (3 × $5000) principal will be in Bruce's estate. If Bruce is in a 40 percent estate tax bracket, 40 percent of $15,000, or $6,000, is saved in federal estate taxes.

Pros and cons

No estate planning tools and techniques are perfect. Each has a cost, and almost all have alternatives. Many of the objectives you would accomplish through the use of a 2503(c) trust can be met through a Uniform Gifts to Minors Act account. So why use a 2503(c) trust?

If you plan to make only one property or cash transfer and you anticipate that gift will be a relatively modest one, use the UGMA or UTMA account. In Dr. Bruce's example, the complexity and expense of creating a 2503(c) trust will probably outweigh its utility. But if you plan on making significant additional gifts in the future, you may want the additional flexibility of a 2503(c) trust (and the guarantee that your child can't take any principal until age 21 at the earliest).

Your decision may be made for you. Certain property can't be held safely inside a 2503(c) trust. For instance, if a gift of stock in an S corporation (see Chapter 16) is given to a 2503(c) trust, the special treatment allowed to such corporations may be inadvertently lost. Conversely, a UGMA account can only hold certain types of property. One common type of property it can't hold in some states is real estate. Fortunately, you can make a gift of real estate to your child through a 2503(c) trust or in many states through an UTMA account.

Another reason you may want to use a 2503(c) trust instead of the UGMA or UTMA account is custodianship. Under UGMA or UTMA laws, you can only name one person as a custodian. When you establish a trust, you can name any number of trustees and have two or more of them acting together. You can even designate a line of successor trustees, but do not name yourself as either trustee or successor trustee. (If you do name yourself as trustee and you die before your child is 21, the value of the assets you put in the trust will be in your estate and become subject to tax even though you transferred them into the trust many years ago.)

One disadvantage of using trusts in which the principal doesn't return is a loss of control over the principal. Consider this technique: Assume you have sold some property and taken back the mortgage. You are now the owner of, say, a fully amortizing 10-year note. The note will be worthless at the end of its term. Transfer it to an irrevocable trust. Another example: Transfer to the trust only the amount that you calculate will be enough to pay for your child's education when interest is added. The trust won't revert to you, but since the money will be totally exhausted whether or not you place it in the trust, the tax savings should outweigh any loss of control.

Thirteen Ways to Shift Income and Save Taxes

There are still many ways to shift both wealth and income and save taxes while setting up a college education fund for your children:

1. Give a series EE U.S. Savings Bond that will not mature until after the donee/child is age 14. No tax will be payable until the bond is redeemed. At that time the gain will be taxed at the child's relatively lower tax bracket. Remember that this strategy will not work if the child already owns Series EE bonds and is already reporting each year's interest accrual as income. Once the election to report income currently is made, it is irrevocable.

    Say you give an EE bond to your 9-year-old. Income from the bond would ordinarily be taxed at your bracket, but there isn't any tax if you elect to defer. The bond can be cashed in after the child reaches 14. At that point, the proceeds will be taxed to him, not you. Your goal of shifting income into a lower tax bracket will have been achieved.

2. Give growth stocks (or growth stock mutual funds) which pay little or no current dividends. The child will, therefore, pay no tax currently and can hold the stock until reaching age 14. Upon a sale, the child will be taxed at the child's bracket.

3. Give *deep discount* tax-free municipal bonds that mature on or after the child's 14th birthday. The bond interest will be tax free to the child, and the discount (face less cost basis) will be taxed to the child at the child's bracket when the bond is redeemed at maturity.

4. Employ your children. Pay them a reasonable salary for work they actually perform. Remember that the new law standard deduction for children is the greater of (a) $500 or (b) earned income (up to a 1987 limit of $2540). Regardless of how much is paid to the child, the business will have a deduction at its tax bracket, and the amount will be taxable to the child at the child's bracket. Furthermore, the child could establish an IRA to shelter income further.

5. Consider the multiple advantages of a *term of years* charitable remainder trust for children over age 14—so the income will be taxed to the child, but the grantor will receive an immediate income tax deduction.

6. In making gifts to your children, consider support obligation cases. These cases hold that parents who can with ease meet the support needs of even an adult college-age child may be considered obligated to provide support. If UGMA or UTMA or 2503(c) trust funds are used to send a child to college, will the parent be taxed? Worse yet, do these cases mean the UGMA custodian (or 2503(c) trustee) violates a fiduciary duty by using such funds to pay for a college education when it's the parent's duty (thus making such funds unavailable for the very purpose for which they were intended)?

7. Emphasis should now be placed on *convertible planning*—the use of a *value shift* followed at the appropriate time by an *income shift*. For example, a GRIT (Grantor Retained Income Trust) would retain for a trust grantor the right to all trust income for a specified number of years. At the end of that time, all income and principal will go to the grantor's child (who by then will be 14 or older). None of the principal or appreciation will be in the grantor's estate if the grantor survives the trust term. (Consider a savings clause that terminates the trust in favor of the grantor if tax law is changed to provide that a completed gift does not occur until the donor's interest is terminated.)

   Consider the split purchase of an asset with the child. The parent buys and keeps an interest (either for life or a specified term of years), while the child buys and keeps the remainder. This can save estate taxes and generate current income tax deductions for the parent. The child's purchase money should come from the other parent, a grandparent, or some source other than the other owner-parent.

8. Life insurance and annuity policies which stay within statutory guidelines (ask for written guarantee from the insurance company

home office) of life insurance should be particularly attractive, assuming *loading* costs are relatively low and/or backended. This includes universal, variable, and traditional whole life of the single, annual, and limited-payment types. In the case of the SPWL (Single Premium Whole Life), the entire single premium paid at purchase starts earning the declared interest rate immediately. The cost of insurance and expenses is recovered by the insurer from the difference between the declared interest rate and the rate the insurer actually earns. If surrendered, any unrecovered expenses are deducted from the policy's cash values. The owner can obtain cash values at any time by (1) surrender (gain over cost is taxable) or (2) loan (loan interest is probably nondeductible). Interest is charged at about the same rate credited on borrowed sums and is free of current tax. Earnings compound free of current taxation. Unlike tax-free municipal bonds, there is no market risk, and SPWL is highly liquid. A parent can purchase the product on his or her own life, which makes college education for the children more likely, and the parent does not have to give up control or make a gift.

9. Concentrate on gift and estate tax savings devices such as the annual exclusion. Parents should consider gifting $10,000–$20,000 a year of non-income-producing assets to a minor's trust or custodial account, which could be converted into income-producing assets slowly after the child turns age 14. The fund can become self-liquidating and exhaust itself by the time the child finishes college/graduate school.

10. Form a family partnership. Suppose you buy a small apartment or office building that's generating taxable income. If you set up a partnership consisting of several members in your family, the tax liability will be spread out among them in proportion to their interests in the partnership.

    According to the tax rules, a family partnership can be used for income-shifting purposes only if the income comes from tangible property, such as a building. But even with that restriction, you have a great deal of flexibility. For instance, you can keep control of the business, even though family members are co-owners. Also, under the law, you may be able to specially allocate some of the tax breaks to yourself if you meet the technical requirements.

11. Transfer ownership of a business. The best kind of business for income-shifting purposes is one in which you yourself perform no services, or only incidental ones. Then you can set up an S corporation (see Chapter 16) and give shares of the corporation to your children. The S corporation would pay no corporate income taxes itself, and your children would pay income taxes on their share of the profits at *their* bracket if they are 14 or over or at *your* bracket

until they reach age 14. Those profits would otherwise have been taxed to you at your bracket.

The S corporation works best when you perform only minimal services—or none. (If you did perform services that produced all the income from the corporation, the IRS would argue that earnings are really yours and, therefore, are taxable to you. That defeats your purpose.) If you're a passive investor, income from the business channeled into an S corporation doesn't result from any services you perform. So your income could be shifted without challenge.

If you're setting up an S corporation for income-shifting purposes, you must follow your attorney's advice carefully. If you issue stock in your children's names, but never invite them to shareholders' meetings or distribute only nominal profits to them, the IRS will likely treat the arrangement as a sham.

12. Borrow money your 14-year-old child has been given by other relatives. Pay a rate of interest higher than he or she was getting before. You increase the child's income. You deduct interest (to the extent of your investment income). And your child reports it on his or her return at his or her tax bracket.

13. Have a UGMA or UTMA custodian purchase *nongovernmental purpose* municipal bonds. Although taxpayers who purchase these bonds after August 7, 1986, must treat the income from them as a preference item for purposes of computing the alternative minimum tax, they are a great buy for funding the college education of children. First, to compensate for the potential minimum tax liability, these bonds will probably be paying 1/2 to 3/4 percent more than public purpose municipal bonds. Second, because there is a $30,000 floor before any AMT is imposed, it's not likely that most children will ever pay a tax on income from these bonds.

20

Sophisticated Planning Techniques

Sophisticated planning techniques are—as the name implies—aggressive leading edge techniques to shift asset values and save hundreds of thousands of dollars of death taxes and other costs. The three techniques discussed—SPLITs (split ownership of property), GRITs (Grantor Retained Income Trusts), and RITs (Remainder Interest Transactions)—should not be attempted without the advice of expert tax counsel.

SPLITs (Split Ownership of Property)

Split ownership of property can:

- Reduce your current income tax.
- Reduce your potential estate tax.
- Enable you to transfer substantial wealth without the imposition of a gift tax.
- Enable you to potentially take as much as $2 in deductions for every dollar that is invested.
- Enable you potentially to convert nondepreciable assets such as stocks and bonds into amortizable assets on which basis may be recovered.

Split ownership consists of a purchase of property in which one party (you) purchases a "life estate" and the second party (your child) buys a remainder interest in income-producing investment property. Ownership of property can be broken down into two elements:

1. The first element, a *life estate,* is the right to use, possess, or enjoy the property and the income it produces for as long as the holder of that life estate lives.
2. The second element, a *remainder interest,* is the balance of the property interest not owned by the life tenant. When the life tenant dies, the holder of the remainder interest, the *remainderman,* receives by operation of law all of the interest in that property.

When there is a split purchase, the senior and junior family members enter into a split purchase arrangement to buy an income-producing asset, securities, or tangible property. The senior family member, for example, the father, acquires the life income interest in the asset. The junior family member, for example, the son, acquires the remainder interest. Each must pay his proportional share of the cost based upon Internal Revenue Service tables that determine the value of life estates and the remainders at different age levels.

Purchasing the investment

For example, assume a 50-year-old father is a wealthy real estate investor and developer who is about to purchase a $1 million office building. The father is already in both the 50 percent estate tax bracket and the maximum income tax bracket. He has a son, to whom he wants to shift wealth. But the father already has exhausted both his annual exclusion and his unified credit. The father also wants to reduce his current income tax burden.

To meet these goals, the father and son purchase the $1 million office building. The father purchases a life estate in the property. At age 50, the father must pay 84.743 percent of the value of the $1 million asset, or $847,430.

The son buys the remainder interest. This includes the right to the building and the land, whatever it is worth, at the father's death. The son must pay $1 million less the $847,430 amount paid by the life tenant. In other words, the son must pay $152,570, 15.257 percent of the purchase price.

Advantages of SPLITs

1. All income, as defined by state law, will be paid to the father as life tenant as long as he lives. Note that the father will receive income on the entire $1,000,000 investment even though he has only invested $847,430. So he receives income on the son's $152,570 investment and, therefore, has *leveraged* his own assets.

Furthermore, the father, as life tenant, pays and, therefore, can deduct all expense and maintenance costs. These payments help "defund" the father's estate and enrich the son. This furthers the asset-shifting potential of this technique.

2. Since the life estate ceases at the life tenant's death, no property interest subject to federal estate tax inclusion is transferred. The $1 million, *plus* appreciation, that might otherwise have been included in the father's estate, is never subject to federal transfer tax. Assuming the father lives to age 78, an additional 28 years, and assuming appreciation in the property at 10 percent per year, at the father's death the property would be worth about $16 million. By utilizing our split purchase technique, the father has saved approximately $8 million in estate taxes.

3. Also, probate costs are significantly reduced because of the automatic ownership shift at the life tenant's death. If the property in question is an out-of-state property, ancillary administration is avoided as well.

4. Since there is no gift, there is no gift tax. The father pays the full fair market value for his interest. The son pays the full fair market value for his interest. Since the price is set by negotiation with a third party and not between father and son, the purchase price is presumably the fair market value.

5. The father has purchased an asset which diminishes in value to zero by the date of his death. Tax law allows recovery of capital in the form of a current amortization deduction as long as the property purchased is held for the production of income.

This deduction is available even if the investment itself is *not* depreciable. A purchaser of a life or other terminable interest may amortize the purchaser's capital investment over the life of the estate so acquired. Therefore, had the father and son purchased even intangible assets (such as a portfolio of stocks or bonds), the father could amortize the cost of that life estate—in this case $847,430—on a straight-line basis over the remainder of the father's projected life expectancy. Also, this amortization deduction can be used to offset income generated by either the split purchased property or income from some other investment property source.

6. The son receives total interest in the asset at the instant of the father's death. If the father dies relatively soon after the split purchase, the son's return on his investment is incredibly high. But even if the parent lives well beyond his life expectancy and if the property continues to appreciate, the continued amortization deductions taken by the father, which translate into capital eventually transferred to the son, will maximize the potential total intrafamily asset-shifting advantage of this technique.

7. Finally, the split purchase technique can be *unwound*. The parties should sign an agreement at the time of the purchase contracting that, upon a specified event or a subsequent joint agreement of the parties, the asset will be sold and each party will receive his actuarially appropriate share of the net proceeds.

Disadvantages and tax traps of SPLITs

There are, as with every planning tool, costs or disadvantages. These include:

1. Unless the split purchased asset is sold, the life tenant has no access to the principal. State law determines the respective rights, powers and duties of the parties unless specified by an agreement as described above. Also, the life tenant cannot mortgage a split purchased property without the consent of the remainderman.

2. With very elderly parents, the joint purchase loses its effectiveness. The reason for this is that the very elderly person pays a relatively lower percentage of the value of the asset. Therefore, the child must pay a much greater amount. For example, if the father were 90, he would pay 28 percent. The son would pay 72 percent of the purchase price of the asset.

This disadvantage can be minimized if the life income beneficiaries are married and the life income interest is structured to last for their joint lives. The value of the remainder interest is reduced because it will become due only upon the death of the surviving income beneficiary.

Assume the father was not 50, but was 65. Under current IRS tables, the father's life interest would be 67.97 percent of the full value of the property, or $679,700. The son's remainder interest would be 32.03 percent, requiring him to contribute $320,300 as his share of the purchase price. This is twice as much as he would have had to pay had the father been only 50 years old.

However, if the father and mother—both aged 65—obtain a joint interest in the specified property that will last until the second of them dies, the value of the remainder factor will be far less than it would be with a single life interest. The value of the son's remainder interest drops from 32.03 percent to 19.18 percent. This means that the son would need to contribute only $191,800 toward the purchase price.

If the father and mother were younger, the value of the remainder interest would continue to shrink. For example, the value of a remainder interest after the death of a 52-year-old husband and a 50-year-old wife will be only 7.23 percent of the face value of the property. Under those circumstances, the son would be required to pay only $72,300 for his remainder interest in the $1,000,000 property.

3. A step-up in basis is lost with this joint purchase technique. At the father's death, the son will not receive a step-up in basis for any asset which was purchased jointly. This increases potential future tax liability upon a sale by the son after the parent's death.

4. If the son used money received as a gift from his father to finance his portion of the joint purchase, the IRS may "collapse" the transaction. It could call the result a gift by the parent to the child of the remainder interest. The result could be the imposition of gift taxes as well as estate tax inclusion. The IRS would argue that the father has made a gift with a retained life estate.

5. Unintended potentially taxable gifts may occur if:

(a) Either party pays more than his share of the initial purchase price; or

(b) Either party makes improvements to the property that enhance its value or extends its useful life and the contribution—computed at time the improvement is made—is more than his share.

(c) Financing is used to purchase the asset, and the proceeds are not shared or repayments are not made in an actuarially correct manner. Life tenant and remainderman should allocate debt proportionally.

Closely held stock is not good property for this technique because it is difficult to value accurately and because it does not pay steady income. The IRS might claim that it is not a life estate if it pays no income.

A property owner who "creates" a life interest in property by selling a remainder interest to a younger family member will not be able to amortize his interest. (It is essential that the split purchased property be acquired in an arms' length transaction from a third party.) If such an interest is sold for less than full and adequate consideration, a potential gift tax liability may arise. Any attempt to convey a preowned asset through third parties for purposes of reacquiring it subject to a split purchase would likely be successfully attacked by the IRS as a step transaction.

Unexpected results

Finally, some assumptions and expectations may not be realized. These assumptions include:

- Asset yield.
- Asset appreciation.
- Parent's marginal tax rate.
- Parent's estate tax bracket.
- Child's opportunity to invest contribution elsewhere at a higher net return.
- Existence or utility of amortization and depreciation deductions.

Terms for Years—Split Interest

Rather than structuring the split purchase as a life estate and a remainder interest, it can be structured as a term for years and a remainder interest. For example, assume the 50-year-old father only wanted income from the property until he retired at age 65. Also, assume that the property was a bond portfolio yielding 9 percent. The father would purchase a 15-year term, and his son would purchase the remainder interest. The value of the remainder interest would be .239392 multiplied by $1 million, or $239,392. Consequently, the father would have to pay $760,608 for his interest.

This $760,608 could then be amortized over the 15-year period providing the father with a yearly deduction of $50,707. Of the $90,000 in yearly income from the portfolio—9 percent of $1 million, the father would only pay taxes on $39,293 ($90,000 minus $50,707). In effect, by purchasing only a term for years, the father has created his own tax shelter.

While the term purchase rather than a life estate magnifies the value of current deductions, it is not without substantial potential cost. With a term split purchase, the father must face at least one Hobson's choice: Either he loses the property and its income prior to death or, if he dies during the term period, the value of his interest will be included in his estate. The amount included would be the present value of the right to the property during his unexpired term. There would be, however, no federal estate tax problem if the right to the property for the unexpired term were left in a qualifying manner to a surviving spouse.

Summary of split purchases

To make this technique work, you must invest in an expert estate planning attorney. That person must evaluate your health, income tax concerns, potential estate tax liability, as well as your desire to effectuate intrafamily value shifting.

GRITs (Grantor Retained Income Trusts)

An irrevocable trust is established. The trustee is directed to pay to the grantor the income from the trust for a specified number of years. When the grantor's interest terminates, the property in the trust is distributed outright to family members, or in some cases, the trust continues for their benefit or makes a distribution to a uniform gifts to minors account or 2503(c) trust.

At the time the trust is funded, a gift is made. The value of that gift is the excess of (a) the value of the property transferred over, or (b) the value of the interest retained by the grantor.

For example, if the trust will run for 11 years and $100,000 was placed into the trust, the value of the (nontaxable) interest retained by the grantor is $64,951.

The value of the (taxable) remainder interest would be the value of the capital placed into the trust ($100,000) minus the value of the nontaxable interest retained by the grantor ($64,951). Therefore, the taxable portion of the grantor retained income trust gift would be $35,049.

Grantor Retained Income Trust (GRIT)

Interest Retained by Grantor	
Number of years trust runs	11
Value of capital placed into trust	$100,000
Term certain factor	0.649506
Value of nontaxable interest retained by grantor	$64,951
Portion Subject to Gift Tax	
Value of capital placed into trust	$100,000
Value of nontaxable interest retained by grantor	$64,951
Gift taxable portion of GRIT	$35,049
After-tax rate at which property grows	0.05
Value of property at end of term	$171,034
Combined federal and state death tax bracket	0.50
Potential death tax savings	$85,517

This remainder interest, by definition, is a future interest gift and will not qualify for the annual exclusion. The donor will have to utilize all or part of the remaining unified credit (or if the credit is exhausted, pay the appropriate gift tax). If the grantor's income interest lasts long enough, however, the value of his or her retained interest would approach—actuarially—100 percent. This would eliminate any gift tax liability. For instance, at age 50, the value of the grantor's retained interest would be $99,148. Therefore, the gift portion would be worth only $852.

Advantage of the GRIT

The advantage of the GRIT is that it is possible for an individual to transfer significant amounts of cash or other assets to children or grandchildren or others but incur little or no gift tax. This leaves the entire amount intact for the ultimate beneficiaries, the remaindermen.

The GRIT is, as its name implies, a *grantor trust*. This means all income, gains, deductions, and credits are treated for income tax purposes as if there were no trust and these items were attributable directly to (and, therefore, taxable currently to) the grantor.

It appears that the perfect funding vehicle would be a very high yielding, tax-free municipal bond so that the grantor would pay no income tax (except for gains realized by the trust upon a sale of the bonds).

Disadvantage of the GRIT

The entire principal must be included in the estate of a grantor who dies during the term of the trust since he has retained a life interest for a period which, in fact, will not end before his death. If any gift tax had been paid upon the establishment of the GRIT, it would reduce the estate tax otherwise payable.

RITs (Remainder Interest Transactions)

It has long been possible to purchase a remainder interest (the right to property at the end of a given period of time such as at the death of the property owner or at the end of a specified term of time such as 10 or 15 years).

A remainder interest is what is left of an estate (typically, but not necessarily, an estate in land) when the prior estate terminates.

The life tenant can use and enjoy the property as long as he or she lives. The purchaser of the remainder interest will own—from the date of purchase—the right to use, possess, and enjoy the property at the death of the life tenant. So the purchase of a remainder interest is the current right to receive property in the future.

Government tables contain factors which state the present value of the right to an asset at the expiration of the life tenant. For example, the present value of a $1,000,000 asset today is $1,000,000. But if the buyer had to wait until the death of the current owner, a person who is currently age 65, the value would be a lot less. In fact, the value is $320,300 according to the government table (which currently assumes a discount rate of 10 percent). So, a son could buy the future right to stock worth $1,000,000 today for a lump sum of $320,300 if he were willing to wait until his father died to possess and vote the stock.

There are, of course, ways other than the payment of a lump sum to purchase an interest in property. For instance, the son could agree to pay his dad an income each year for the rest of his life. The son would have to pay his father (if the parties wanted to avoid gift tax implications) an annuity, starting at once, that was the actuarial equivalent of $320,300. To purchase the remainder interest in a $1,000,000 asset, the son, in this example, would be obligated to pay his father $47,124 a year for as long as his father lived.

If the father dies any time after the transfer, assuming a proper valuation and the government tables were followed accurately, there should be no estate tax on the transferred property. Why no estate tax? Because the property was sold for full and adequate consideration for what had been received. The father (aside from payments which had been received from the son and still held at death) had retained no property interest subject to tax.

The IRS has ruled privately that, if the sale of the remainder by a property owner is for full value of the remainder, as determined under the Treasury's actuarial tables, the property will not be includable in the seller's estate.

Only the portion of the basis allocated to the remainder interest may be subtracted from the consideration received in order to compute the gain or loss in the sale.

Even after the sale, the transferor will be entitled to all the depreciation on the property unless a trust is used. If a trust is used, the allocation specified in the trust agreement will control. If the agreement does not address this point, all of the depreciation can be taken by the life tenant (up to the life tenant's basis).

If the father dies prior to reaching life expectancy, it is obvious that the son has purchased the property for a considerable discount. Conversely, if the father outlives his life expectancy, the son will still have made a good investment if the property has been appreciating.

The numbers that follow illustrate the effect of a 65-year-old who sells a remainder interest in property worth $1,000,000 to his son who agrees, instead of paying a lump sum, to pay his father an income each year for as long as the father lives. This is called a *private annuity*.*

---

*The combination of a sale of a remainder interest coupled with payments in the form of a private annuity was popularized by attorney, Stephan R. Leimberg, and Memphis, Tennessee, attorney, A. Stephen McDaniel, in an article entitled "The Private Annuity Time Grab" revisited.

Annuitant's age	65
Basis of property	$600,000
Fair market value of entire assets	$1,000,000
Remainder factor at given age	0.32030
Remainder value	$320,300
P.V. factor of annuity at given age	6.7970
Annual payment to purchase remainder interest	$47,124

Tax-Free Portion of Each Payment

Basis of portion sold	$192,180
Life expectancy of transferor annuitant	20.0
Tax-free portion of each payment received	$9,609

Ordinary Income Portion

Annual payment		$47,124
Less:		
Tax-free portion	$9,609	
Equals:		
Ordinary income portion		$37,515

21

Protecting Yourself from the Problems of Old Age

Some problems seem to grow larger as we grow older. It is important to recognize the problems associated with old age and take whatever action is indicated now to prevent these problems from adversely affecting our future.

Problems Associated with Old Age

1. *Protection against disability.* Improved health care and longer life expectancies make disability planning especially important for older people. Ask yourself these questions. Do I have adequate disability insurance? What income will I receive from Social Security, my employer, and from other benefits if I am no longer capable of working? Can my investments provide me with adequate income?

2. *The need for someone to help manage your property.* Have I set up a trust or given a Durable Power of Attorney for someone to manage my money for me if I am physically or mentally incapable of taking care of it myself?

3. *Personal health care decisions.* What will happen to me if I am not capable of caring for myself? Have I given someone the right to make medical decisions for me if I am incapable of doing so? (Some states permit you to do so in a Power of Attorney.) Do I have a "Living Will?"

4. *Is your estate plan in order?* Are my wills up to date, my bank accounts set up properly, and are my life insurance beneficiary provisions exactly the way I want them?

5. *Are your assets set up to minimize death and other transfer taxes?* Tax laws have changed dramatically in the last 10 years. A well-drafted estate plan prepared just a few years ago may not be tax efficient today and should be reviewed.

6. *Last minute estate planning.* What can you do if you are aware that death is imminent?

How Disability Can Affect Your Personal Security

Consider the case of Sally who had been a longtime valued employee of the Ajax Insurance Company. She was now retired, with a pension and $60,000 in the bank. Sally had a few close friends with whom she played cards and went to the movies, but her only close relative was a brother who lived 2000 miles away. When Sally suffered a stroke, she was found in her apartment by the building superintendent and taken to the hospital. Although Sally had a will leaving all of her assets to her brother's children, she had made no plans to take care of herself in the event of disability.

How was Sally to receive the benefit of her pension and other assets if she was not physically capable of handling her money? Since she had not designated anyone to act on her behalf, someone had to be appointed to act for her. There was, however, a real problem as to who would institute the appropriate court proceedings to have someone appointed to manage Sally's property. The Orphans' Court (or other appropriate court in the state where Sally lived) could permit the director of the hospital where Sally was a patient to ask the court to appoint someone to take care of Sally. Or the court could insist that Sally's brother petition the court to name someone to take care of Sally, since he was her closest relative.

In order for the court to appoint someone to act for Sally (most states call that person a "guardian" or a "committee"), Sally would have to be declared legally incompetent. How does a court go about deciding if someone is legally incompetent? It must have professional testimony, most likely from a psychiatrist, that Sally was incapable of handling her own money. Once appointed, Sally's "guardian" would be responsible for accounting to the court as to their use of Sally's money.

What could Sally have done to avoid this situation? As a matter of fact, Sally had several very important options available to her.

The living trust

Sally could have set up a revocable living trust, (discussed in Chapter 7). If Sally had sat down with a trust officer at the bank where she deposited her pension checks, for example, he could have explained the advantages to Sally of the revocable living trust. If Sally had permitted the trust department of the bank to handle her investments for her, she could have put a provision in the trust for the bank to be "trustee" and to apply the income from her trust for her benefit if she became disabled. She also could have given her Trustee the right to use principal for Sally's benefit if it was necessary. Then, when she was hospitalized, someone from the bank would have been in touch with Sally, would have advised the hospital that the bank was the trustee for Sally, and that all bills should be forwarded to it. Sally's doctors could have been assured that there were funds available for Sally to receive the finest care. Arrangements could have been made for Sally to be placed in a health care facility so that her convalescence could be accelerated. Since the bank was already handling

Sally's money, Sally's disability would have no negative effect on Sally's investments.

Stand-by trust

If Sally wanted to have the bank handle her affairs only in the event she became disabled, but did not want to turn over control of her investments to the bank at the present time, she could have prepared a *standby* or *step-up* trust with the bank. Under this trust, the bank only takes over Sally's investments when Sally is no longer able to handle them herself. How does the bank know when Sally can no longer handle her own funds? Either Sally tells the bank, or the trust provides for Sally's doctor or a member of Sally's family or a friend to advise the bank to activate Sally's trust.

The durable power of attorney

If Sally wanted to invest her own money while she was capable, but wanted to have someone else—a relative, friend, or bank—act for her if she became disabled, Sally could have given that person a power of attorney.

Another case: Ben was in his midfifties and always enjoyed good health. He owned a very successful men's clothing business and personally supervised every phase of the business himself. He did the buying for the business, was his own best salesman, wrote all of the checks and even kept the books himself. He provided very well for his wife, Betty, and their three children. When Ben suffered a stroke on the way home from work, both Betty's and Ben's business were in serious trouble. Since all of the bank accounts for the business were in Ben's name, Betty could not sign the checks to take care of the payroll at the end of the week or to pay for any of the merchandise. When Betty consulted a lawyer, she was told that, since Ben was not competent to take care of his own affairs, it would be necessary for Betty to go to court and have a guardian appointed for Ben and have him declared incompetent.

You are perfectly healthy and have no reason to think you'll be anything but healthy for years to come. Yet Sally, Ben, and you may at some time all have a common need—a need for someone to act on your behalf if you can't.

One of the most effective methods by which an individual can protect himself against the possibility of future mental incompetency is the durable power of attorney. You have the right to designate someone to act for you and to give that person permission to perform just about any legal acts that you could otherwise do for yourself. Technically, a durable power of attorney is a power of attorney by which a person designates another his "attorney-in-fact." In order to make a power of attorney *durable,* the writing must contain the words, "this power of attorney shall not be affected by my subsequent disability or incapacity" (or words with similar meaning).

In many states, it is also possible to appoint someone as your attorney-in-fact only at some future date if you become disabled. This is called a *springing power of attorney,* which does not go into effect immediately, but will only become effective if the person giving the power of attorney becomes disabled in the future.

There are many instances where a power of attorney can be valuable even if you are not disabled. For instance, you may be out of the country, and complex financial affairs may require immediate decisions in your absence. A power of attorney is an expedient and inexpensive method of appointing someone to act for you, in the event that you are unable for any reason to act for yourself.

But because it involves a transfer of your authority to someone else, it should only be given to a person in whom the donor (the person who gives the power of attorney) has complete confidence. Because of the many different powers that can be contained in the power of attorney, and the necessity to conform to the wording of the various states' statutes in order to make certain that the power of attorney will be durable (continue to be effective despite future disability), it should definitely be prepared by an attorney.

Perhaps the best way to illustrate how broad or how many different individual powers you may want to consider using is to examine the provisions of an actual power of attorney.

POWER OF ATTORNEY*

KNOW ALL MEN BY THESE PRESENTS, that I, ERIC JASON ROSEN-BLOOM, hereby revoke any general power of attorney that I have heretofore given to any person, and by these Presents do constitute, make and appoint BRETT ALAN ROSENBLOOM my true and lawful attorney:

1. To ask, demand, sue for, recover and receive all sums of money, debts, goods, merchandise, chattels, effects and things of whatsoever nature or description which are now or hereafter shall be or become owing, due, payable, or belonging to me in or by any right whatsoever, and upon receipt thereof, to make, sign, execute and deliver such receipts, releases or other discharges for the same, respectively, as he shall think fit.

2. To sign checks, drafts and other instruments or otherwise make withdrawals from any checking, savings, transaction or other deposit account in my name, and to endorse checks payable to me and receive the proceeds thereof in cash or otherwise; to open and close checking, savings, transaction or other deposit accounts in my name; to purchase and redeem savings certificates, certificates of deposit or similar instruments in my name; to execute and deliver receipts for any funds withdrawn or certificates redeemed; and to do all acts regarding any checking account, savings account, savings certificate, certificate of deposit or similar instrument which I now have or may hereafter acquire, the same as I could do if personally present.

---

*Adapted from *The Tools and Techniques of Estate Planning,* 6th Edition: The National Underwriter Company, Cincinnati, Ohio.

3. To borrow money for my account on whatever terms and conditions may be deemed advisable, including the right to borrow money on any insurance policies issued on my life for any purpose without any obligation on the part of such insurance company to determine the purpose for such loan or application of the proceeds, and to pledge, assign, and deliver the policy or policies as security.

4. To make loans, secured or unsecured, in such amounts, upon such terms, with or without interest and to such firms, corporations, and persons as shall be appropriate.

5. To have access to and control over the contents of any safe deposit box rented by me, to rent safe deposit boxes in my name, to close out and execute and deliver receipts for safe deposit boxes in my name, and to do all acts regarding any safe deposit box which I now have or may hereafter acquire, the same as I could do if personally present.

6. To invest in my name in any stock, shares, bonds (including U.S. Treasury Bonds referred to as "flower bonds"), securities or other property, real or personal, and to vary such investments as he, in his sole discretion, may deem best.

7. To purchase, sell, repair, alter, manage and dispose of personal property at private sale or public sale of every kind and nature, and to sign, seal, execute and deliver assignments and bills of sale therefor.

8. To purchase or otherwise acquire any interest in and possession of real property and to accept all deeds for such property on my behalf; and to manage, repair, improve, maintain, restore, build, or develop any real property in which I now have or may have an interest.

9. To lease, sublease, sell, transfer, convey and mortgage any real property owned by me, including my residence, or in which I have an interest, upon such terms and conditions and under such covenants as he shall think fit, and to sign, seal, execute and deliver deeds and conveyances therefor.

10. To vote at meetings of shareholders or other meetings of any corporation or company in which I have an interest and to execute any proxies or other instruments in connection therewith.

11. To continue the operation of any business belonging to me or in which I have an interest for such time and in such manner as my attorney may deem advisable or to sell or liquidate or incorporate any business, or interest therein, at such time and on such terms as he may deem advisable and in my best interest.

12. To commence, prosecute, discontinue or defend all actions or other legal proceedings pertaining to me or my estate or any part thereof; to settle, compromise, or submit to arbitration any debt, demand or other right or matter due me or concerning my estate as he, in his sole discretion, shall deem best and for such purpose to execute and deliver such releases, discharges or other instruments as he may deem necessary and advisable.

13. To prepare, sign and file federal, state or local income, gift or other tax returns of all kinds, claims for refund, requests for extensions of time, petitions to the tax court or other courts regarding tax matters and any and all other tax related documents, including, without limitation, receipts, offers, waivers, consents, powers of attorney, closing agreements; to exercise any elections I may have under federal, state or local tax law; and generally to act in my behalf in all tax matters of all kinds and for all periods before all persons representing the Internal Revenue Service and any other taxing authority, including receipt of confidential information and the posting of bonds.

14. To employ lawyers, investment counsel, accountants, physicians and other persons to render services for or to me or my estate and to pay the usual and reasonable fees and compensation of such persons for their services.

15. To make gifts to my parents in such amounts as my attorney deems proper.

16. To make additions to an existing trust for my benefit, to create a trust for my benefit, and to withdraw and receive the income or corpus of a trust for my benefit.

17. To disclaim any interest in property and to renounce or resign from fiduciary positions.

18. To authorize my admission to a medical, nursing, residential or similar facility and to enter into agreements for my care; and to authorize, arrange for, consent to, waive and terminate any and all medical and surgical procedures on my behalf, including the administration of drugs, or to withhold such consent.

19. To procure, alter, extend or cancel insurance against any and all risks affecting property and persons, and against liability, damage or claims of any sort.

20. To execute, deliver, and acknowledge deeds, deeds of trust, covenants, indentures, agreements, mortgages, hypothecations, bills of lading, bills, bonds, notes, receipts, evidences of debts, releases and satisfactions of mortgage, judgments, ground rents and other debts.

In addition to the powers and discretion herein specifically given and conferred upon my attorney, and notwithstanding any usage or custom to the contrary, my attorney shall have the full power, right and authority to do, perform and to cause to be done and performed all such acts, deeds and matters in connection with my property and estate as he, in his sole discretion, shall deem reasonable, necessary, desirable and proper, as fully, effectually and absolutely as if he were the absolute owner and possessor thereof.

In the event of my disability or incompetency, from whatever cause, this power of attorney shall not thereby be revoked.

IN WITNESS WHEREOF, I have hereunto set my hand and seal this
day of   , 1988.

WITNESSED:

_____   _____ (SEAL)
                                 ERIC JASON ROSENBLOOM

_____

STATE OF   :
                                 :   SS
COUNTY OF   :

Before me, the undersigned, a Notary Public within and for the County of   , State of   , personally appeared ERIC JASON ROSENBLOOM, known to me to be the person whose name is subscribed to the within instrument, and acknowledged that he executed the same for the purposes therein contained.

IN WITNESS WHEREOF, I have hereunto set my hand and official seal this　　　　day of　　　　, 1988.

How a Power of Attorney Can Save Taxes

There are no adverse tax implications to setting up a power of attorney as it does not shift any property rights; it merely authorizes someone to perform certain acts on your behalf.

But tax savings may result. Larry was extremely ill. Shortly before lapsing into a coma, Larry signed a power of attorney that authorized his son to make gifts up to $10,000 each to a number of related donees on Larry's behalf. These were all beneficiaries Larry had named in his will. It also authorized the son to purchase flower bonds, government bonds that could be purchased at a discount and used to help pay Larry's federal estate tax.

The son immediately used $100,000 from Larry's checking and savings accounts to make gifts of $10,000 each to the ten children and grandchildren Larry had named in his will. Since Larry was still alive on January 2nd of the following year, his son liquidated a number of nonappreciated assets, put the proceeds into Larry's checking account, and repeated the gift, giving $10,000 each to ten donees on Larry's behalf.

Even if Larry died within a day or two of the second round of gifts, not one penny of the $200,000 total would be in Larry's estate. Because of the $10,000 per donee annual gift tax exclusion, the entire $200,000 of gifts would be federal gift-tax free as well. If Larry's estate were in the 40 percent federal estate tax bracket, the savings in federal estate tax would be 40 percent of $200,000 or $80,000.

The son also used his power of attorney right to buy flower bonds on Larry's behalf. This made it possible to pay $100,000 of federal estate tax at a cost of only $85,000 of cash. Still further tax dollars and aggravation were saved by the power of attorney which gave Larry's son the right to prepare and sign Larry's income and gift tax returns on his behalf.

Naturally, as is the case with every other planning device, the durable power of attorney should not be considered a panacea or a solution to all of your problems. But in many cases, a power of attorney will be a powerful yet inexpensive estate planning tool. Ask your lawyer if you should have a power of attorney.

A Living Will

Consider a living will. In this era of modern technology, we all have thought about our right to die. Many people have expressed a desire that extraordinary means should not be employed to prolong their lives. Some states (including Arkansas, California, Idaho, New Mexico, North Carolina, Oregon, and Texas) have already enacted laws making it easier for doctors or family members to honor your wishes. In other states, a specimen document will have no legal effect. But certainly, the declaration of desires (see opposite page), if properly executed while you are competent, will help a physician and relatives follow your wishes more readily than if you had signed no such document, even in states that have not passed right-to-die laws. Give a copy of the signed living will (our specimen is based on one designed in a project of the Yale Law School) to your personal physician and to appropriate family members and discuss your thoughts and desires with them (and your attorney).

Proposed Living Will

DECLARATION MADE THIS _____ DAY OF _____
I, _____ being of sound mind, willfully and voluntarily make known my desire that my dying shall not be artificially prolonged under the circumstances set forth below, do hereby declare:

If at any time I should have an incurable injury, disease or illness certified to be a terminal condition by two physicians who have personally examined me, one of whom shall be my attending physician, and the physicians have determined that my death will occur whether or not life-sustaining procedures are utilized and where application of life-sustaining procedures would serve only to artificially prolong the dying process, I direct that such procedures be withheld or withdrawn and that I be permitted to die naturally with only the administration of medication or the performance of any medical procedures deemed necessary to alleviate pain and provide me with comfort care.

In the absence of my ability to give directions regarding the use of such life-sustaining procedures, it is my intention that this declaration shall be honored by my family and physicians as the final expression of my legal right to refuse medical or surgical treatment and accept the consequences from such refusal.

I understand the full import of this declaration and I am emotionally and mentally competent to make this decision.

Signed _____

City, County, _____

State of Residence _____

The declarant has been personally known to me and I believe him or her to be of sound mind.

Witness _____

Witness _____

What to Do When Your Time Is Limited

There are a great many things you can do if you are aware that the death of a family member—or yourself—is imminent. An incredible amount of tax and administration expense dollars can be saved if you are willing to act decisively:

1.   Certain bank loans for automobile loans, home mortgages, home improvements, and other business and personal loans permit or may even require the purchase of group (no exam required) creditor life insurance. Borrow the money, obtain the insurance, and spread out the repayment of the loan over as long a period as possible.

2.   If you own permanent life insurance and you are disabled, call your agent to see if you have a disability waiver of premium. If you do, and you've met the requirements to have your premiums waived, the insurer will repay every dollar of premium you've paid after you became totally disabled. It will also take over the premium payments for you, and your policy will stay in full force. Dividends and cash value will continue to increase as though you were still paying premiums.

3.   If you don't have waiver of premium or it doesn't apply, talk to your insurance agent and other counselors about extended term. You can stop paying premiums and still be covered for the full death benefit under the policy.

4.   Buy flower bonds if your advisors have guesstimated there will be significant federal estate taxes to be paid. Flower bonds (see Chapter 14) are special U.S. government bonds you can buy even on your deathbed (or have the person with your power of attorney purchase for you). These bonds can be bought at a discount and are redeemable at their face value in payment of the federal estate tax. Keep in mind that these bonds must be purchased while you are alive; your executor can't do it for you.

5.   Increasing your salary may enlarge death benefits under certain fringe benefit plans. If you control your business and your pension, group insurance to other benefits are based on a multiple of salary, an increase in salary could have a multiplier effect. In other words, if your group insurance, for example, is two times your salary, every dollar of increased salary increases your group coverage by two dollars.

How to Reduce Transfer Taxes

6.   If you haven't changed your will since September 13, 1981, your estate may not be eligible for the unlimited federal estate marital deduction. Roughly half of your estate may be subjected to federal estate tax— needlessly! Call your attorney to review your will and/or trust.

7.   Repay life insurance policy loans. Why? Because in most states, a dollar of life insurance is worth more to your beneficiaries than a dollar of cash in the bank (or anyplace else). The reason is that most states treat life insurance more favorably than other assets. Some states exclude life insurance totally from state death taxes. Many other states exempt a large part of insurance proceeds. Repaying policy loans will also reduce the size of your probate estate and help save on administrative expenses.

8. If you've named your estate as beneficiary of your life insurance, change it—*Now!* You may have needlessly subjected the insurance to state inheritance taxes as well as to the claims of creditors.

9. If you plan to make gifts to a charity in your will, don't wait—do it *Now!* A lifetime gift results in an income tax reduction that you wouldn't have had otherwise. You are probably in a higher (lifetime income) tax bracket than your estate's tax bracket. That means a current deduction will be more valuable.

Personal Touches

There are a number of things you can do to make it easier for your executor and other family members. These include:

10. Tell the appropriate people where your safe deposit box is and the location of your keys.

11. Arrange for successor management-or-sale-of your business. (It's far easier for you to do these things than your uninformed and emotionally distraught successors.)

12. Prepare a list of advisors (names, addresses, phone numbers) and discuss with your family which ones can be relied upon for various advice and assistance.

13. Prepare a letter to various family members (some people call these *letters of instruction*). This is a personal nonlegal document explaining your wishes with respect to how family heirlooms are to be distributed, your thought about the remarriage of your spouse, and other highly personal matters that you don't want (or that shouldn't be) disclosed in your will or other public documents.

14. Make an up-to-date list of all your investments and be sure all important documents (wills, trusts, deeds, birth certificates, and so forth) are in your safe deposit box. Be sure the right person has the key and knows where the box is located.

22

Special Planning for the Handicapped

We have said it many times: Everyone needs estate planning. But if you have a physically, mentally, or emotionally handicapped person in your family, then you absolutely must have a carefully prepared plan. Not only is it important for the handicapped individual, but in many cases, if one family member is under a physical, mental, or emotional handicap, the effects will be felt by everyone in the family. Let's look at the special problems that handicapped people face and how you can plan to ease them.

George and Debbie had two healthy children, Jimmy and Karen. George had a good job with a large corporation, and now that both children were in school, Debbie was planning to resume teaching. Unfortunately, Jimmy was struck and injured when getting off the school bus by an automobile that ignored the flashing lights on the bus. As a result, Jimmy was left with permanent injuries that made it necessary for him to have full-time care, and Debbie had to stay home and care for him.

The Need for a Guardian

The first problem to be considered in a case like Jimmy's is the question of determining mental capacity. There's really no gray area when it comes to determining the competency of an individual. According to law, a person is either competent to handle his or her own affairs or is legally incompetent. Parents usually have the right to act for a minor, but once the child reaches the age of majority (18 to 21 depending upon the state law), then he or she will be legally competent unless declared otherwise by a court. When should a guardian be appointed? Certainly where a large sum of money might be available to an injured child (like collecting from the automobile driver who hit Jimmy), a guardian of the child's property would be needed.

How is a guardian of a minor's property appointed? A petition is filed in the Orphans' Court, or the court which supervises these proceedings, giving the history of the injured person, the reason for the petition and information as to the injured person's property. The petition may be filed by anyone interested in the injured person's welfare. It is also necessary to give notice to relatives or anyone who has an interest in the welfare of the injured person. At the hearing, which may be closed to the public, medical and other testimony is presented to the court. If the court is satisfied that the welfare of the injured person would not be served by having him or her present, then their presence may not be required.

How does a judge decide whether someone is competent? They use a legal standard (their state's definition of incapacity). If the court is satisfied that the injured person is unable to manage his or her own property, the court will (by using a standard such as determining that the injured person is "liable to dissipate his or her funds" or "become the victims of designing persons," or that he or she "lacks sufficient capacity to make or communicate responsible decisions concerning his or her person") appoint a guardian to handle the property of the incompetent person. In every case, a lawyer familiar with this type of proceeding should be retained by the parents of the injured child.

Insurance and Government Benefits

What remedies and benefits are available to the family of an injured person? In Jimmy's case, the first remedy might be pursuing a personal injury claim against whomever was responsible for his injury. Insurance benefits should be carefully reviewed, such as hospitalization, automobile insurance, workers' compensation insurance, catastrophic loss benefits, and all other possible insurance coverage.

Many seriously and permanently injured and disabled persons are eligible for benefits under federal or state programs. Some programs are based on need, such as Supplemental Security Income (SSI) and Medicaid. Other programs that provide benefits do not have income or asset eligibility requirements such as Social Security, veteran's benefits, and Medicare.

We strongly recommend that you contact the local Social Security office, or other state or governmental agency, as soon as possible after a serious injury or disability to make application for benefits and to find out to what benefits you are entitled.

The Parents' Estate Plan

What plans should George and Debbie make for Jimmy if either or both of them died? If their estate is modest and the expenses for caring for Jimmy are high, they should immediately increase the size of their estate by purchasing additional life insurance. If they cannot afford to set aside money today to care for Jimmy if George should die, he should, at the very least, purchase an inexpensive term life insurance policy to provide the money necessary for Jimmy's care at George's death.

How should parents of handicapped children set up their wills?

How your estate plan is structured depends, in part, upon the government benefits available for the child's care. For example, if George and Debbie were to make wills leaving everything to each other, and then equally to their children, Jimmy and Karen, the money paid to Jimmy *might disqualify him* from receiving government benefits to which he is entitled. This is one of the most serious problems faced by parents of handicapped children.

Disinheriting the handicapped child

How can you provide for handicapped children and still not disqualify them from receiving government benefits? One solution might be to disinherit them. If George and Debbie were to leave all of their property to Karen, then Jimmy could still receive government benefits. The money that otherwise would have been paid to Jimmy will not cause him to lose his government benefits. This prevents the needless "wasting" of estate assets since Jimmy will still be properly cared for by the governmental benefits. Karen will be able to use the money she receives at her parents' deaths for her college education or other purposes. An "outright bequest" or gift to a severely disabled child may, therefore, not be practical in many situations, even if the child could handle or invest the money.

Morally obligated gift

Another option is to leave property to another person and ask him or her to use the money for the handicapped child. This is called a *morally obligated gift*. It can be effective where a direct bequest could affect other benefits being received by the handicapped child. But there are obvious problems with this approach. The income will be taxed to the person receiving it. The biggest potential drawback is that there will be no guarantee that whoever receives the property will comply with the deceased parents' request that the funds, in fact, be used for the handicapped child.

Trust for handicapped children

The most effective manner to transfer funds for the use of handicapped children is by placing the funds in a trust. This is one area in which it is extremely important to have an attorney in your state who specializes in setting up trusts for handicapped children.

How should the trust be set up? The laws of your state will be the ultimate test. Suppose, for example, that a parent provided in his will for a trustee to hold property in trust for the benefit of a disabled child following the death of the parent. The trust might provide that the income and principal will be used for the child's care, maintenance, support, or education. While this type of trust might be excellent for normal healthy children, it could have unfortunate results for a handicapped child.

The availability of the trust assets may disqualify the child from receiving the governmental benefits essential to his or her daily care and maintenance. *Therefore, it is absolutely essential that the trust be drafted so that the handicapped child will have the use and benefit of the trust assets without disqualifying him or her from receiving government aid and assistance.*

How can this be accomplished? The trustee should have the decision-making power to distribute income and principal among a number of beneficiaries (one of which will be the handicapped person). The trustee should have the absolute discretion to control the amount of the distributions and to decide whether there is a need to make a distribution. If, for example, the trustee was given the right, in the trustee's discretion, to use income or principal from the trust for Jimmy and Karen, it is more difficult for the government to argue that the property and the availability of the trust assets for Jimmy should disqualify him from receiving benefits. Specific language could also be included that any funds used for the handicapped person are to supplement other benefits received by that person, and in no event would any trust monies be used where it would disqualify the beneficiary from receiving governmental funds.

If the handicapped person is only one of a class of beneficiaries, and if the trustee has discretion in making payments to or for the use of any beneficiary, and the trust indicates that the handicapped person's distributions are only to supplement their benefits, it will be difficult for the governmental agency to claim that they are entitled to any share of the trust assets.

Many states also recognize *spendthrift trusts.* These are trusts with provisions which clearly state that the trust assets cannot be reached by a creditor of the beneficiary. This provision should also be considered in any trust for a handicapped person.

Where to Go for Help

There are many nonprofit organizations such as "The National Head Injury Foundation" that will make information available to you, free of charge, concerning the benefits and alternatives available to the family of handicapped persons. Governmental agencies such as Social Security, Medicare, the Veterans' Administration, state rehabilitation services, and local school districts with an individualized educational program all should be consulted.

In addition to nonprofit organizations, there are now organizations which, though operated for profit, are designed to help families with handicapped children. Trust companies and trust departments of commercial banks can be of considerable help in formulating an estate plan that includes trusts for handicapped persons and in furnishing the names and addresses of attorneys and private agencies.

There are numerous highly qualified persons, often with a professional designation of CLU (Charter Life Underwriter), ChFC (Charter Financial Consultant), or CFP (Certified Financial Planner) who can be of considerable benefit to you.

Names and addresses of attorneys can be obtained by contacting your local estate planning counsel. It is essential that you use an attorney who specializes in *estate planning for handicapped persons* to help you coordinate your estate plan.

23

Charitable Gifts

If we don't plan to get where we are going, we'll probably wind up someplace else. The main purpose for estate planning is not to save taxes but to achieve personal objectives.

Many of us have charitable objectives. We'd like to repay society for many of its blessings and fulfill our moral obligations to give to those from whom we have taken so much.

If you have such a desire, you should know that the tax laws encourage such gifts. So why not take those favorable laws into account in your planning?

The tax laws regarding charitable contributions are highly complex and technical. Because so much is at stake, it is extremely important to "go by the book" in this area. The comments that follow are general and merely summarize the most basic and essential of the key rules and available tools. We urge you to consult with your attorney and CPA before making large charitable gifts.

Advantages of Outright Lifetime Gifts

One of the greatest pleasures is the joy of seeing your gift in action. To add to that enjoyment, if you make an outright gift to a qualified charity, you'll receive an income tax deduction.

The income tax law can't limit how much you can give—you could give every dollar that you have. But tax law does limit the size of the deduction you'll obtain from your lifetime gift and whether or not you'll be allowed a deduction.

Here are five requirements for an income tax deduction: First, charitable contributions are deductible only if they are made to organizations which are *qualified*. A donee will be considered qualified only if it meets three conditions: (a) it must be operated exclusively for religious, charitable, scientific, literary, or educational purposes, or to foster national or international amateur sports competition, or to prevent cruelty to children or animals; (b) no part of the organization's earnings can benefit any private shareholder or similar individual; and (c) the organization cannot be one disqualified for tax exemption because it attempts to influence

278

legislation or participates in, publishes or distributes statements for, or intervenes in, any political campaign on behalf of any candidate seeking public office.

The Internal Revenue Service publishes a list of qualified charities. Examples of "qualified" organizations are nonprofit schools and hospitals, churches and synagogues, the United Fund, Community Chest, YMCA, YMHA, the American Red Cross, the Boy Scouts, Campfire Girls, the American Cancer Society, and the Heart Association.

Second, "property" must be the substance of the gift. Therefore, the value of your time or services, even if contributed to a qualified charity, is not deductible. For example, if you were a carpenter and spent ten hours building chairs for your daughter's public high school, you could not deduct your normal hourly wage as a charitable contribution. However, you could deduct the cost of any materials you purchased in producing the finished product.

The donation of the "use" of property to a charity is *not* a contribution of property. This means the rent-free use of an office, or even an office building, will not be considered a charitable contribution any more than will a contribution of personal services.

Third, you must make a contribution in excess of the benefit you receive. For example, you donate cash to a charity. The charity in turn might pay you (and perhaps your survivors) an annuity income for life. Only the difference between the contribution you made and the value of a similar commercial annuity payable to you would be deductible.

Likewise, if the charity is selling tickets to a first showing of a movie, your contribution is deductible only to the extent you pay more than the regular commercial value of your ticket. So, if a ticket would normally sell for $6, and you paid $10, the $4 amount in excess of the normal price would be deductible.

Fourth, your gift to a charity must actually be paid in cash or other property before the close of the tax year in question.

Fifth, if your lifetime transfer to a charity is a gift of a "partial interest" (where your gift will be split between noncharitable and charitable beneficiaries), very strict rules apply. Generally, if a charity's interest in the transfer of property is a remainder interest (the charity receives what remains after your noncharitable income beneficiaries have received income for a specified time), a transfer in trust will qualify only if it is a so-called "annuity" or "unitrust" or a "pooled income" fund. (These terms are defined and described later in this chapter.)

If you have met these five requirements, the tax implications are:

1. A charitable contribution to a qualified charity reduces your current income and, therefore, your taxes. So, if you have donated property other than cash, a charitable gift may result in more spendable income.

2. You pay no federal gift taxes regardless of the size of your gift.
3. The charity itself will pay no tax upon the receipt of your lifetime gift.
4. Generally, no income tax will be payable by a qualified charity on income earned by property you have donated to it.

A gift to a charity can be one of the simplest estate planning techniques. While you are alive, you make a charitable gift merely by writing a check, assigning stock, transferring life insurance policies, signing a deed to real estate or conveying property to charity in any other normal outright manner.

You can figure the cost of your gift, after your tax deduction, by this formula:

Tax savings = Amount of deductible gift times effective tax bracket

For example, a $2000 gift by a taxpayer in a combined federal and state tax bracket of 40 percent equals $800 in tax savings.

Stated another way, the out-of-pocket cost of the gift equals:

Amount contributed − Tax savings

For instance, the $2000 gift less the $800 in tax savings equals the out-of-pocket cost of the gift, $1200.

What a charitable contribution really costs

This table shows the after-deduction cost of a $10,000 contribution to a qualified charity at various tax brackets:

If Your Tax Bracket Is	A $10,000 Contribution Costs about	If Your Contribution Is Property Other Than Cash, You Increase Your Spendable Income By about
15%	$8500	$1500
28%	$7200	$2800
33%	$6700	$3300

Your income tax charitable deduction is limited by the type of property you give:

(a) Rent free occupancy.
(b) Cash.
(c) Ordinary income property.
(d) Capital gain property.
(e) Tangible personal property where the use of that property by the donee *is* related to the exempt functions of the donee.
(f) Tangible personal property where the use of that property is *un*-related to the exempt purposes of the donee.

If the gift you make is merely to allow the charity to occupy the premises of property you own, or if your gift entitles the charity to your services, you will receive no deduction no matter how valuable a right it is. To receive any deduction, you must actually donate property.

Cash gifts to *public* charities generate a deduction of up to 50 percent of your adjusted gross income. So if your adjusted gross income is $100,000 this year, you could contribute and currently deduct as much as $50,000. If you give more than $50,000, you could carry over the excess deduction for up to five future years and use it to offset income in those years. Most churches and synagogues, hospitals, nonprofit schools, and other charities are considered public charities and, therefore, qualify for this 50 percent deduction.

Ordinary income property is property that would produce ordinary income rather than capital gain if you sold it. Examples of ordinary income property include capital assets you've held six months or less, inventory or stock-in-trade, and works of art, books, letters, and musical compositions (if you are the person who created or prepared them or for whom they were prepared).

What is your deduction if you give ordinary income type property? Your deduction is limited to your cost (tax basis) for the property. For example, suppose you contribute real estate that you bought three months ago. You paid $15,000 for it, and now it's worth $20,000. Your deduction is limited to your cost, or $15,000. The percentage limits and carry-over rules for this type of property are the same as for cash gifts. That means you can't take a current deduction for an amount in excess of one-half of your adjusted gross income.

Capital gain property is a contribution of a capital asset held for more than 6 months. The rules here are complex. The amount of your deduction depends on whether the charity is a public charity and (if your gift is tangible personal property) how the charity will use your gift.

If a public charity will use your tangible personal property in a manner related to its tax-exempt functions and activities (for example, if you donate a painting to an art museum that will display it to the public), the deduction is *use-related*. A use-related gift means the full value of what you donate is deductible (up to 30 percent of your adjusted gross income).

For instance, Lara has $60,000 of adjusted gross income. She contributes stock worth $30,000 to the Girl Scouts of America. Assume the stock cost her $10,000. Her $30,000 contribution is deductible—up to 30 percent of her $60,000 adjusted gross income. In other words, she can deduct $18,000 this year. The $12,000 difference ($30,000 less $18,000) can be carried over and used as a deduction in future years.

Not all gifts of tangible personal property are use-related. For example, if the art museum intended to sell the painting rather than display it, or the donor donated a diamond necklace that was not a work of art the museum intended to display, the gift would not be use-related. Here the donor's deduction is limited to 50 percent of his or her adjusted gross income—but a deduction can be taken only for the donor's cost. So, if Lara donated a diamond necklace worth $20,000 that cost her $12,000, and the museum sold it and used the proceeds to purchase art, since the museum's use of the gift is unrelated to its exempt purpose of displaying art to the public, Lara's deduction would be limited. She could only deduct her $12,000 cost. If the gift was use-related, her deduction could have been the fair market value of her gift, $20,000, currently deductible up to 30 percent of Lara's adjusted gross income.

What's the moral? First, you get more tax saving mileage from giving appreciated capital gain property than from giving cash or other assets. Why? Because (with the exception of unrelated-use tangible personal property), you can deduct the full value of the property (up to the current maximum limit of 30 percent of your adjusted gross income) and escape regular income tax on the appreciation. That means the gift may cost less than if you sold the same property, paid your tax, and then contributed the proceeds.

The Tax Reform Act of 1986 provides that the appreciation element (built in gain) in charitable gifts of capital gain assets will be considered a *preference* for purposes of computing the alternative minimum tax. This means that a person who contributes capital gain property worth $30,000 that cost $10,000 has a *preference* of $20,000 ($30,000 less $10,000). This preference is added to other preferences, and the alternative minimum tax is then computed if the total exceeds the appropriate exemption (essentially $40,000 for married individuals filing jointly and surviving spouses and $30,000 for individuals who are not married).

Second, it pays to hold substantially appreciated stock or other investment property for more than six months before donating it. That makes it eligible for more favorable treatment than if it were not held for more than 6 months (where a donor contributes a capital asset which has been held for 6 months or less, the amount of charitable deduction is limited to the donor's cost).

Third, leave ordinary income property to a charity in your will so you'll receive a full estate tax deduction. (The estate tax law doesn't treat ordinary income property any differently from capital gain property.)

Fourth, leave ordinary income property, including works of art you have created, to your children, who receive a new cost basis. They can then receive an income tax charitable deduction for the full fair market value of their gift when they contribute that asset to charity.

Fifth, if the property you would like to contribute is worth less than you paid for it, sell it, take a tax deductible loss and contribute the proceeds.

Sixth, if the property you would like to give is tangible personal property, obtain a written commitment from the donee specifying that the donated property will be used in a manner related to its (the organization's) exempt purpose.

Here is a table capsulizing those charitable deduction rules:

Charitable Contribution Deduction Limitations

Type of Property	Donee*	Adjusted Gross Income Limit (%)	Deduction Limitation Carryover (Years)	Tax Treatment
(a) Rent free occupancy or services	—	—	—	No deduction
(b) Cash	Public	50	5	Full deduction
(c) Ordinary income property	Public	50	5	Deduction limited to basis
(d) Capital gain property (except for tangible personal property	Public	30	5	Full deduction for fair market value (potential gain is preference)
(e) Tangible personal property				
(1) "use related"	Public	30		Full deduction for fair market value (potential gain is preference)
(2) "non-use related"	Public	50	5	Deduction limited to donor's cost

*Regardless of the type of property given, the deduction for an individual's contributions to private foundations is limited to the lesser of (a) 30 percent of the taxpayer's adjusted gross income or (b) 50 percent of adjusted gross income less any charitable contribution deduction allowed for contribution to public type charities. Appreciated property gifts—other than publicly traded stock—made to a private foundation will be deductible only to the extent of the donor's basis.

Future Interest Gifts

You can receive a current deduction even if you give the charity only a *future interest*. A future interest is any interest or right that the charity will possess or enjoy at some time in the future. Future interest includes situations where a donor purports to give tangible personal property to a charitable organization but has made a written or oral agreement with the organization reserving to a noncharitable beneficiary (himself, a member of his immediate family, or a friend) the right to use, possess, or enjoy the property. For example, suppose Dave donates an Ansel Adams photograph to an art museum but arranges with the museum to keep the photograph in his home as long as he lives. The museum has a future interest in the photograph.

One of the basic general rules governing charitable contribution deductions is that contributions must (a) actually be paid, (b) in cash or other property, (c) before the close of the tax year. (Generally, no deductions are allowed for an outright contribution of less than the donor's entire interest in property.) Since the museum's enjoyment of the photograph was deferred, no current tax deduction would be allowed. The implication is that typically a deduction will not be allowed until the charity receives actual possession or enjoyment of the work of art.

A gift of tangible personal property must be complete, in the sense that the charity must have all interests in and rights to the possession and enjoyment of the property. Generally, this means that a transfer of a future interest in property to a charity is not deductible until all intervening interests in and rights to possession held by the donor or certain related persons or organizations have expired (or unless the gift is in the form of a future interest in trust that meets the requirements discussed next).

Deductions for certain remainder interests

If the general rule is that a donor receives no deduction if the charity has to wait, how can I receive a current tax deduction for such a gift? (How can I have my cake and eat it, too?) The answer is, because of certain favorable exceptions to that general rule, you can receive a current deduction if you:

1. Make a gift of your house or farm. For example, you could give your farm to the Boy Scouts but stipulate that you have the right to live on it as long as you live. You'd receive an income tax deduction now for the present value of the farmland that would someday be received by the Scouts.
2. Make a gift in trust that the charity will not receive until you (and/or your spouse or other designated relative) die(s). It is possible to put property into a trust, receive income from that property for as long as you (and/or other noncharitable beneficiaries you name) live and still obtain a deduction—today. How? By using a charitable remainder trust.

A charitable remainder trust is one in which the charity receives what remains after a specified number of years or after the lifetimes of specified individuals (which may include yourself).

This means there's a way to provide income for yourself and someone you love, increase your income through favored treatment, and, at the same time, fulfill your charitable objectives. How? Let's say you are in a 40 percent combined federal and state income tax bracket. You would like to retire next year. You know at that time your income tax bracket will drop substantially. Assume also that years ago you bought securities that have appreciated substantially. If you sold them in order to reinvest your proceeds in some investment yielding more income, you'd have to pay an immediate tax. That tax would reduce the amount remaining to earn income for you significantly.

So, instead of selling the securities, you contribute them to a charitable remainder trust. That gives you an immediate tax deduction. That deduction, in turn, puts money in your pocket—now. The trustee of your trust could sell the stock and reinvest the proceeds in higher yield assets. Since you have retained the right to the income for life, and since no tax is paid on the sale by the trust, the principal and, therefore, the income it produces for you is not reduced by any tax (except, in some cases, the AMT on preference items).

Suppose you want to provide income to your spouse after your death. You can also provide that income from the trust is to be paid to him for life if he survives you. That extra security has a cost, of course. Since the charity has to wait longer for its money, the value of its interests—and, therefore, the value of your current deduction—is reduced.

Charitable Remainder Unitrust

One popular type of remainder trust is the *charitable remainder unitrust*. You can create a unitrust by transferring money or securities to a trustee. The gift is irrevocable. The trustee, in turn, pays you (and perhaps your spouse) an income each year you live. At your death(s), the assets in the trust become the sole property of the charitable donee.

You receive payments based on a fixed percentage of the fair market value of the trust assets. The percentage stays the same, but the assets are revalued each year. For instance, if you decide on a 10 percent return, each year you'll be paid an amount equal to 10 percent of the value of the trust (in that year). So if the trust has increased in value, your income increases. If the trust has decreased in value, you'll receive less.

You receive an immediate income tax charitable deduction in the year you create the trust and transfer the assets to it. The deduction is measured by the present value of the charitable organization's right to eventually receive the assets of the trust; that is, the deduction is affected by your age at the time of the gift, the amount involved, and what percentage of the trust's assets you choose to receive each year.

If $300,000 is transferred into a charitable remainder unitrust for a 60-year-old, and a payout rate of 9 percent is selected, the donor will receive an immediate deduction of $111,410. (This is the present value of the charity's right to receive the trust assets.)

You pay no tax when you contribute property to the trust, even if the stocks you transfer to the trust have appreciated substantially. (But the untaxed appreciation may be considered a tax preference item, which could subject it to the alternative minimum tax.) If the trust should sell assets at a gain, those gains are taxed neither to you nor to the trust.

When you receive your income payments from the trust, some of the payment may be tax free and the balance ordinary income. The exact percentages depend on how the assets of the trust are invested.

Charitable Remainder Annuity Trust

Another popular type of remainder trust is the *charitable remainder annuity trust*. Here's how the annuity trust works: You transfer money or securities to a trust. The trustee, in turn, pays you a fixed dollar amount for the rest of your life, regardless of whether the assets in the trust increase or decrease in value. At your death, the remaining principal of the trust goes to the charitable beneficiary.

Your deduction is based on the present value of the charity's right to receive the trust assets upon your death (determined by reference to IRS tables).

If a 60-year-old donor transferred $300,000 to a charitable remainder annuity trust and took a 9 percent annuity, he would receive $27,000 a year. The present value of that retained right to a yearly annuity of $27,000 a year is worth $201,126. So, the charity's remainder interest is worth $300,000 less $201,126, or $98,879. That's the current deduction that would be allowed to the donor.

Charitable Lead Trust

You could also reverse the process. You could set up a trust, put income-producing assets in it and give the charity the right to the income for a specified period of time. At the end of that time, your beneficiary would receive the property. This is called a charitable *income* or *lead trust* and has a number of tax advantages especially useful for individuals who have particularly high-income years followed by low-income years (as is common in retirement).

Using Corporate Stock as a Charitable Gift

Giving a charity shares of stock in your closely held business may yield substantial dividends.

First, you donate some of your stock to a charitable organization you have selected. You receive a charitable contribution deduction measured by the current fair market value of the stock you contributed. Then your corporation buys the stock back from the charity. (Had the corporation redeemed the stock directly from you, dividend treatment would probably have resulted.)

One person who used this device was a controlling shareholder who gave a school about 200 shares of his corporation's stock each year. He took a deduction for the value of the stock, about $25,000. The terms of the gift provided that the university could not dispose of the shares without first offering them to the corporation at their fair market value. The corporation was not required to purchase the stock but did have a 60-day option in which to purchase any stock offered to it. Within a year or two after the shares were received by the school, they were offered to the corporation, which purchased them. The proceeds of these redemptions were then invested by the school.

If you do it properly, you can siphon funds from your business free of income tax by making a charitable contribution of your personally owned stock (which yields personal tax deduction), followed by an unrelated redemption of that stock by your corporation. This technique may eliminate or reduce the threat of a corporate accumulated earnings tax problem, generate a current income tax deduction for you, and provide cash for your favorite charity with no out-of-pocket outlay on your part (except, perhaps, an AMT tax).

The keys for success of this charitable stock bailout are (1) make your gifts of stock complete and irrevocable, (2) don't insist upon any formal or informal agreement that your charitable donee will sell the stock back to your corporation, and (3) don't promise the charity either directly or indirectly that your business will buy the stock you've given to it.

You could leverage the benefits of this technique. Take the tax savings you have realized and give it to a child. The child could use it to purchase life insurance on your life. At your death, the child could use the proceeds to buy assets from your estate (thereby providing liquidity for your executor to pay estate taxes) or buy stock under a buy-sell agreement. This latter approach makes the funding of the buy-sell tax deductible. Ask your insurance agent about *vanishing premium* life insurance which would require only a half dozen or so charitable gifts to fully fund the buy-sell.

How to Use Life Insurance for Charitable Giving

Many successful and charitably minded people use life insurance on their lives as a way to make their charitable contributions. Why?

First, the death benefit going to the charity is guaranteed as long as premiums are paid. This means that the charity will receive an amount that is fixed in value and not subject to the potential downside risks of securities.

Second, life insurance provides an "amplified" gift that can be purchased on the installment plan. Through a relatively small annual cost (premium) on your part, you can provide a large future benefit for the charity. A significant gift can be made without impairing or diluting the control of your family business interest or other investments. Assets earmarked for your family can be kept intact.

Third, life insurance is a self-completing gift. If you live, guaranteed cash values, which can be used by the charity currently, grow constantly from year to year. If you become disabled, the policy will remain in full force through the waiver-of-premium feature. This guarantees both the ultimate death benefit to the charity and the same cash values and dividend build-up that would have been earned had you not become disabled. Even if your death occurs after only one premium payment, the charity is assured of your full gift.

Fourth, the death proceeds can be received by your designated charity free of federal income and estate taxes, probate and administrative costs and delay, brokerage fees or other transfer costs. This means the charity receives "one hundred percent" dollars. Compare this prompt and certain cash payment with the payment of a gift to the selected charity under the terms of your will. In that case, administrative costs reduce amounts the charity will receive, and probate delays of up to several years are not uncommon.

Fifth, because of the contractual nature of the life insurance contract, large gifts to charity are not likely to be subjected to attack by disgruntled heirs. Life insurance proceeds also do not run afoul of the so-called state *mortmain statutes,* which prohibit or limit gifts made to charities within a short time before death.

Finally, a substantial gift may be made with no publicity. Since the life insurance proceeds on your life that are paid to charity can be arranged so they will not be part of your probate estate, the proceeds can be paid confidentially. Of course, if you want publicity, you can have it.

Here's how to obtain a current income tax deduction. Have the charity own the policy on your life and name itself the beneficiary. The premiums you pay can then be fully and currently deductible as charitable contributions. How? We suggest that you make your check out directly to the charity. Have it pay the premiums to the life insurance company. That will insure the most favorable tax results.

Your cancelled check will serve as proof of (1) the fact that your gift was made to the charity, (2) the date the gift was made, and (3) the amount of your gift. It will also assure you of a full deduction up to 50 percent of your adjusted gross income. (When an indirect gift is made to a charity, the annual deduction limit is lowered to 20 percent of the taxpayer's income. A gift in trust is one such example. Another example of an indirect gift is where premiums on a policy owned by a charity are remitted directly to the life insurance company instead of to the charity itself.)

Records, Records, Records

When you make a gift to charity, be sure to keep records of your gift. Keep all receipts, cancelled checks or other evidence of the date of the actual payment, the name of the charity, the amount, and the type of gift you've made. Your receipts should be held at least three years from the date your tax return is due or filed, or two years from the time you paid your tax if that date was later. Keep your tax returns and tax payment checks permanently.

Gifts at Death

Not everyone can or wants to give up either income or principal while they are alive—even if the recipient will be a charity that is near and dear. Many, however, would like to make a meaningful and significant gift upon death.

The estate tax law (and most states' death tax laws) favor charitable gifts by providing an unlimited charitable deduction. In other words, you could provide in your will that you leave your entire estate—no matter how large or what type of assets are in your estate—to charity and not have to pay one nickel in federal estate taxes.

If there is a charity you love, or feel you "owe," we suggest that you contact the charity directly. It probably has a person or department in charge of fund-raising who can assist you in deciding what to give and how to give it.

Many colleges, universities, and other charities can provide your attorney with helpful and cost-saving specimen documents or will provisions.

PART FIVE

HOW TO PUT
YOUR PLAN INTO ACTION
Finding the Right Person
at the Right Price

24

How to Choose
Your Advisors

One of the stories used to illustrate an estate planning idea or one of the tax savings special situations in this book was applicable to your specific needs. You have increased your knowledge of where you stand in regard to planning for the future, regardless of your previous technical background. You have probably learned a lot about yourself, your property, and your family that were not evident before. What is more important, by now, you probably have some definite goals that you now feel are attainable. What next?

Where to Go for Information

If you haven't already done so, now is the time to fill in your Financial Firedrill Form. Accumulate as much information as you can about yourself.

There is a great deal of helpful information and advice you can obtain at no cost. Your local IRS office can provide you with booklets on estate, gift, and income tax laws. Your bank's trust department is an important source of information on wills, trusts, and state property laws.

Many insurance agents and financial planners are highly trained in computing the probable costs of dying and the income and capital needs of your survivors. We recommend a CLU, ChFC, or CFP.

Obtain the deed to property you own, and make sure it is set up in accordance with your overall plans. In most cases, married couples will want to check to see if the survivor will own the entire property at the death of the first spouse.

Be certain that the stock that was supposed to be set up in a custodian's name for your child has been set up that way and was not put in your name by mistake. That custodian should typically be someone *other* than the donor.

Make absolutely certain that you have named contingent beneficiaries in your life insurance policies. Write to the insurance company for written confirmation.

All of these steps may seem basic, but they are several of the most frequently occurring "oversights" that only become apparent following death.

Once you've done all you can for yourself, then it is time to find professionals with whom you want to work.

Credentials of a Competent Attorney

The keystone of the estate planning team is the lawyer. If you do not think you will have any of the serious death tax problems discussed and perhaps only need a will and to rearrange your life insurance, then your only expense might be your legal fees. A will that spells out your wishes for your family and at the same time distributes your assets as efficiently as possible, while being completely coordinated with your insurance and other benefits, should not be an expensive undertaking.

In most cases, it is to your advantage to utilize the services of an experienced lawyer who specializes in taxes and estate planning. Most lawyers are competent and have experience in preparing simple wills. But in the age of specialization, all lawyers cannot be experts in all areas of the law.

Ask the attorney about his or her tax background or what special estate planning courses he/she has taken. (The Advanced Estate Planning Course of the American College is a particularly useful background.)

Look on the office walls to see if he/she belongs to an estate planning council—or ask. Check credentials. Some states certify attorneys in selected areas. Texas, for example, examines an attorney's credentials by a panel of experts and administers a rigorous additional bar examination in the estate planning area.

Finding the Attorney

There are other ways to find competent estate planning attorneys. Go to your local library and look for attorneys who write or lecture on estate planning to other attorneys or CPA's. Magazines to scan for such people include *Taxation for Accountants, The Practical Lawyer, Estate Planning Magazine, The Journal of Accountancy* and *Trusts and Estates Magazine.*

Practicing lawyers who also teach courses on Estate Planning and Taxation at local law schools or for Chartered Life Underwriters or Certified Financial Planners are also good choices. You may want to ask the trust department of several banks in the area to give you the names of three attorneys. Ask your CLU, ChFC, CFP, or CPA for suggestions.

Call your county estate planning council; ask them to send you a (free) directory of their members.

Go to a lecture or continuing education class taught by an attorney. After visiting just one lecture, you can quickly tell how he or she explains complex legal matters. If an attorney can't communicate in class, how will he or she communicate with you or your family?

Interview the attorney

How do you know you have the right lawyer? Make certain that at the initial interview the lawyer understands what you have and what you want to do with it. Has the attorney explained the law to you as it applies to your situation, what the tax consequences will be, and how best to achieve your goals in the most efficient manner possible?

A good attorney will question you at length about (1) the members of your family, (2) the facts concerning your occupation, (3) your present and anticipated income—both before and after taxes, (4) your personal goals, and (5) the estate planning steps you have already taken. (If the attorney doesn't take the time or show the interest or insight to ask these kinds of questions, you have the wrong person.)

Demand a written estimate of what the charges will be and how they are calculated. Give the attorney a chance to understand your situation and what type of work will have to be done for you before quoting a fee. A lawyer cannot quote a price for services before it is known what type of services he or she will be called on to perform.

The CCCA test

As with *all* professionals whom you ask to work for you, make sure that the person you have selected passes the CCCA test—competent, caring, compassionate, and accessible. If your phone calls aren't returned promptly early in the relationship, don't count on things getting better. An unanswered call or ignored request may be symptomatic of a failure to care (or office inefficiency or even overload).

Walk out if you find the attorney has strong opinions on what you should or should not do—*before* he or she takes the time to get to know you.

Is a big firm better than a one person operation? That depends. Larger firms make it possible to have specialists. That's good. But if your work will be turned over to a new associate, that's bad. The general practitioner is fine to draw your simple will—but if things are more complicated than that you need someone who spends the bulk of his or her time in the estate planning area. In any event, be sure the person you select will personally handle your estate plan.

The Accountant—An Essential Member of an Estate Planning Team

Do you require the services of an accountant? If you own your own business, or don't take standard deductions on your income tax return, you probably have—or should have—your own accountant. Most people with moderate to high incomes find that the expense of having a qualified accountant review their tax returns is more than made up by the ideas and tax savings they realize. The need for a qualified accountant is even greater when you are doing your estate planning.

In many cases, an estate planning lawyer is competent to review the tax implications of your situation and make recommendations and draw the appropriate instruments. But we feel that you should insist that the attorney contact and discuss your situation with your accountant before drafting any instruments.

Here are just a few reasons: (1) In estimating the value of a business, the input of your accountant is often essential. (2) What you can or can't afford to save, whether you are or are not utilizing the most efficient retirement savings plans available to you, and how best to provide funds for the death or disability of a business partner or associate are some of the kinds of information that are within the knowledge of your accountant. (3) Even if you think your income is too modest to have an accountant review or prepare your returns, it is often a good idea, at least every few years, to secure some professional advice in this area. There might be one to two easily available tax savings plans that you are not utilizing solely because no one has ever told you about them. The accountant is an invaluable member of the estate planning team.

How do you choose the services of an accountant if you do not already have one? If your purpose is to assist in your estate plans, then it is obviously best to have an accountant who specializes in estate planning situations and death taxes. There is a national organization, the National Association of Estate Planning Councils, which is comprised of local estate planning councils throughout the country. They include accountants, attorneys, banking officers from the estate planning and trust departments, and representatives of the life insurance industry. Accountants belonging to this organization have indicated by their membership that they specialize in estate planning and would be prime candidates to assist in your estate plan. Membership lists can be obtained from the trust officer or estate planning officer of your commercial bank or by looking in your phone book under Estate Planning Councils. Your attorney, CLU, ChFC, or CFP, as well as your banker, might also be in the position to recommend a qualified accountant.

How to Pick a Life Insurance Agent

Quite often, the professional who first gets you thinking about estate planning is your insurance agent. Life insurance, as has been indicated, is a key and integral part of most estate plans and one of the most effective, inexpensive, simplest, and surest ways to provide income to and financial security for your heirs. Choosing whom you buy your insurance from is an important decision, especially if the life insurance will be an integral part of your estate plan.

Question the qualifications of an insurance representative. A person holding the designation of Chartered Life Underwriter (CLU) can be of considerable help to you. Likewise, a Chartered Financial Consultant (ChFC) or Certified Financial Planner (CFP) will have studied the tax laws in much greater detail than the average person marketing financial products and services. We recommend you search for someone with these credentials to work with your attorney, CPA, and trust officer.

Initials Alone Are Not Enough

Formal qualifications alone do not guarantee satisfactory results. You should apply the CCCA test as well as your own intuition in determining whether the individual with whom you are doing business has considered your overall situation and your best interest in making recommendations to you.

Ask your agent how recently he or she took a course in estate planning. Look for a certificate on the wall. Ask if he/she belongs to an estate planning council.

How to Pick a Trust Officer

Most commercial banks have estate planning and trust departments, with qualified people ready to give both advice and assistance with your personal estate plans. Quite often, if you are a customer of the bank, there will be no charge for conferring with the bank representative. This is sometimes a desirable starting point for you in attaining some initial advice or in following through with some of the ideas presented in this book.

Obviously, the bank involved would be more than pleased if you decided to include it in your estate plan—as executor or co-executor of your will, or as a trustee or co-trustee under one or more trusts that might be indicated. Usually, no charge is imposed by a bank upon being named executor of a will or trustee of a trust that will not begin until your death. Until the bank actually begins work, there are no charges for merely appointing it now to act after your death.

As in the case of the purchase of any other service, banks charge fees. Ask what these fees are. Ask your advisors to explain the pros—and cons— of using the bank as your executor or trustee (or co-executor or co-trustee). Ask them to show you how their bank's investment experience compares to other banks. Be sure fees as well as all terms and conditions are in writing and signed by a bank officer.

One more point. Shop around for a bank the same way you'd shop for any other service. All trust departments are *not* equally equipped to help your estate plan. Ask if their personnel have taken estate planning courses or a comparable post-graduate law school course.

Your Executor—An Important Appointment

Being an executor involves a tremendous amount of responsibility. Before naming someone to be your executor in your will, or volunteering to act as an executor for someone, you should be aware of the nature of the job.

When a person dies, the law requires that his or her property must be collected. After debts, taxes, and expenses are paid, the remaining assets are distributed to whoever is entitled to that property. That distribution is determined by the person's will, if there is one, or the intestate laws of the state in which death occurred, if there is no will. It is the executor's responsibility to collect and distribute the assets and to pay the death taxes and expenses of the deceased.

In trying to accomplish all of this, the executor can run into a number of problems. For example, if there was a business in the estate, and the executor handles it improperly, he/she can be sued by the beneficiaries of the estate for certain mistakes or omissions. In many cases, businesses are continued following a person's death by the executor, without authority in the will to continue the business and without court authorization. The executor can be held personally liable for any loss to the estate suffered by continuation of the business in those cases. Executors have also been held responsible for not investing the proceeds properly, for filing tax returns late, and for failing to exercise options that were available to them for the benefit of the estate. The executor may have to make decisions that can have serious death tax consequences.

Here is a checklist that will help you select an executor or executrix (or female executor):

1. Does the person I am considering *care* about my beneficiaries and care about the handling of my estate assets?
2. Is the person I am considering legally and emotionally as well as intellectually *competent?*
3. Can the person I am considering be *objective* and deal with all parties concerned fairly?
4. Does the person I am considering have *knowledge of* my *beneficiaries,* their circumstances and needs, *and* of the *subject matter* (the assets) *of my estate?*
5. What *experience* does the person I am considering have? Has he ever made decisions of major significance?
6. Does the person I am considering *know my business?*
7. What *business or investment management experience* does this person have?
8. Does the person I am considering have the *time* it takes to accomplish the job?
9. What is the physical *proximity* of the person I am considering *to the beneficiaries and the estate?*
10. Do I absolutely and without question *trust* this person with the principal product of my lifetime?

Attorney as executor

Should your attorney name himself or herself as executor of your will, *without* your express request, we suggest (a) you fire the attorney and (b) you send a copy of the will to your local bar association's disciplinary committee for immediate action. We feel it is almost as unethical for an attorney to write himself into the will as executor as it would be if he named himself your beneficiary.

The next question is, should *you* name your attorney as executor? We feel the answer should be no. Why not? It is the executor who hires the estate's attorney and negotiates on behalf of the estate's beneficiaries with that attorney for fees and terms.

If the attorney is the executor, who represents the beneficiaries? Who negotiates the fees to be charged for the legal advice the executor will need? Who can fire the estate's attorney if he doesn't answer the calls or letters of the estate's beneficiaries? Who can question the estate's attorney on actions taken or not taken? Who can challenge the attorney if he hires his law partner as the estate's attorney? Who can dismiss the estate's attorney if, for any reason, he is or becomes incompetent?

We feel that in most cases (there are always exceptions) there should be a system of checks and balances which is not present when the attorney who draws the will is named as the estate's executor.

Consider the beneficiary with the largest share of the estate as the executor. That person has more to gain by a careful selection of the estate's attorney and even more careful scrutiny of the attorney's progress—and the most to lose if a poor choice is made or allowed to continue.*

Selecting a Trustee

Our choice for most trusts is to use a professional (typically a bank) trustee, unless: (a) there is a small amount involved; or (b) where there is a close family situation where a specific individual clearly has the interest of the beneficiary at heart, the time, skill, and inclination to properly invest the funds, and is in a position to systematically pay the proceeds to the beneficiaries or else apply it for them, by payment either directly to a college, hospital, or for rent, or for other purposes. Sometimes there is an individual who will fit these requirements, such as a brother who has had experience as a stockbroker or accountant. But more often than not, the best interest of the estate, yourself, and your beneficiaries will be served by using the services of someone who does this on a regular basis and has the time, skill, and patience to act accordingly.

Trust companies, usually commercial banks with a trust department, are best situated to act where a trust is involved unless the amount involved is so small as to not warrant your paying the bank its minimum fees. We recommend that you appoint an individual or several individuals to work as co-trustees with the bank.

An alternative is to appoint an individual as trustee who will hire counsel and/or bank to assist him in his or her duties.

*Before you make any decisions or take any action regarding an executor or the administration of an estate, we strongly suggest you read our book, *The Executor's Manual* (Doubleday and Company, Garden City, N.Y., 1986).

Selecting Guardians

Where you are appointing someone to act as guardian of the *property* of a child or an incompetent, basically the same rules will apply as indicated for trustees.

However, where you want someone to act as guardian of the *person* of your minor children and to more or less stand in the position to your children that you were at the time of your death and actually take care of them personally, as opposed to merely handling money for them, an individual would be the proper choice.

Factors to consider in selecting a personal guardian

Relatives should usually be the first persons to consider in selecting a guardian for your children. But remember that your parents are much older than your children. Their personal health might not warrant them acting as guardians and caring for your children until your children attain their majority. If, in fact, your parents are the logical or only natural choice available at the time, then definitely name alternative guardians in your will in the event that your parents, for any reason, become incapable of assuming the responsibility of caring for your minor children. Brothers and sisters are sometimes logical choices, and quite often, close friends with whom your children have warm personal relationships should be considered.

Be certain that you discuss your selection with the proposed persons or institutions so you will be sure that they will accept this serious responsibility and what, in fact, can be a prolonged and significant financial imposition.

Many friends and relatives, aware of the serious implications that the death of both parents can cause, have reciprocal arrangements. Ann and John and Stan and Sue each have two children and have been friends and neighbors for ten years. Ann and John left their property and a special additional insurance policy to a trust with the Great Valley Bank. If Ann and John both die in an accident, Stan and Sue will raise their friends' children. The bank as trustee will provide Stan and Sue with the necessary extra money to care for the children and to facilitate their moving in with Stan and Sue. In that way, the children can be assured of a home in which they can be well cared for, in circumstances that are not much different than their former home. In such cases, your will or trust should specifically provide for additional money to be available to these guardians, in the event that any additions or renovations are necessary to their home, to accommodate your children.

We sometimes recommend provisions in our clients' wills under which it is mutually agreed that the other family can move into your home to live with your children, in the event that you and your spouse die in a common accident or within a short time of each other's death.

Remember also that only the surviving spouse can name the personal guardian for your children. As long as one parent is alive, then of course he/she is the natural parent and guardian of any minor children.

Educate Your Survivors—Before They Are Survivors

Not only is it necessary to select your professional advisors and those persons or institutions who will take an active part in handling your affairs after your death, but you should also let everyone know what plans have been made, what you want done, and who can be relied upon for assistance.

Years ago, when husbands worked and wives stayed home, serious problems occurred when the husband died and the wife was forced to come to grips for the first time with the world of business and economics. Today, this is hardly the normal case. But there can be unfortunate results if your beneficiaries are not aware of the plans you have made or don't have the training or experience to execute those plans.

The amount, extent, and location of your assets should be made available to your executor, so that time will not be lost or assets not uncovered because no one knew where they were. Why have a conflict caused by having an executor or trustee who is not familiar to your beneficiaries or start because of a lack of communication? Why not tell your beneficiaries—and certainly discuss with your spouse—your plans and desires, so that any accommodation can be made at this time, rather than at a time of emotional stress? Educate those you love now so they'll know how to act and what to do if . . .

Do It—Now!

Even though it is often a sacrifice, there is a good feeling in knowing you have money in the bank, insurance protection for your family, and peace of mind caused by the security of proper planning. Don't make a lot of mental notes that this and that must be done and then conveniently put this book away for that sometime in the future when you know you must get to it.

Put yourself on your own payroll now! Take the time now or in the immediate future to take care of those things that must be done. Then you can relax without the pressure of what an unsecured future can mean to those people or those organizations that have meaning to you.

Most of us like the additional bonus we get every time we can remove a little more pressure from our daily lives. With the information in this book, you can institute a plan that definitely can remove some of the problems and unknowns that create insecurity. By planning in advance, you can have a more secure future for yourself and for your family plus the pleasure of knowing you have lived a full and happy life and have been successful in keeping your money for the people you love.

Take One Step at a Time

Don't become discouraged by what must seem like an overwhelming task. You have made a lot of progress if you manage to review and update your present will, update your life insurance coverage and beneficiaries, and put all your important papers in a safe (deposit box) place with a list of the people who can be relied upon by your survivors.

Be sure, no matter what, that you own enough life and disability insurance to pay your (or your family's) fixed expenses. Then go from there.

Oh yes, before you close the book, consider this ancient thought. We feel it is the single most important estate planning concept we can share:

> "If I am not for myself,
> who will be for me?
> Being only for myself,
> what am I?
> If not now,
> when?"
>
> Hillel—
> *Ethics of the Fathers*

APPENDIXES

Appendix A
Your Present Financial Picture

Your Family Profile and Financial Picture
(A Quick Review of Your Present Assets)

Family record:

Name	Relationship	D.O.B.	Married	No. of Children	Social Security No.
_____	_____	_____	_____	_____	___/___/___
_____	_____	_____	_____	_____	___/___/___
_____	_____	_____	_____	_____	___/___/___
_____	_____	_____	_____	_____	___/___/___
_____	_____	_____	_____	_____	___/___/___
_____	_____	_____	_____	_____	___/___/___

Home address: _____

Home phone: _____

Business address(es): _____

Business phone no.(s): _____

Financial Record:

Asset Category:	Joint/Survivor	Current Market Value and Ownership		Liabilities
		Husband	*Wife*	
Personal Residence				
Other Real Estate				
Household Contents				
Personal Effects (Furs, Jewelry)				
Automobiles				
Other Vehicles (Motorcycles, Boats)				
Collectibles (Stamps, Coins, Antiques)				
Savings, Checking, Money Mkt. Funds				
Securities (Stocks, Bonds, Mut. Fds.)				
Tax Shelters				
Life Insurance				
Annuities				
Business Interests				
Pension				
Profit Sharing				
I.R.A.s - Keogh				
Stock Options				
Deferred Compensation				
Other				
Totals:				

Appendix B
Income Tax Tables

1987 Rates

	Taxable Income	Rate (%)
Married individuals filing joint returns	$ 0–$3,000	11
	$ 3,001–$28,000	15
	$ 28,001–$45,000	28
	$ 45,001–$90,000	35
	over $90,000	38.5
Heads of households	$ 0–$2,500	11
	$ 2,501–$23,000	15
	$ 23,001–$38,000	28
	$ 38,001–$80,000	35
	over $80,000	38.5
Single taxpayers	$ 0–$1,800	11
	$ 1,801–$16,800	15
	$ 16,801–$27,000	28
	$ 27,001–$54,000	35
	over $54,000	38.5
Married individuals filing separate returns	$ 0–$1,500	11
	$ 1,501–$14,000	15
	$ 14,001–$22,500	28
	$ 22,501–$45,000	35
	over $45,000	38.5

Rates for 1988 and Thereafter

	Taxable Income	Rate (%)
Married individuals filing joint returns	$ 0–$29,750	15
	$ 29,751–$71,900	28
	$ 71,901–$149,250	33
	over $149,250	28
Heads of households	$ 0–$23,900	15
	$ 23,901–$61,650	28
	$ 61,651–$123,790	33
	over $123,790	28
Single taxpayers	$ 0–$17,850	15
	$ 17,851–$43,150	28
	$ 43,151–$89,560	33
	over $89,560	28
Married individuals filing separate returns	$ 0–$14,875	15
	$ 14,876–$35,950	28
	$ 35,951–$113,300	33
	over $113,300	28

Appendix C
Unified Rate Schedule
for Estate and Gift Taxes

If the amount with which the tentative tax to be computed is:	*The tentative tax is:*
Not over $10,000	18% of such amount
Over $10,000 but not over $20,000	$1,800 plus 20% of the excess over $10,000
Over $20,000 but not over $40,000	$3,800 plus 22% of the excess over $20,000
Over $40,000 but not over $60,000	$8,200 plus 24% of the excess over $40,000
Over $60,000 but not over $80,000	$13,000 plus 26% of the excess over $60,000
Over $80,000 but not over $100,000	$18,200 plus 28% of the excess over $80,000
Over $100,000 but not over $150,000	$23,800 plus 30% of the excess over $100,000
Over $150,000 but not over $250,000	$38,800 plus 32% of the excess over $150,000
Over $250,000 but not over $500,000	$70,800 plus 34% of the excess over $250,000
Over $500,000 but not over $750,000	$155,800 plus 37% of the excess over $500,000
Over $750,000 but not over $1,000,000 . . .	$248,300 plus 39% of the excess over $750,000
Over $1,000,000 but not over $1,250,000 . .	$345,800 plus 41% of the excess over $1,000,000
Over $1,250,000 but not over $1,500,000 . .	$448,300 plus 43% of the excess over $1,250,000
Over $1,500,000 but not over $2,000,000 . .	$555,800 plus 45% of the excess over $1,500,000
Over $2,000,000 but not over $2,500,000 . .	$780,800 plus 49% of the excess over $2,000,000

For 1984-1987—*In the case of decedents dying and gifts made in 1984, 1985, 1986, and 1987:*

Over $2,500,000 but not over $3,000,000 . .	$1,025,800 plus 53% of the excess over $2,500,000
Over $3,000,000	$1,290,800 plus 55% of the excess over $3,000,000

For 1988 and Later Years

Over $2,500,000	50%

Appendix D
Glossary

Accidental death benefits. The accidental death, or double indemnity, feature of a life insurance policy that will provide a larger additional benefit, often twice the face amount of the policy, if death arises from accidental means.

Adjustable life. An adjustable life insurance policy permits the insured to change from term to permanent, apportion premium dollars and change the type of coverage without cancelling the policy. This flexibility is subject to the limitations of the specific policy in question.

Administration. The management of the estate of a deceased person. It includes collecting the assets, paying the debts and taxes and making distribution to the persons entitled to the decedent's property.

Administrator (m)/administratrix (f). The person appointed to manage the estate of a deceased person if decedent had no valid will, or when the will did not provide for an executor (m) or executrix (f) to settle the decedent's estate.

Alternate value date. For federal estate tax purposes, the value of the gross estate six months after the date of death, unless property is distributed, sold, exchanged or otherwise disposed of within six months. In that case the value of such property is determined as of the date of disposition.

Annual exclusion. For federal gift tax purposes, an exclusion of $10,000 is allowed the donor each year provided the gift is one of a present interest in property. (The donee must be given an immediate right to use, possession or enjoyment of the property interest.)

Attestation clause. The paragraph at the end of a will indicating that certain persons by their signatures have heard the testator (testatrix) declare the instrument to be his (her) will and have witnessed the signing of the will.

Automatic premium loan. A provision in permanent life insurance policies which permits the company to borrow from the cash value of the policy to pay the premium, if the insured has elected this provision.

Beneficiary. The person who inherits a share or part of the decedent's estate. One who receives a beneficial interest under a trust or insurance policy is also called a beneficiary.

Bequest. A gift of property by will. A specific bequest is a gift of specified property (my watch or automobile). A general bequest is one that may be satisfied from the general assets of the estate (I give $100 to my brother, Sam). If the specific bequest (my watch) was sold before the decedent died, the gift will fail.

Buy-sell agreements. A buy-sell agreement, or business purchase agreement, is an arrangement for the disposition of a business interest in the event of the owner's death, disability, retirement or upon withdrawal from the business at some earlier time. Business purchase agreements can take a number of forms: (1) an agreement between the business itself and the individual owners (a stock redemption agreement); (2) an agreement between the individual owners (a cross-purchase agreement); and (3) an agreement between the individual owners and key person, family member or outside individual (a third party) business buy-out agreement.

Charitable contribution. A charitable contribution is a gratuitous transfer of property to charitable, religious, scientific, educational, and other specified organizations. If the donee of the gift falls within a category designated by the law, a charitable deduction may be taken for income, gift, or estate tax purposes. Charitable contributions have tax value, therefore, because they result in a current income tax reduction, may reduce federal estate taxes, and can be made a tax-free gift.

Charitable deductions. A deduction allowed against a reportable gift to a charitable organization (equal to the value of the gift). For estate tax purposes there is no limit on the amount of the deduction.

Charitable remainder annuity trust. A charitable remainder annuity trust is a trust that permits payment of a fixed amount annually to a noncharitable beneficiary, with the remainder going to charity.

Charitable remainder unitrust. A charitable remainder unitrust is a trust that is designed to permit payment of a periodic sum to a noncharitable beneficiary, with the remainder going to charity.

Codicil. A supplement or addition to an existing will to effect some revision, change or modification of that will. A codicil must meet the same requirements regarding execution and validity as a will.

Community property. Property acquired during marriage in which both husband and wife have an undivided one-half interest. Not more than half can be disposed of by the will. In some Community Property States, the husband can control and dispose of community property during marriage. There are currently eight (8) Community Property States: Arizona, California, Idaho, Louisiana, New Mexico, Nevada, Texas, and Washington.

Contingent interest. A future interest in real or personal property that is dependent upon the fulfillment of a stated condition or the happening of an event that may or may not occur.

Contingent remainder. A future interest in property dependent upon the fulfillment of a stated condition before the termination of a prior estate. For example, husband leaves property in trust to pay the income to his wife during her lifetime. After his wife's death the trustee is to transfer the property to his son if the son is then living. Otherwise, the property is to go to his daughter. The son has a remainder interest which is contingent upon his outliving his mother. The daughter has a contingent remainder interest which she will only receive if the son does not outlive their mother.

Convertible term. A right to exchange your term policy for a whole life or endowment type of policy without evidence of insurability.

Corporation. A separate and distinct legal entity whose exact nature and status are determined by the state of incorporation. For federal tax purposes, a corporation is an organization that has a preponderance of the following elements: (1) associates; (2) limited liability; (3) free transferability of interests; (4) centralized management; (5) continuity of life; and (6) an objective to carry on business and divide the gains therefrom.

Corpus. A term used to describe the principal or trust estate as distinguished from the income. When we speak of the corpus of a trust we are talking about the assets in the trust.

Credit estate tax. A tax imposed by a state to take full advantage of the amount allowed as a credit against the Federal Estate Tax.

Decedent. The person, either man or woman, who died.

Decreasing term. Similar to mortgage insurance in that the death benefit decreases over the specific period of time in which the insurance is in effect.

Defined benefit pension plan. A type of pension plan under which definitely determinable retirement benefits are computed using a predetermined benefit formula established when the plan is created. Each employee is promised a specific amount of retirement benefits. The employer's contribution to provide that benefit is based on an actuarial determination of the cost of benefits promised.

Disclaimer. The refusal to accept property that has been devised or bequeathed. It's a renunciation by the beneficiary of his or her right to receive the property in question.

Dividend options. Options available to owners of "participating" insurance policies in which the insured can elect to take dividends in any of the following ways: (1) in the form of cash; (2) to reduce the premium; (3) to buy "paid up" additional insurance; (4) to leave the dividends with the company to earn interest; (5) to purchase one year term insurance; (6) to pay off the policy at an earlier date; and (7) to use a combination of the above.

Domicile.   An individual's permanent home. The place to which, regardless of where he or she is then living, an individual has the intention of returning.

Donee.   The person who received a gift. The term also refers to the person who is the recipient of the power of appointment from another person.

Donor.   The person who makes a gift. The term also refers to the person who grants a power of appointment to another person.

Durable power of attorney.   A "durable" power of attorney is a power of attorney which is not terminated by subsequent disability or incapacity of the principal.

Endowment insurance.   Endowment insurance pays the face amount at the sooner of the time of "endowment"—the maturity of the contract, or at the death of the insured prior to the endowment date.

Estate tax.   A tax imposed upon the right of a person to transfer property at death. This type of tax is imposed not only by the federal government but also by a number of states.

Executor (m) executrix (f).   The person named by the deceased in his or her will to manage the decedent's affairs. This personal representative of the decedent stands in the shoes of the decedent, and collects the assets of the estate, pays the debts and taxes, and makes distribution of the remaining property to the beneficiaries or heirs.

Fair market value.   The value at which estate property is included in the gross estate for federal estate tax purposes. The price at which property would change hands between a willing buyer and a willing seller, neither being under a compulsion to buy or sell and both having knowledge of the relevant facts.

Federal estate tax.   An excise tax levied on the right to transfer property at death, imposed upon and measured by the value of the estate left by the deceased.

Fiduciary.   One occupying a position of trust. An executor, administrator, trustee and guardian all stand in a fiduciary relationship to those persons whose affairs they are handling.

Flower bonds.   Flower bonds are certain U.S. Treasury obligations (which are traditionally traded at a discount) owned by a decedent at death that can be redeemed at par value (plus accrued interest) in payment of federal estate taxes. They are called flower bonds because they "blossom" at death, and while purchased at a discount, can be redeemed at their full par value in payment of federal estate taxes.

Generation-skipping transfer tax (GSTT).   Tax law on transfers to grandchildren or younger generations. A flat rate tax equal to the highest current estate or gift tax bracket is imposed on every generation skipping transfer. The tax applies to transfers in trust or arrangements having substantially the same effect as a trust, such as transfers involving life estates and remainders, estates for years and insurance and annuity contracts.

Gift.   For tax purposes, property rights or interests voluntarily and gratuitously passed on or transferred during lifetime for less than an adequate and full consideration in money or money's worth to another, whether the transfer is in trust or otherwise, direct or indirect.

Gift splitting (for federal gift tax purposes).   A provision allowing a married couple to treat a gift made by one of them to a third person as having been made one-half by each, provided it is consented to by the other.

Gift tax.   A tax imposed on the lifetime voluntary gratuitous transfer of property. There is a federal gift tax, and some states also impose a tax on gratuitous transfers during lifetime.

Gift tax exclusion (for federal gift tax purposes).   Anyone, married or single, can give up to $10,000 in cash or other property each year to any number of persons (whether or not they are related to the donor) with no gift tax liability.

Grace period.   A safety device provision included in life insurance policies which permits the insured to have an extra period of time (usually thirty days) in which to pay the premium without losing the benefits of the policy.

Grantor.   A person who creates a trust; also called a settlor, creator, donor, or trustor.

Gross estate.   An amount determined by totaling the value of all property in which the decedent has an interest and which is required to be included in the estate by the Internal Revenue Code for federal estate tax purposes.

Guaranteed insurability rider.   An additional benefit that can be added to a life insurance policy guaranteeing the insured the right to purchase additional life insurance without evidence of insurability on certain option dates—usually available only up to certain ages.

Guardian.   There are two classes of guardians. A guardian of the person is appointed by the surviving spouse in his or her will to take care of the personal affairs of their minor children. Since each parent is the natural guardian of the minor children, only the surviving parent can name the guardian of the person. A guardian of the property of a minor or incompetent is a person or institution appointed or named to represent the interests of a minor child or incompetent adult. A guardian of property can be named in a will, or will be appointed by a court.

Heir. A person designated by law to succeed to the estate of the person who dies intestate (without a will). Sometimes an heir is designated as next of kin.

HR-10 (Keogh retirement plan). Under HR-10 (Keogh Plan) a self-employed individual is allowed to take a tax deduction for money he or she sets aside to provide for retirement. The HR-10 plan is also a means of providing retirement security for employees working for the self-employed individual.

Incontestable clause. A provision contained in life insurance policies which prevents the insurance company from denying a claim because of any error, concealment or misstatement after the contestable period has expired (usually two years).

Individual retirement account (IRA). A provision in the tax laws which permits individuals who are not covered by a qualified pension or profit sharing plan or tax deferred annuity to set aside and deduct the lesser of $2,000 a year or 100 percent of compensation, in the form of an individual retirement account. Even covered employees can have an IRA, but their deductions may be severely limited. The earnings of the IRA account, between the time they are deposited and the time they are received, accumulate tax free. An individual must be at least 59 years old (unless disabled) to receive an IRA payment without tax penalty.

Inheritance tax. A tax levied on the rights of the heirs to receive property from a deceased person, measured by the share passing to each beneficiary, sometimes called a succession tax. The federal death tax is an estate tax. Some states have estate taxes but most have inheritance taxes.

Installment payments of estate tax under Section 6166. Section 6166 of the Internal Revenue Code provides for the payment of federal estate tax in installments in certain cases in which the deceased had an interest in a closely held business that represented a considerable part of his estate. To receive special tax treatment under 6166, the value of the business interest must comprise *more* than 35 percent of the adjusted gross estate.

Installment sale. The installment sale is an elective device for spreading out the taxable gain and thereby deferring income tax from the sale of property. Essentially, the major ingredient is that the seller agrees to accept the purchase price in installments over a period of years (or agrees to accept no payment in the year of the sale and one or more payments in later years).

Insurance trust. A trust composed partly or wholly of life insurance policy contracts.

Intangible property. Property that does not have physical substance. The item itself is the only evidence of value. Examples are certificate of stock or bond, and goodwill or an oral contract.

Interpolated terminal reserve. The reserve on any life insurance policy between anniversary dates, regardless of whether further premium payments are due. It is determined by a pro rata adjustment upward (or downward in the case of certain long duration term policies) between the previous terminal reserve and the next terminal reserve.

Inter vivos trust. A trust created during the grantor's lifetime. It becomes operative during lifetime as opposed to a trust under a will, called a testamentary trust, which does not go into effect until the testator's death.

Intestacy laws. Individual state laws that provide for distribution of property of a person who has died without leaving a valid will.

Intestate. Without a will—a person who dies without a valid will dies intestate.

Irrevocable trust. A trust that cannot be revoked or terminated by the grantor. To qualify as irrevocable for tax purposes, the grantor cannot retain any right to alter, amend, revoke or terminate.

Joint tenancy. The holding of property by two persons in such a way that on the death of either, the property would go to the survivor. If the persons are husband and wife, then the property is said to be held "by the entireties." This is contrasted to tenancy in common in which each of the owners has an undivided interest, which upon the death of one is passed by probate to heirs specified in a valid will or under intestacy laws.

Lapse. The failure of a testamentary gift due to the death of the recipient during the life of the testator (the person who made the will).

Legacy. Technically a gift of personal property by will, but in practice it includes any disposition by will.

Legatee. A person to whom a legacy is given.

Letters of administration. A written document issued to the administrator, administratrix (if no will) or to the executor named in a will authorizing him to act as such. After the will is probated or is taken to the appropriate office for formal approval (Register of Wills, Probate,

Orphans' or Surrogate Court), the letters of administration (no will) or letters testamentary (will) are granted. They serve as official recognition of the fact that the administrator or administratrix or the executor or executrix has the right to take any action that the deceased would have taken in regard to handling and disposing of the decedent's property.

Life estate. The title of the interest owned by a life tenant. A person whose interest in property terminates at his or her death.

Life tenant. The person who receives the income from a legal life estate or from a trust fund during his or her own life. This right terminates at death.

Liquid assets. Cash, or assets which can be readily converted into cash without any serious loss (bank accounts, life insurance proceeds, government bonds).

Living will. A living will is a written expression of an individual's desire that extraordinary means should not be employed to prolong his or her life. Living wills are legal in some states. In other states, where the living will itself has no legal effect, it can be of help to physicians and relatives by enabling them to know of a patient's wishes.

Marital deduction. For federal estate tax purposes, the portion of a decedent spouse's estate that may be passed to the surviving spouse without its becoming subject to the federal estate tax levied against the decedent spouse's estate under present federal estate law. The marital deduction is unlimited, provided that the property passes to the surviving spouse in a qualified manner.

Marital trust. A trust set up to take advantage of the marital deduction provisions of the federal estate tax. It can take the form of a Q.T.I.P. trust or a general power of appointment (GPOA) trust, defined elsewhere in this glossary. The trust property that will pass outside the marital trust will be a "non-marital" or residual trust. Typically, the beneficiaries of the non-marital trust will be the children of the spouse setting up the trust. Assets in the marital trust are taxed when the surviving spouse dies, while assets in the non-marital trust are not in the surviving spouse's estate and therefore not taxed when the spouse dies.

Medical expense reimbursement plan. A medical expense reimbursement plan (MERP) is an agreement provided by an employer to reimburse one or more employees for dental expenses, cosmetic surgery and other medical expenses which are not covered under a medical plan available to all employees. Typically, a medical expense reimbursement plan reimburses employees for medical expenses incurred by the employee, his or her spouse and dependents.

Money purchase pension plan. A type of pension plan which bases the retirement benefit upon an employer's commitment to make an annual contribution. Benefits are directly dependent upon the length of time an employee participates in the plan and the amount of money contributed on his or her behalf each year, plus interest and appreciation on such funds.

Non-cancellable and guaranteed renewable. A provision in a disability policy under which the premium is guaranteed and the coverage guaranteed for the length of the renewable period. The company has no right to cancel the policy or change the amount of the premium. This is contrasted with policies that are only "guaranteed renewable" under which the insurance company retains the right to change the amount of the premiums on a class basis, and policies that are "renewable only at the option of the insurance company." Under these latter policies, the company has the right to refuse to renew the policy on its anniversary date.

Non-forfeiture values. Options in an insurance policy which give the insured the right to elect "reduced paid-up" life insurance, or "extended term" life insurance, as well as receiving the cash value of the policy, at any time that the insured no longer wishes to continue paying premiums.

Non-liquid assets. Assets that are not readily convertible into cash for at least nine (9) months without a serious loss. (Real estate and business interests).

Non-probate property. Property that passes outside the administration of the estate. It passes other than by will or the intestacy laws (jointly held property, pension proceeds and life insurance proceeds paid to a named beneficiary are examples of non-probate property, as is property in an inter vivos trust).

Pension plan. A pension plan is a retirement plan established and maintained by an employer for the benefit of employees and their beneficiaries. The primary purpose of a pension plan must be to provide benefits for the employees upon their retirement because of age or disability.

Personal holding company. A personal holding company is a corporation which meets two particular tests (and is not specifically excluded from such status). These two tests are: (1) a stock ownership test; and (2) an income test. Such tests must be met in the same taxable year so that it is possible for a corporation to attain personal holding company status in one year and not in the next.

Pour over. A term referring to the transfer of property from an estate or trust to another estate or trust upon the happening of an event that is provided in the instrument. For example, a provision in a will can provide that certain property be paid (poured over) to an existing trust.

Power of appointment. A property right given to a person to dispose of property that he or she does not fully own. There are two types of powers of appointment. A general power of appointment is a power over the distribution of property exercisable in favor of any person the donee of the power may select, including himself, his estate, his creditors or the creditors of his estate. A limited power of appointment is the power granted to a donee that is limited in scope. This is sometimes called a special power. An example of a limited power would be giving the donee of the power the right to distribute the property at his death to any of his sister's children that he designates.

Power of attorney. A power of attorney is a written document which enables an individual, or "principal," to designate another person or persons as his or her "attorney in fact," that is, to act on the principal's behalf. The scope of the power can be severely limited or quite broad.

Present interest. An immediate, unfettered, and actuarially ascertainable legal right to use, possess, or enjoy property.

Principal. The property comprising the estate or fund that has been set aside in trust, or from which income has been expected to accrue. The trust principal is also known as the trust corpus or res.

Private annuity. A private annuity is an arrangement between two parties, neither of whom is an insurance company. One party, the transferor, conveys complete ownership of property to the other, the transferee. In return, the transferee promises to make periodic payments to the transferor for some period of time—usually for the transferor's life or for the life of the transferor and his or her spouse.

Probate. The process of proving the validity of the will and executing its provisions under the guidance of the appropriate public official. The title of the official varies from state to state. Wills are probated in the Register of Wills office, in some states called the Probate or Surrogate Court. When a person dies, the will must be filed before the proper officer and this is called filing the will for probate. When it has been filed and accepted, it is said to be "admitted to probate." The process of probating the will involves recognition by the court of the executor named in the will (or appointment of an administrator if no executor has been named or the person named cannot or will not serve).

Probate property. Property that can be passed under the terms of the will, and if no will under the intestacy laws of the state, is probate property. Property held in the individual name of the decedent, or in which the decedent had a divisible interest, is probate property.

Profit sharing plan.   A profit sharing plan is a plan for sharing employer profits with employees. A profit sharing plan does not have to provide a definite, predetermined formula for determining the amount of profits to be shared. Profits to be shared can arbitrarily be determined on a year-to-year basis. However, there must be a definite formula for allocating these profits to each participant. But without a definite contribution formula, an employer must make recurring and substantial contributions to a profit sharing plan.

Q.T.I.P. trust.   The Q.T.I.P. trust (qualified terminal interest property trust) is a trust that can qualify for the marital deduction under current tax laws, even though under the trust a spouse is given only the income of the trust for life. Assets at death pass to the beneficiaries named by the spouse who set up the trust. Under prior law, only a trust in which the spouse had a general power of appointment over the trust property would have qualified for the marital deduction. This latter type of trust is called a general power of appointment trust.

Reinstatement.   A privilege contained in life insurance policies which enables the insured to reinstate the policy when it has lapsed for nonpayment.

Residuary estate.   The remaining part of the decedent's estate, after payment of debts and bequests. Wills usually contain a clause disposing of the residue of the estate that the decedent has not otherwise bequeathed or devised.

Reversionary interest.   A right to future enjoyment by the transferor of property that is now in the possession or enjoyment of another party. For example, a son creates a trust under which his father is to receive the income for life with the principal of the trust to be paid over to the son at his father's death. The son's interest is the reversionary interest.

Revocable trust.   A trust that can be changed or terminated during the grantor's lifetime and the property in the trust recovered by him.

Sale/gift-leaseback.   A sale-leaseback involves one party selling property (or in the case of a gift-leaseback, giving property) to another party and then leasing back the same property. This type of transaction is usually intended to secure a number of income and/or estate tax advantages.

Section 303 stock redemption.   Section 303 of the Internal Revenue Code establishes a way for a corporation to make a distribution in redemption of a portion of the stock of a decedent that will not be taxed as a dividend. A Section 303 partial redemption can provide cash and/or other property from the corporation without resulting in dividend treatment and provides cash for the decedent, share-holders or executor to use to pay death taxes and other expenses.

Short term trust (also known as a Clifford trust). An irrevocable trust running for a period of at least ten years or the life of the beneficiary, whichever is shorter, in which the income was typically payable to a person other than the grantor and established under the provisions of the Internal Revenue Code under prior law. The income is taxable to the income beneficiary and not to the grantor. The agreement provided that on the date fixed for termination of the trust, or on the prior death of the beneficiary, the assets of the trust would be returned to the grantor. Unless the trust was established and funded on or before March 1, 1986, this type of trust will no longer shift income taxation from the grantor to the trust or its beneficiary.

Shrinkage. The reduction in the amount of property that passes at death caused by loss of capital and income resulting from the sale of assets to pay death costs.

Simplified employee pension plan (S.E.P.P.). A simplified employee pension plan is a retirement savings program with most of the same rules, but higher limits than a regular IRA. Unlike the IRA, the S.E.P.P. is available only to employees. As in the case of an IRA, earnings grow income tax free and you pay no tax until you begin to receive benefits.

Single premium whole life. The entire premium is paid upon the purchase of a life insurance policy and credited immediately with the declared rate of interest. The purpose of the policy is to attempt to allow the policy owner to enjoy interest income free of current taxation without jeopardizing the tax advantaged status of the policy.

Sole ownership. Holding of property by one person in such a manner that upon death it passes either by the terms of the person's will or if there is no valid will, then according to intestacy laws.

Sprinkling or spray trust. A trust under which the trustee is given discretionary powers to distribute any part or all of the income among beneficiaries in equal or unequal shares, and direction to accumulate any income not distributed.

Stock option. A stock option is a right to buy stock in the company you work for within a certain period of time and at a fixed price regardless of what the stock is selling for at the time the option can be exercised.

S corporation. An S corporation (previously called a subchapter S corporation) is a corporation that elects not to be taxed as a corporation for federal income tax purposes. Income is taxed directly to shareholders. In all non-tax respects it is a typical corporation.

Survivor's income benefit plan. A survivor's income benefit plan (S.I.B.P.) often called a death benefit only plan, or "D.B.O.," is an agreement between a corporation and an employee. The corporation agrees that if the employee dies before retirement, it will pay a specified amount, or an amount determinable by a specified formula, to the spouse of the employee or another employer-designated class of beneficiary such as employee's children. Typically, the amount may be a multiple of salary such as two or three times the average base pay in the three years preceding death.

Tangible property. Property that has physical substance—may be touched, seen or felt. The thing itself has value (a house, car or furniture).

Taxable estate. An amount determined by subtracting the allowable deductions from the gross estate.

Tenancy by the entireties. The holding of property by husband and wife in such a manner that, except with the consent of each other, neither husband nor wife has a disposable interest in the property during this lifetime of the other. Upon the death of either, the property goes to the survivor.

Tenancy in common. The holding of property by two or more persons in such a manner that each has an undivided interest which, upon the death of one, is passed by probate. It does not pass to the surviving tenant in common.

Terminal reserve. The reserve on a life insurance policy at the end of any contract year and, for policies on which premiums are still due, the amount of the reserve prior to the payment of the next premium.

Term insurance. Under this type of coverage, you must die before the term expires in order for your beneficiaries to collect the insurance. Several forms of term insurance include annual renewable term or yearly renewable or "YRT" term. This type of policy is renewable each year while at the same time the premiums also increase.

Testamentary. The disposition of property by will. A testamentary document is an instrument disposing of property at death, either a will in fact or in the nature of a will.

Testate. A term used when a person dies having left a will.

Testator. A person who leaves a will in force at death.

Transfer for value rule. The income tax rule that taxes otherwise exempt life insurance proceeds when a life insurance policy (or any interest in a policy) has been transferred for any kind of valuable consideration. There are specific exceptions to this rule, but a transfer of a policy for value should never be made to anyone without consulting an attorney or accountant.

Trust.   A fiduciary arrangement whereby the legal title of the property is held, and the property managed, by a person or institution for the benefit of another.

Trustee.   The holder of legal title to property for the use or benefit of another.

2503(c) trust.   A 2503(c) trust is a gift tax tool that enables someone to make a gift to a minor in trust and still obtain the $10,000 annual exclusion. The use of this irrevocable funded trust for gifts to minors eliminates many of the practical objections to giving young children outright gifts.

Unfunded insurance trust.   An insurance trust that is not provided with cash or securities to pay the life insurance premiums. Such premiums are paid by someone other than the trustee.

Unified credit (for federal gift and estate tax purposes).   The unified credit is a dollar-for-dollar reduction against the federal estate and gift tax. In 1983 the credit was $79,300 and protected an estate of $275,000. In 1984 the credit was $96,300 and protected an estate of $325,000. In 1985 the credit was $121,800 and protected an estate of $400,000. In 1986 the credit was $155,000 and protected an estate of $500,000. In 1987 and thereafter, the unified credit became $192,800 and now protects an estate of up to $600,000 from federal estate taxation.

Uniform gift to minors' act.   The Uniform Gift to Minors' Act (U.G.M.A.) provides that an adult, while he or she is alive, may make a gift of certain types of property, such as securities, money or a life insurance contract to a minor, by having it registered in the name of and/or delivering it to the donor or another adult person or trust company as custodian for the minor. The minor acquires equitable title to the subject matter of the gift. This method avoids many of the problems and expenses of other methods of transferring property to a minor such as outright gifts, trusts or guardianship arrangements. A similar but more flexible statute—in terms of the assets it can hold—is the UTMA, Uniform Transfers to Minors Act which has been adopted by many states.

Universal life.   A form of life insurance under which the cash values are generally invested by the insurer in equities and other securities to provide a better rate of return than a typical cash value life insurance policy. Features include flexibility in the amount of premium payments, and adjustments in the amount of death protection without the necessity of taking out a new contract.

Variable life.   A form of life insurance under which the premium is fixed, and the death benefit is guaranteed to be not less than the face amount, but can increase considerably if investment earnings exceed the assumed rate of interest. The policyowner can direct the investment by selecting among several accounts held by the insurer.

Vested interest.   An immediate fixed interest in real or personal property, although the right to possession and enjoyment may be postponed until some future date or until the happening of some event. For example, if a husband leaves real property and securities to a trustee in trust to pay the income to his wife during her lifetime and at her death to transfer the property to his son and his heirs, the wife has a present vested life interest in the right to the income, and the son has a future vested interest in the right to property.

Whole life insurance.   Permanent insurance in which the face amount of the insurance and the premium remain level throughout the life of the contract. A reserve is built into the policy that can be borrowed, or received in cash or in the form of other non-forfeiture values at the option of the insured.

Will.   Technically, a legal expression of what you want to happen to your property when you die. Formal requirements vary by states, but usually at a minimum a will must be in writing and signed at the end. Requirements for witnesses vary according to states.

Index